™

References for the Rest of Us!

BESTSELLING BOOK SERIES

Are you intimidated and confused by computers? Do you find that traditional manuals are overloaded with technical details you'll never use? Do your friends and family always call you to fix simple problems on their PCs? Then the ...*For Dummies*® computer book series from IDG Books Worldwide is for you.

...*For Dummies* books are written for those frustrated computer users who know they aren't really dumb but find that PC hardware, software, and indeed the unique vocabulary of computing make them feel helpless. ...*For Dummies* books use a lighthearted approach, a down-to-earth style, and even cartoons and humorous icons to dispel computer novices' fears and build their confidence. Lighthearted but not lightweight, these books are a perfect survival guide for anyone forced to use a computer.

> "*I like my copy so much I told friends; now they bought copies.*"
>
> — Irene C., Orwell, Ohio

> "*Quick, concise, nontechnical, and humorous.*"
>
> — Jay A., Elburn, Illinois

> "*Thanks, I needed this book. Now I can sleep at night.*"
>
> — Robin F., British Columbia, Canada

Already, millions of satisfied readers agree. They have made ...*For Dummies* books the #1 introductory level computer book series and have written asking for more. So, if you're looking for the most fun and easy way to learn about computers, look to ...*For Dummies* books to give you a helping hand.

IDG
BOOKS
WORLDWIDE

1/99

WORD 2000
FOR WINDOWS®
FOR
DUMMIES®

by Dan Gookin

IDG Books Worldwide, Inc.
An International Data Group Company

Foster City, CA ♦ Chicago, IL ♦ Indianapolis, IN ♦ New York, NY

Word 2000 For Windows® For Dummies®

Published by
IDG Books Worldwide, Inc.
An International Data Group Company
919 E. Hillsdale Blvd.
Suite 400
Foster City, CA 94404
www.idgbooks.com (IDG Books Worldwide Web site)
www.dummies.com (Dummies Press Web site)

Library of Congress Catalog Card No.: 99-61124

ISBN: 0-7645-0448-7

Printed in the United States of America

10 9 8 7 6 5 4 3 2 1

1B/ST/QU/ZZ/IN

Distributed in the United States by IDG Books Worldwide, Inc.

Distributed by CDG Books Canada Inc. for Canada; by Transworld Publishers Limited in the United Kingdom; by IDG Norge Books for Norway; by IDG Sweden Books for Sweden; by Woodslane Pty. Ltd. for Australia; by Woodslane (NZ) Ltd. for New Zealand; by TransQuest Publishers Pte Ltd. for Singapore, Malaysia, Thailand, Indonesia, and Hong Kong; by ICG Muse, Inc. for Japan; by Norma Comunicaciones S.A. for Colombia; by Intersoft for South Africa; by Le Monde en Tique for France; by International Thomson Publishing for Germany, Austria and Switzerland; by Distribuidora Cuspide for Argentina; by Livraria Cultura for Brazil; by Ediciones ZETA S.C.R. Ltda. for Peru; by WS Computer Publishing Corporation, Inc., for the Philippines; by Contemporanea de Ediciones for Venezuela; by Express Computer Distributors for the Caribbean and West Indies; by Micronesia Media Distributor, Inc. for Micronesia; by Grupo Editorial Norma S.A. for Guatemala; by Chips Computadoras S.A. de C.V. for Mexico; by Editorial Norma de Panama S.A. for Panama; by American Bookshops for Finland. Authorized Sales Agent: Anthony Rudkin Associates for the Middle East and North Africa.

For general information on IDG Books Worldwide's books in the U.S., please call our Consumer Customer Service department at 800-762-2974. For reseller information, including discounts and premium sales, please call our Reseller Customer Service department at 800-434-3422.

For information on where to purchase IDG Books Worldwide's books outside the U.S., please contact our International Sales department at 317-596-5530 or fax 317-596-5692.

For consumer information on foreign language translations, please contact our Customer Service department at 1-800-434-3422, fax 317-596-5692, or e-mail rights@idgbooks.com.

For information on licensing foreign or domestic rights, please phone +1-650-655-3109.

For sales inquiries and special prices for bulk quantities, please contact our Sales department at 650-655-3200 or write to the address above.

For information on using IDG Books Worldwide's books in the classroom or for ordering examination copies, please contact our Educational Sales department at 800-434-2086 or fax 317-596-5499.

For press review copies, author interviews, or other publicity information, please contact our Public Relations department at 650-655-3000 or fax 650-655-3299.

For authorization to photocopy items for corporate, personal, or educational use, please contact Copyright Clearance Center, 222 Rosewood Drive, Danvers, MA 01923, or fax 978-750-4470.

About the Author

Dan Gookin got started with computers back in the post slide rule age of computing: 1982. His first intention was to buy a computer to replace his aged and constantly breaking typewriter. Working as slave labor in a restaurant, however, Gookin was unable to afford the full "word processor" setup and settled on a computer that had a monitor, keyboard, and little else. Soon his writing career was under way with several submissions to (and lots of rejections from) fiction magazines.

The big break came in 1984 when he began writing about computers. Applying his flair for fiction with a self-taught knowledge of computers, Gookin was able to demystify the subject and explain technology in a relaxed and understandable voice. He even dared to add humor, which eventually won him a column in a local computer magazine.

Eventually, Gookin's talents came to roost as he became a ghostwriter at a computer book publishing house. That was followed by an editing position at a San Diego computer magazine, at which time he also regularly participated in a radio talk show about computers. In addition, Gookin kept writing books about computers, some of which became minor best-sellers.

In 1990, Gookin came to IDG Books Worldwide, Inc., with a book proposal. From that initial meeting unfolded an idea for an outrageous book: a long overdue and original idea for the computer book for the rest of us. What became *DOS For Dummies* blossomed into an international bestseller with hundreds and thousands of copies in print and many foreign translations.

Today, Gookin still considers himself a writer and computer "guru" whose job it is to remind everyone that computers are not to be taken too seriously. His approach to computers is light and humorous yet very informative. He knows that the complex beasts are important and can help people become productive and successful. Yet Gookin mixes his knowledge of computers with a unique, dry sense of humor that keeps everyone informed — and awake. His favorite quote is, "Computers are a notoriously dull subject, but that doesn't mean I have to write about them that way."

Gookin's titles for IDG Books include: *DOS For Dummies,* Windows 95 Edition; *PCs For Dummies,* 6th Edition; and *Discovering Windows 95*. Gookin holds a degree in Communications from the University of California, San Diego, and lives with his wife and four boys in the rare and gentle woods of Idaho.

ABOUT IDG BOOKS WORLDWIDE

Welcome to the world of IDG Books Worldwide.

IDG Books Worldwide, Inc., is a subsidiary of International Data Group, the world's largest publisher of computer-related information and the leading global provider of information services on information technology. IDG was founded more than 30 years ago by Patrick J. McGovern and now employs more than 9,000 people worldwide. IDG publishes more than 290 computer publications in over 75 countries. More than 90 million people read one or more IDG publications each month.

Launched in 1990, IDG Books Worldwide is today the #1 publisher of best-selling computer books in the United States. We are proud to have received eight awards from the Computer Press Association in recognition of editorial excellence and three from Computer Currents' First Annual Readers' Choice Awards. Our best-selling ...*For Dummies*® series has more than 50 million copies in print with translations in 31 languages. IDG Books Worldwide, through a joint venture with IDG's Hi-Tech Beijing, became the first U.S. publisher to publish a computer book in the People's Republic of China. In record time, IDG Books Worldwide has become the first choice for millions of readers around the world who want to learn how to better manage their businesses.

Our mission is simple: Every one of our books is designed to bring extra value and skill-building instructions to the reader. Our books are written by experts who understand and care about our readers. The knowledge base of our editorial staff comes from years of experience in publishing, education, and journalism — experience we use to produce books to carry us into the new millennium. In short, we care about books, so we attract the best people. We devote special attention to details such as audience, interior design, use of icons, and illustrations. And because we use an efficient process of authoring, editing, and desktop publishing our books electronically, we can spend more time ensuring superior content and less time on the technicalities of making books.

You can count on our commitment to deliver high-quality books at competitive prices on topics you want to read about. At IDG Books Worldwide, we continue in the IDG tradition of delivering quality for more than 30 years. You'll find no better book on a subject than one from IDG Books Worldwide.

John Kilcullen
Chairman and CEO
IDG Books Worldwide, Inc.

Steven Berkowitz
President and Publisher
IDG Books Worldwide, Inc.

Eighth Annual Computer Press Awards ➤1992

Ninth Annual Computer Press Awards ➤1993

Tenth Annual Computer Press Awards ➤1994

Eleventh Annual Computer Press Awards ➤1995

Author's Acknowledgments

Sincere thanks and appreciation continue to go to the French, who have enjoyed past editions of this book so much. (Honestly, I should simply acknowledge the translator, who does such a superior job.)

Thanks also go to Ray Werner and Lauren Straub who helped on earlier editions of the book. For this edition, thanks to my beloved wife, Sandra. Without her input I literally would not know how to dress. And editor Kyle has been a real kick to work with. Kyle! Lie low. I like you.

Publisher's Acknowledgments

We're proud of this book; please register your comments through our IDG Books Worldwide Online Registration Form located at http://my2cents.dummies.com.

Some of the people who helped bring this book to market include the following:

Acquisitions, Editorial, and Media Development

Senior Project Editor: Kyle Looper
(Previous Edition: Bill Helling)

Acquisitions Editor: Mike Kelly

Copy Editor: Kathleen Dobie

Technical Editor: Lee Musick

Editorial Manager: Leah P. Cameron

Editorial Assistant: Beth Parlon

Production

Project Coordinator: Valery Bourke

Layout and Graphics: Linda M. Boyer, J. Tyler Connor, Angela F. Hunckler, Brent Savage, Kate Snell, Michael A. Sullivan, Brian Torwelle

Proofreaders: Kelli Botta, Sharon Duffy, Jennifer Mahern, Rebecca Senninger

Indexer: Johnna VanHoose

General and Administrative

IDG Books Worldwide, Inc.: John Kilcullen, CEO; Steven Berkowitz, President and Publisher

IDG Books Technology Publishing: Brenda McLaughlin, Senior Vice President and Group Publisher

Dummies Technology Press and Dummies Editorial: Diane Graves Steele, Vice President and Associate Publisher; Mary Bednarek, Director of Acquisitions and Product Development; Kristin A. Cocks, Editorial Director

Dummies Trade Press: Kathleen A. Welton, Vice President and Publisher; Kevin Thornton, Acquisitions Manager

IDG Books Production for Dummies Press: Michael R. Britton, Vice President of Production and Creative Services; Cindy L. Phipps, Manager of Project Coordination, Production Proofreading, and Indexing; Kathie S. Schutte, Supervisor of Page Layout; Shelley Lea, Supervisor of Graphics and Design; Debbie J. Gates, Production Systems Specialist; Robert Springer, Supervisor of Proofreading; Debbie Stailey, Special Projects Coordinator; Tony Augsburger, Supervisor of Reprints and Bluelines

Dummies Packaging and Book Design: Patty Page, Manager, Promotions Marketing

◆

The publisher would like to give special thanks to Patrick J. McGovern, without whom this book would not have been possible.

◆

Contents at a Glance

Cartoons at a Glance

By Rich Tennant

Table of Contents

Introduction

●●●

*W*elcome to *Word 2000 For Windows For Dummies,* and let's all hope with this, the 2000th edition of Word, Microsoft finally got things right. Seriously, this is a tight, fast, better version of Word and you're holding in your hands the tightest, fastest, and bestest book for that product.

Word is a massive program. It does a lot. But the truth is that you don't need to know everything about Word to use it. A better question is: Do you *want* to know everything about Microsoft Word? Probably not. You don't want to know all the command options, all the typographical mumbo-jumbo, or even all those special features that you know are in there but terrify you. No, all you want to know is the single answer to a tiny question. Then you can happily close the book and be on your way. If that's you, you've found your book.

This book informs and entertains. And it has a serious attitude problem. After all, I don't want to teach you to love Microsoft Word. Instead, be prepared to encounter some informative, down-to-earth explanations — in English — of how to get the job done by using Microsoft Word. You take your work seriously, but you definitely don't need to take Microsoft Word seriously.

About This Book

This book is not meant to be read from cover to cover. It's not a novel and if it were then I'd kill off all the characters at the end, so it would be a bad read anyway. Instead, this book is a reference. Each chapter covers a specific topic or task that Word does. Within a chapter, you find self-contained sections, each of which describes how to perform a specific task or get something done. Sample sections you encounter in this book include

- ✔ Saving your stuff
- ✔ Cutting and pasting a block
- ✔ Quickly finding your place
- ✔ Aligning paragraphs
- ✔ A quick way to cobble a table together
- ✔ A caption for your figure
- ✔ Step-by-step mail merging guide

There are no keys to memorize, no secret codes, no tricks, no pop-up diora-
mas, and no wall charts. Instead, each section explains a topic as if it's the
first thing you read in this book. Nothing is assumed, and everything is cross-
referenced. Technical terms and topics, when they come up, are neatly
shoved to the side where you can easily avoid reading them. The idea here
isn't for you to learn anything. This book's philosophy is to help you look it
up, figure it out, and get back to work.

How to Use This Book

This book helps you when you're at a loss over what to do in Word 2000. I
think that this situation happens to everyone way too often. For example, if
you press Ctrl+F9, Word displays a {} thing in your text. I have no idea what
that means, nor do I want to know. What I do know, however, is that I can
press Ctrl+Z to make the annoying thing go away. That's the kind of knowledge you find in this book.

Word uses the mouse and menus to get things done, which is what you would
expect from Windows. Yet there are times when various *key combinations,*
several keys you may press together or in sequence, are required. This book
shows you two different kinds of key combinations.

This is a keyboard shortcut:

> Ctrl+Shift+P

This shortcut means that you should press and hold Ctrl and Shift together,
and then press the P key, and release all three keys.

Menu commands are listed like this:

> File➪Open

This command means that you open the File menu (with the mouse or the
keyboard — it's your choice) and then choose the Open command.

If I describe a message or something you see on-screen, it looks like this:

```
Cannot find hard drive, save elsewhere?
```

This book never refers you to the Word manual or — yech! — to the Windows
manual. Even so, it helps if you have a good book as a reference. *PCs For
Dummies,* 6th Edition, published by IDG Books Worldwide, Inc., contains lots
of supplemental information you'll find useful.

What You're Not to Read

Special technical sections dot this book like chicken pox on an eight-year-old. They offer annoyingly endless and technical explanations, descriptions of advanced topics, or alternative commands that you really don't need to know about. Each one of them is flagged with a special icon or enclosed in an electrified, barbed wire and poison ivy box (an idea I stole from the Terwilliker Piano Method books). Reading this stuff is optional.

Foolish Assumptions

Here are my assumptions about you. You use a computer. You use Windows, either Windows 95 or Windows 98. There is little difference between them as far as this book is concerned. If there's anything special in Windows 98, I flag it in the text (which maybe happens twice in this entire book).

Your word processor is Microsoft Word 2000. I refer to it as "Word" throughout this book. Word may have come with your computer, you may have purchased it as a stand-alone program, or it may be a part of a larger suite of programs called Microsoft Office 2000. Whatever. Same program, same Word.

How This Book Is Organized

This book contains seven major parts, each of which is divided into several chapters. The chapters themselves have been sliced into smaller, modular sections. You can pick up the book and read any section without necessarily knowing what has already been covered in the rest of the book. Start anywhere.

Here is a breakdown of the parts and what you can find in them:

Part I: Breaking into Word

This is baby Word stuff — the bare essentials. Here you discover how to giggle, teethe, crawl, walk, burp, and spit up. Then you can move up to the advanced topics of moving the cursor, editing text, searching and replacing, marking blocks, spell checking, and printing. (A pacifier is optional for this section.)

Part II: Letting Word Do the Formatting Work

Formatting is the art of beating your text into typographical submission. It's not the heady work of creating a document and getting the right words. No, it's "You will be italic!" "Indent, you moron!" and "Gimme a new page *here*." Often, formatting involves a lot of yelling. This part of the book contains chapters that show you how to format characters, lines, paragraphs, pages, and entire documents without raising your voice (too much).

Part III: Sprucing Up Your Document

Beyond formatting is the realm of adding things to your document to make it look nice. This part of the book is a potpourri of esoteric doodads and thingies you can add to your text: boarders, shading, tables, figures, columns, footnotes, and other interesting goobers.

Part IV: Land of the Fun and Strange

This part covers some general and miscellaneous topics, items that others might consider to be too borderline bizarre to be found in a "beginners" book on Word.

Part V: Creating Lotsa Stuff in Word

Word's very own cookbook of sorts. Though I didn't have the space to include *everything*, this part of the book gives you some hints and tips on creating various fun and interesting (and unexpected) things in Word.

Part VI: The Part of Tens

How about "The Ten Commandments of Word"? Or consider "Ten Truly Bizarre Things." Or the handy "Ten Things Worth Remembering." This section is a gold mine of tens.

What's Not Here

This book can be only so big. The book's author, on the other hand, can grow to immense sizes! To keep them both in check, the Powers That Be at IDG Books have taken some of this book's excess and placed it up on the World Wide Web for easy access. That way they can keep the book small and still offer you information and help keep the author large. (Or something like that.)

If you have Internet access and a Web browser, you can visit this book's bonus pages at:

```
http://www.dummies.com/word2000/bonus/
```

If you don't have Internet access, don't worry. The information on the Web page isn't essential to running Word. The Web page merely contains bonus information, plus some random thoughts. It's entirely optional reading.

Icons Used in This Book

This icon flags useful, helpful tips or shortcuts.

This icon marks a friendly reminder to do something.

This icon marks a friendly reminder not to do something.

This icon alerts you to overly nerdy information and technical discussions of the topic at hand. The information is optional reading, but it may enhance your reputation at cocktail parties if you repeat it.

Where to Go from Here

Start reading! Observe the Table of Contents and find something that interests you. Or look up your puzzle in the Index.

If you're new to Word, start off with Chapter 1.

If you're an old hand at Word, consider checking out Part V for some inspiration.

Read! Write! Produce!

By the way, I am available on the Internet for any questions you may have about this book or Microsoft Word 2000. While I cannot answer every question (you should use the Microsoft Technical Support for that), I might be able to offer a suggestion. I'm open to input and, in fact, several parts of this book have come from reader input:

dang@idgbooks.com

I answer all my own e-mail and respond to everyone who writes. Enjoy the book. And enjoy Word 2000. Or at least tolerate it.

Part I
Breaking into Word

The 5th Wave · By Rich Tennant

"We're concerned—Brian doesn't seem to be bonding with the Word 2000 Help Assistant like the other kids."

In this part . . .

The old image of computers was one of overgrown calculators. Computers did numbers and math. And on early science-fiction TV shows, computers were oracles: Mr. Spock would ask a question about some remote planet and the computer would offer some vague answer equal to any prophecy ever divulged at Delphi (though not in rhyme). Today, however, computers are different.

In addition to crunching numbers, computers are equally deft at working wonders with words. To make that happen, you need a computer tool for working with words. That tool is Microsoft Word. This part of the book introduces you to Word and how you can use it to help you compose words on a computer. There's no math, and what little mysticism occurs is carefully explained throughout the text.

Chapter 1

The Big Picture

I remember the very first time I sat down at a word processor. I bought myself a nice pair of sturdy, rubber pants — the kind trout fishermen wear. And though it's hard to sit down in sturdy rubber pants, I did it anyway. For some reason, I felt the computer may — if I mistreated it — suddenly spew water all over me. And my fear was justified; I was actually sitting in front of an aquarium. And in the long run, aquariums make for lousy computers.

There are right and wrong ways to do everything. With a PC and Microsoft software, there are actually about 800 right ways and only a handful of wrong ways to do anything. This chapter helps you set your bearings, offering you the Big Picture overview of Word, your PC's word processing software.

How Do I Start Thee, Word? Let Me Count the Ways . . .

O! Fair Word. How might I woo thee?

Time and time again, it's been proven that the best way to start Word is to use the trusty Windows Start button. Heed these steps:

1. **Make sure your computer is on and toasty.**

   Refer to *PCs For Dummies,* 6th Edition, by yours truly (IDG Books World-wide, Inc.) for quick and accurate turning-on-the-computer instructions.

Any computer that's on is, in fact, toasty. The only way to make it more toasty is to actually insert bread, which is not recommended.

2. Prepare yourself.

Inhale deeply. Crack your knuckles. Make sure you're seated, with a nice, upright, firm posture. Are you fingers ready to dance on the keyboard? Then you're physically ready to use Word.

To prepare mentally, close your eyes. Relax. Think of calm blue waters. Prepare to let your thoughts flow into the computer. Remember, you are the master. (Keep muttering that over and over: *I am the master.*)

3. Click the Start button.

The Start button lives to the left of the taskbar, on the bottom of the screen. (You can typically find it there, although it's been known to wander.)

If you cannot locate the Start button, press the Ctrl+Esc key combination or, if your keyboard has one, press the Windows key (between the Ctrl and Alt keys).

Successfully pressing the Start button yields the Start menu.

4. Stop muttering *I am the master.*

Really, now.

5. Choose <u>P</u>rograms⇨Microsoft Word.

Point the mouse at the word Programs on the Start menu. Soon a sub-menu appears, similar to the one shown in Figure 1-1.

Click the Microsoft Word menu item. (It may also say "Word" or possibly "Word 2000" or even "Word 9.")

Watch in amazement as your computer whizzes and whirs. Before too long, a screen that looks like Figure 1-3 appears (look ahead a few pages). Word is stumbling into town! I discuss the whatzits of the screen in the section, "Word on the Screen."

✔ If you don't see Microsoft Word right there on the menu (as in Figure 1-1), look for a menu item that reads "Microsoft Office." Point the mouse at that item and up pops another submenu, where Microsoft Word lurks.

✔ Your computer can be set up to run Word automatically every time you turn it on. Think of the time that can save! If you want your computer set up in this manner, grab someone more knowledgeable than yourself — an individual I call a computer guru. Tell your guru: "Make my computer always start in Word." If your guru is unavailable, frantically grab other people at random until you find someone bold enough to obey you.

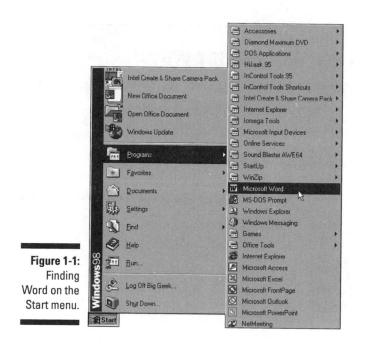

Figure 1-1:
Finding
Word on the
Start menu.

> ✔ I prefer to run Word full screen, maximizing its window so that nothing
> else bugs me when I'm writing. To run Word in the full-screen mode, click
> the box button (the middle one) in the upper-right corner of the window.
> This button maximizes Word to fill the entire screen. If Word is already
> maximized, two overlapping boxes appear on the button; you don't need
> to click anything in that case.

Another way to charm Word into being

Microsoft
Word

My favorite way to run Word is by opening a shortcut icon pasted to the
desktop. The Start thing is just too silly for me to make a habit of. So I locate
the Word shortcut icon (shown in the margin), double-click, and Word rushes
to the screen. If you don't have a shortcut to Word on the desktop, then you
can paste one there yourself. Heed the instructions in the "Finding and pasting the Word icon somewhere" sidebar.

In Windows 98, the very bestest way to start Word is to put a Word icon on
the Quick Launch bar, and then click that icon.

1. **Coax the Quick Launch bar into existence by right-clicking the taskbar
   and choosing <u>T</u>oolbars➪Quick Launch from the pop-up menu, as
   shown in Figure 1-2.**

Starting Word (the many ways)

Here is a summary of various ways to start Word:

✔ Choose Programs⇨Microsoft Word from the Start menu.

✔ Open (double-click) a Word icon on the desktop.

✔ Open (single-click) a Word icon on the Quick Launch bar.

✔ Choose a Word document from the Documents menu on the Start menu.

✔ Open (double-click) any Word document.

Figure 1-2:
Summoning
the Quick
Launch
bar in
Windows 98.

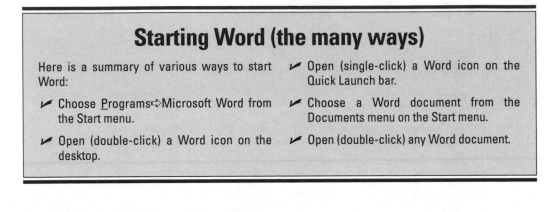

2. **Paste a Word shortcut icon on the Quick Launch bar.**

   Now, Word is only one quick click away from in-your-face word processing.

Starting a project you've been working on

If you're a Word maven, then a quick way to get back into the writing mode is to just pluck your currently hot document from the Start menu's Documents submenu.

1. **Click the Start button.**

   Up pops the Start menu.

2. **Point at the Documents menu item.**

   The Documents sub-menu appears. That menu lists the last 16-or-so files or documents that you opened in Windows. (Though not every file is listed there because the Moon is out of phase with Venus.)

TECHNICAL STUFF

Finding and pasting the Word icon somewhere

Creating a shortcut to Word, either on the desktop or on the Quick Launch bar, requires that you follow two confusing and over-simplified steps: First, locate the original Word icon and second, drag that icon to the desktop or Quick Launch bar.

To find the original Word icon, open the My Computer icon on the desktop. Open drive C. Open the Program Files folder, then the Microsoft Office folder. Inside that folder lives the Word icon.

To copy the icon from the folder to the desktop, press the Ctrl key (which ensures that Windows copies the icon and does not move it), and drag the icon from the folder, releasing the mouse when the icon is over the desktop. (You may

need to move the windows around so that you can see the desktop.)

To put the icon on the Quick Launch bar, first make sure the Quick Launch bar is big enough for another icon; if you need to, drag the separator between the Quick Launch bar and the taskbar so that the Quick Launch bar has room for one more icon. Then drag the Word icon down to the bar and release the mouse button. You don't need to press the Ctrl key this time because Windows won't move files to the Quick Launch bar.

When you're done, be sure to close the window(s) you opened.

---

3. Locate your document in the list and click it.

Choose your document by clicking the mouse. Click. The document wakes up Word, and you're busy on your favorite document. Again.

Documents appear in the Documents window in alphabetical order. Newer documents you open bump the older ones off the list. So if you just edited 16 graphics files, they bump off any Word documents that were once there.

Honestly, any Word document icon you open starts Word. In fact, if you've been working on the Great American Novel for several years now, consider pasting its icon on the desktop and just opening that icon to start your day.

At the top of the Documents menu is the My Documents folder where Word automatically stores the documents you create. Choosing the My Documents folder opens a window in which you can locate other Word documents that may not be on the Documents menu.

Documents, documents, and documents. All of the sudden the word "documents" has lost its meaning.

Word on the Screen

Follow along with this text and Figure 1-3 to locate the many fresh and exciting items on the typical blank Word screen.

Gizmos and gadgets

Writing is Word's primary job. Well, not "writing" in the Earnest Hemingway sense. Actually, it's processing words that Word does best. That's why the largest portion of the Word screen is for composing text (refer to Figure 1-3).

Surrounding the text-composing area you'll find various bells, whistles, switches, and doodads that would be interesting only if they were edible. And the good news is that with Word 2000, all of that stuff is totally customizable by you. (Better know what it all means before you go changing everything.)

- ✔ **The Title bar,** which says `Document 1 - Microsoft Word` until you save your document to disk.
- ✔ **The Menu bar,** which contains a full list of Word's various and sundry commands.
- ✔ **The Standard and Formatting toolbars,** which are shown side-by-side in Figure 1-3, although you can rearrange them at your whim.
- ✔ **The Ruler,** which helps you set margins and tabs.

Below the writing area are two items.

- ✔ **The View buttons,** located to the left of the horizontal scroll bar, control how your document is displayed.
- ✔ **The Status Bar,** which dishes up lots of trivia about your document, some of which is interesting.

What each of these various buttons, bars, and menus does and whether or not it's important is covered elsewhere in this book. Right now you just need to know the names of things so you don't get lost later.

Control menu
Menu bar
Standard toolbar
Toothpick cursor
Insertion pointer (mouse)
Blank space to write in   Ruler

Formatting toolbar
Close (quit)
Maximize
Document close button   Minimize
Title bar

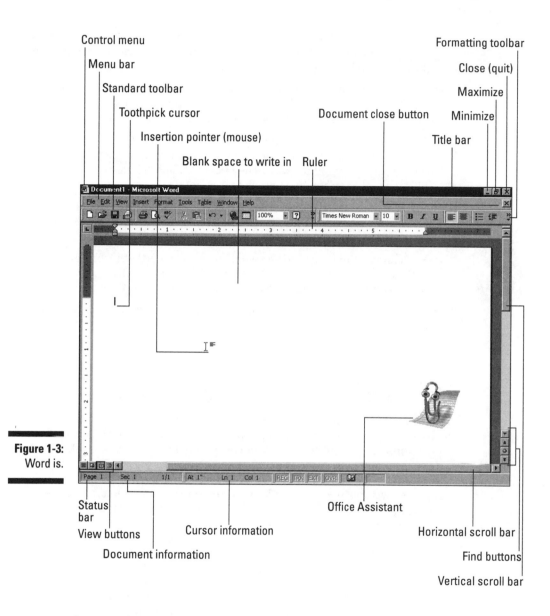

Figure 1-3:
Word is.

Status bar
View buttons
Document information
Cursor information

Office Assistant

Horizontal scroll bar
Find buttons
Vertical scroll bar

I cover what each of these various buttons, bars, and menus does and whether or not it's important elsewhere in this book. Right now you just need to know the names of things so you don't get lost.

✔ The Office Assistant (an animated paper clip) is covered in the section, "Your assistant," later in this chapter.

✔ The Status Bar is not a yuppie hang-out. It contains cubbyholes into which random and often cryptic information is displayed. This book explains when the information is useful to you.

✔ Figure 1-3 shows Word in the "Print Layout" view. If it looks different on your screen, choose <u>V</u>iew⇨<u>P</u>rint Layout from the menu. (Some people prefer to use Word in the "Normal" view.)

✔ The Windows taskbar, located at the bottom of the screen, is a part of Windows itself and not Word. However, as you open documents in Word, buttons representing those documents appear on the Windows taskbar.

✔ Notice the mouse pointer in Figure 1-3? It's the *insertion* pointer, shaped like an I-beam. That's the way the mouse pointer appears when it's sliding over your document in Word. The I-beam means "I beam the insertion pointer to this spot when you click the mouse."

✔ The lines next to (or beneath) the insertion pointer are part of Word's click-and-type feature. Using click-and-type is covered in Chapter 18, "Automatic Formatting Tricks."

✔ You can use the mouse to see what some of the little buttons and things with pictures on them do in Word. Just hover the mouse pointer over the button and voilà! It's like Folger's Instant Information Crystals.

✔ If you don't actually see the Standard or Formatting toolbars or the ruler, or you want to change the way the Word screen looks *right now*, hop on up to Chapter 29, "Modifying Word's Appearance."

The blank place where you write

After Word starts, you are faced with the electronic version of "The Blank Page," the same idea-crippling concept that induced writer's block in several generations of typewriter users. It makes you wonder if cave-people ever had "stone block."

The key to writing in Word is to look for the blinking *insertion pointer* — a blinking toothpick in your text that shows you where your typing will appear on the screen.

The flat, bold line at the end of your text is the *End-of-Text marker*. Below this line is a vast, vacuous, void of a place. Nothing exists in the white space below this marker, not even blank pages — only infinite nothingness. The End-of-Text marker is the steel beam that supports your text, keeping it from harm's way, in the evil nothingness that exists below your text.

✔ Writing (or typing, depending on how good you are) is covered in the next chapter. That would be Chapter 2.

✔ Any weird stuff you see on-screen (a ¶, for example) is a Word secret symbol. Chapter 2 tells you why you may want to view those secret symbols, and how to hide them if they annoy you.

 ✔ The exact spot where the text appears is called the cursor. It's also called an insertion pointer because traditional computer cursors are underlines that slide under what you type. I prefer the term *toothpick cursor* because *insertion pointer* is just too medically geometric for my tastes. Characters you type appear immediately to the left of where the toothpick cursor is flashing, and then the cursor moves forward and waits for the next character.

Your assistant

When you need help in Word, you're supposed to turn your attention to the little animated character — your Office Assistant. Normally this character looks like a paper clip with bulging eyes, but you can change the character to something else if you like (I tell you how in the "Various other Office Assistants" sidebar). The paperclip is shown in Figure 1-4.

Figure 1-4:
The paper
clip.

The Office Assistant is there to help you. Most of the time, however, it just sits there watching while you type or getting bored while you rummage for a thought.

Here are Office Assistant musings:

 ✔ To see the Office Assistant if it's not currently displayed, choose Help⇨ Show the Office Assistant.

 ✔ You can move the Office Assistant around by dragging it with the mouse. I put my assistant (the Dog) down in the lower-right corner of the screen where he won't get into any trouble.

 ✔ Right-click the Office Assistant to see a list of its menu options. My favorite menu Item is "Animate," which makes the Office Assistant do something interesting.

 ✔ If you detest the Office Assistant, right-click on his nose and choose the Hide menu option. (I hated the Office Assistant for previous versions of Word, but actually like this new incarnation.)

 ✔ The Office Assistant hides when you switch from Word to other applications.

 ✔ Using the Office Assistant to get help is covered in Chapter 2.

Various other Office Assistants

You're not limited to the paperclip as your Office Assistant. There is an entire rogues gallery of animals, minerals, and vegetables you can have as an assistant. They all offer help. They all do tricks. They all look different. They all annoy in different ways.

To choose another assistant, or to just view the gallery, right-click the Office Assistant and click the Choose Assistant option. (Choose Help⇨Show the Office Assistant to see the Office Assistant if it's not currently visible.)

Use the Back and Next buttons in the Office Assistant dialog box to see the gang, or just view the images below for an idea of what's available.

Assistant	*Name*	*Assistant*	*Name*
	"Rocky" (Also known as The Dog — My favorite assistant.)		"The Genius" (Not Mark Twain.)
	"Mother Nature" (Can also look like a volcano.)		"F1" (You F1, I'll F2. Actually F1 is the help key on your keyboard.)
	"Office Logo" (Like we would enjoy Microsoft's marketing that much.)		"The Dot" (I am not Bob.)
			"The Cat " (Not compatible with the dog.)

Microsoft may make other types of office assistants available. I would suppose they'd be available on the Internet somewhere, but I've been unable to find them. Refer to your favorite Windows or Internet book for more information on finding such things.

Click OK to close the Office Assistant dialog box and choose a new assistant. (Word may require its original CD to copy the assistant to your hard drive.)

A Look at Your Keyboard

As your office fills with water, you climb onto your desk. As you float away, you notice that your keyboard would make an adequate paddle. You can row to safety! Until that time, using your keyboard properly is an important part of using Word.

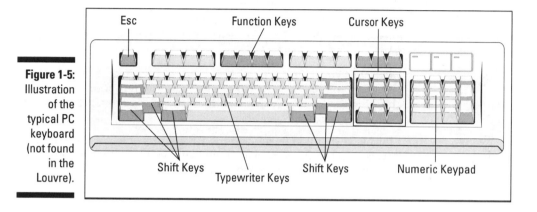

Figure 1-5: Illustration of the typical PC keyboard (not found in the Louvre).

Figure 1-5 shows the typical PC keyboard used during the turn-of-the-century. (Turn-of-the 20th to the 21st century, not the 19th to 20th centuries, when "keyboard" typically implied a piano.)

Notice how the keyboard is divided into separate areas, each of which has a special function? In Word, you use the keys in these groups either alone or in combination with other keys:

✔ **Function keys:** These keys are located along the top row of the keyboard, labeled F1 through F12. You can use them alone or in cahoots with the Ctrl, Alt, and Shift keys.

✔ **Typewriter keys:** These are the standard alphanumeric keys you find on any typewriter: A through Z, 1 through 0, plus symbols and other exotic characters.

✔ **Cursor keys:** These arrow keys move the toothpick cursor around the screen. Also lumped in are the Home, End, PgUp (or Page Up), PgDn (or Page Down), Insert, and Delete keys. Oh, and the big plus and minus keys on the number pad are counted as well.

✔ **Don key:** A domesticated ass. Like a little, stupid horse.

- ✔ **Numeric keypad:** These keys toggle (meaning that they can't make up their minds) between cursor keys and number keys. The split personality is evident on each key cap, which displays two symbols. The Num Lock key and its corresponding light are on if the numeric keypad (1, 2, 3) is active. If the cursor keys (arrows, Home) are active, Num Lock is off.

- ✔ **Shift keys:** These keys don't do anything by themselves. Instead, the Shift, Ctrl, and Alt keys work in combination with other keys. Here are some individual keys worth noting:

  - **Enter:** Marked with the word "Enter" and sometimes a cryptic, curved arrow-thing: ↵. You use the Enter key to end a paragraph of text.

  - **F4:** The F4 key is the "repeat" key in Word. Pressing F4 repeats the last thing you did, whether it was typing or finding something, or changing the format. F4 is a very handy key, and I remind you of its usefulness over and over again.

  - **F1:** This key should be labeled HELP! The F1 key is Word's help key. It wakes up the Office Assistant, allowing you to type in a question, or it gives you help on a specific item in a dialog box.

Depressing the keys

When I tell you to "depress the Enter key," you should look at your keyboard, stare the Enter key squarely in the eye and say, aloud, "You, you funny-looking key. You're worthless. All the other keys hate you. My right pinky hates you. You're despised! You should leave the keyboard right now and hide in shame, you worthless key, you!" There, now the Enter key is quite depressed.

Seriously, you don't "depress" any key on your keyboard. You press keys. Press them down, and then release them. Actually, any swift tapping motion will do. And the better keyboards pleasingly click for you, making your typing as noisy as it would be on an old manual Olympia.

Typing key combinations

Aside from regular typing, you need to use various key combinations to tell Word how to carry out certain commands. For example:

Ctrl+P

Or if you can palm a basketball in one hand, you can try:

Ctrl+Shift+F12

Both keyboard shortcuts open the Print dialog box — which isn't really important right now. What is important is what these key combinations tell you to do, namely: Press and hold the Ctrl key while you press P, then release both keys; or press and hold the Ctrl and Shift keys and then press the F12 key. Release all three keys.

These key combinations appear all the time. Always press and hold the first key (or keys) and then press the last key: Press and release.

✔ This key combination method works just like pressing Shift+F to get a capital F. It's the same thing, but with the odd Ctrl (Control) and Alt (Alternate) keys.

✔ Yeah, you have to really reach to get some of those key combinations.

✔ You don't need to press hard. If you're having trouble working a keyboard shortcut, pressing harder doesn't make the computer think, "Oh, Lordy, she's pressing really hard now. I think she means it. Wake up, wake up!" A light touch is all that's required.

✔ Remember to release the keys: With Ctrl+P, for example, press and hold the Ctrl key, press P, and then release both keys. If you don't know which one to release first, release the second key and then the Shift key (Shift, Ctrl, Alt) last.

✔ Click the Cancel or Close button if you accidentally open the Print dialog box; you can also press the Esc key on the keyboard. See Chapter 9 for more information on canceling printing.

Quitting Word When You're All Done

Knowing when to leave is the height of proper etiquette. And sometimes it pays to not even show up. But Word cares not for social things. When the writing is done, or you're done writing, it's time to quit Word.

1. **Choose File⇨Exit.**

   Click File. A menu drops down. Click the Exit command (toward the bottom of the menu).

2. **Save any files, if Word prompts you to do so.**

   Word always warns you before it leaves; if you have any unsaved work, you're prompted to save it to disk. The Office Assistant (if visible) prompts you, as shown in Figure 1-6.

Figure 1-6:
Don't leave
just yet!

Click Yes to save your file. You may be asked to give the file a name if you haven't yet done so. (Chapter 2 tells you how this is done.)

If the slop you typed isn't worth saving, click No.

You can click Cancel to "quit" the exit command and return to Word for more word processing delight.

If you elect to quit, Word leaves the screen and you're returned to the Windows desktop, where you can busy yourself with yet another game of FreeCell.

✔ If you've hidden the Office Assistant, then a regular old cruddy dialog box replaces the cutesy Dog message shown in Figure 1-6.

✔ The File➪Exit command is the proper way to exit Word. Do not, under any circumstances, reset or turn off your PC to quit Word! Doing so can potentially scramble files on your computer's hard disk. Computers are troublesome enough by themselves. No point in your contributing to that madness by doing something sloppy.

✔ Exiting Word returns you to the Windows Desktop. If you want to turn your machine off, choose the Shutdown command from the Start button's menu, or press Ctrl+Esc+U, and then click the OK or Yes button. Only turn off your computer when Windows says that it's safe to do so.

✔ You can find more information on turning off your computer in *PCs For Dummies,* 6th Edition from the bosom of IDG Books Worldwide, Inc.

How to Quit What You're Doing without Quitting Word

If you're finished with a document, you can make it vanish from your screen and start on something new without quitting Word. You do this by "closing" a document, which is similar to ripping a sheet of paper out of your type-writer — without the satisfying *SSHHHHHTHWP!* sound that makes.

To close a document, choose File⇨Close. This step closes the document window and makes it vanish from the screen. The "white space" in the window disappears.

To start a new document, choose File⇨New, select Blank Document from the New dialog box, and click OK.

To start a new document, choose File⇨New.

You can open a document on disk using the File⇨Open command, which I introduce in the next chapter.

- ✔ Why close a document? Because you're done working on it! Maybe you want to work on something else or quit Word after closing. The choices are yours, and I explain them in the next chapter.

- ✔ There is no need to close a document, really. In fact, I work on a document over a period of days and keep it open (and my PC on) the entire time. Doesn't hurt a thing. (Now I do save it to disk, which *is* important.)

- ✔ If you try to close a document before it has been saved, Word displays a warning dialog box. Click the Yes button to save your document. If you want to continue editing, click the Cancel button and get back to work.

- ✔ If you're working on several documents at once, closing one makes another one appear on-screen in place of the document you just closed.

- ✔ You don't have to quit Word when you just want to start working on a new document.

Chapter 2

How Most Folks Use Word

In This Chapter

▶ Starting a new document in Word

▶ Typing tips

▶ Watching the screen

▶ Formatting

▶ Getting help

▶ Saving your document to disk

▶ Printing

▶ Closing your document

*T*he journey of 10,000 miles starts off with a single step. And if you have a bunion, then it's a single, painful step. You get the point: For everything you do, there are basic steps to take. From driving the car to changing a baby's diapers to dropping your car keys down a sewer grate, there are steps for everything. Word processing is no exception.

This chapter gives you the basic steps to take as you use Word every day. In fact, if this book were a pamphlet, this chapter would be it. (The rest of the book just offers more details and highly useful information, as well as justification for the hefty cover price.)

Overview (For the Impatient)

The Word word processing process goes like this:

1. **Start a new document in Word.**

2. **Type.**

3. **Format.**

4. **Save.**

5. **Preview.**

6. **Print.**

7. **Close.**

Everyone follows these steps in one way or another. A good Word user repeats Steps 2, 3, and 4, sometimes varying the order. (Most of the time you're typing in Word. Toward the end of the process you should start formatting, though many people format as they type.)

If you saved a document earlier and want to work on it again, replace Step 1 with "Open a document on disk." (See Chapter 8 for more information on the Open command.)

Steps 5 and 6 are only necessary when you're done and plan on printing your work. (Chapter 9 discusses Preview and Print.)

The rest of this chapter elaborates on these steps.

Starting a New Document

When Word starts, it presents you with a blank document, suitable for typing. Your next step, logically, is to type.

If you need to start a new document while you're already editing something in Word (such as when you're writing a letter to a friend and realize that you forgot to type up that urgent business letter), choose File⇨New from the menu. The new document appears in another window right inside of Word's main window, blank and ready for typing.

 ✔ Clicking the New button on the toolbar also starts up a new document should you need one in a hurry.

 ✔ See Chapter 10 for more information on working with more than one document in Word.

 ✔ Another way to start your work is to open a document on disk. (See Chapter 8, "Basic Document Tricks," for more information.) After the document is open, it appears in a window just like any other document you've created. Work away!

Typing (Or Hunting and Pecking)

Forget all the gizmos and fancy features! Most of your time in Word is spent typing.

> _Clackity-clack-clack-clack._

Go ahead, type away; let your fingers dance upon the keycaps! What you type appears on-screen, letter for letter — even derogatory stuff about the computer. (Your PC doesn't care, but that doesn't mean that Word lacks feelings.)

New text is inserted right in front of the blinking toothpick cursor. For example, you can type this line:

    Farming is the world's oldest profession.

To change this sentence, move the toothpick cursor to just after the _S_ in "world's." Type a space and the following text:

    second

The new text is inserted as you type, with any existing text marching off to the right (and even to the next line), happily making room.

The whole sentence should now read:

    Farming is the world's second oldest profession.

✔ Every character key you press on the keyboard produces a character on-screen. This fact holds true for all letter, number, and symbol keys. The other keys, mostly gray on your keyboard, do strange and wonderful things, which the rest of this book tries hard to explain.

✔ Don't be afraid to use your keyboard! Word always offers ample warning before anything serious happens. A handy Undo feature recovers anything you accidentally delete. See Chapter 4, "Basic Editing."

✔ The Shift key produces capital letters, just like on a typewriter (if you've ever used one).

✔ The Caps Lock key works like the Shift-Lock key on a typewriter. After you press that key, everything you type is in ALL CAPS.

✔ Sorry for all the typewriter analogies.

✔ The Caps Lock light on your keyboard comes on when you're in All Caps mode.

"Do I need to learn to type?"

No one needs to learn to type to use a word processor, but you'll do yourself a favor if you learn. My advice is to get a computer program that teaches you to type. I can recommend the *Mavis Beacon Teaches Typing* program, even

though I don't get any money from them. I just like the name "Mavis," I suppose.

Knowing how to type makes a painful experience like Word a wee bit more enjoyable.

✔ The number keys on the right side of the keyboard are on the numeric keypad. To use those keys, you must press the Num Lock key on your keyboard. If you don't, the keys take on their arrow key function. See Chapter 3, "Basic Movement."

✔ The Num Lock light on the keyboard comes on when you press the Num Lock key to turn the numeric keypad on. Most PCs start with this feature activated.

✔ If you're a former typewriter user, then you're probably pushing 40! Man you're old! Seriously, don't use the L or I key for a number one or the O (oh) key for a zero in a word processor. This is wrong. Please type **1** for the number one and **0** for the number zero.

✔ The world's oldest profession is most likely herding.

When to press that Enter key

Press the Enter key only when you reach the end of a paragraph.

No, that was too easy. Let me ramble on about this for a few more paragraphs:

The Enter key on your computer's keyboard does not work the same way as the Return key on a typewriter. Back in those days (when TV was black-and-white and Dad wore a hat to work), you pressed the Return key at the end of each line, usually after a "ding!" With a word processor, however, you don't need to do that.

For example, type the following text. Just type it all and don't bother pressing the Enter key, nope, not at all:

> In an effort to find the best typists in the universe, the
> Federation enlisted the help of 7th grade typing instructor
> Maxine Kornhieser. Traveling the galaxy, Ms. Kornhieser almost
> found the perfect match; the Dolesori of Plantax 9 could type
> rapidly with their 12 double-jointed fingers on each hand.
> Alas, the Dolesori lacked any backbone whatsoever and, thus,
> Ms. Kornhieser disapproved of their posture.

Notice how the text *wraps*? The last part of the text on the end of one line
moves down to the start of the next line. It's automatic! There's no "ding!" —
nor is there any need to press Enter at the end of the line.

Press Enter only at the end of a paragraph.

- ✔ This feature (wrapping text from one line to the next), is called "word wrap." It was something to boast about in the early days of the PC, but is totally accepted today.

- ✔ Some people end a paragraph with two presses of the Enter key; others use only one press. If it's extra space you want between paragraphs, you should use Word's paragraph formatting commands, as I describe in Chapter 12 of this book.

- ✔ Double-spacing your lines is *also* done with a paragraph formatting command. Do not press Enter if you want double-spacing! See Chapter 12, "Formatting Paragraphs," for more information.

- ✔ If you want to indent the next paragraph, press the Tab key after pressing Enter.

- ✔ If you press the Enter key in the middle of an existing paragraph, Word makes a new paragraph. The rest of your text moves to the beginning of the next line.

   This works like any other key inserted in your text. The difference is that you insert an Enter character, which creates two paragraphs where you had one before.

   The Enter key works like any other key — pressing it inserts an Enter character and creates two paragraphs where you had one before.

- ✔ You can delete the Enter character by using the Backspace or Delete keys. Removing Enter joins two paragraphs together or, if you press Enter more than once, cleans up any extra blank lines.

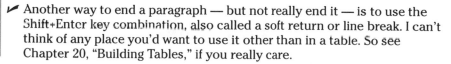

- ✔ Another way to end a paragraph — but not really end it — is to use the Shift+Enter key combination, also called a soft return or line break. I can't think of any place you'd want to use it other than in a table. So see Chapter 20, "Building Tables," if you really care.

When to whack the spacebar

You use the spacebar shown in Figure 2-1 to insert spaces between words or sentences. Unlike typing, in a word processor you put only one space between sentences. (If you're a touch-typist, this is a tough habit to break, but it's possible.)

Figure 2-1:
The spacebar.

The only peeve I have about the spacebar is that too often folks use spaces to line up columns of information or to indent. This is terribly wrong and, as those folks discover, the output on paper looks tawdry. Yes, cheap and tawdry.

Instead of using the spacebar to indent or line up text, use the Tab key. The Tab key is the best way to organize information on the screen. Unlike the spacebar, the Tab key indents text to an exact position so that when you print, everything lines up nice and neatly. (See Chapter 13, "Formatting Tabs," for more Tabby information.)

✔ Use that spacebar to put spaces between words and sentences.

✔ If you're a touch-typist, remember to put only one space between sentences when you're word processing.

✔ I hear that typing teachers still teach students to put two spaces between sentences. Hey: You're wrong. Get over it. The typewriter is dead. Okay? Move on. . . .

✔ Use the Tab key to indent or arrange text in columns.

✔ In fact, any time you're tempted to use more than two spaces in a row, use a Tab instead.

✔ The Romans couldn't put spaces between words on buildings because the Chiselers Union didn't know how to charge for it.

Things to notice whilst you type

Lots of interesting things go on while you type, some of which may puzzle you, others of which may annoy you, and a few that may cause you undue consternation.

The status bar

The first thing to notice while you type is the status bar at the bottom of the screen. The information there tells you something about your document and where you're typing in it. Figure 2-2 explains everything, although the only items I refer to are the Page (current page you're editing), and the total pages in document (the last number in item "C" in Figure 2-2).

A) Page the toothpick cursor is on

B) Ignore

C) Currently page/total pages in document

D) Toothpick cursor's position from the top of the page

E) Line on the page the toothpick cursor is on

F) Toothpick cursor's column, going left to right

Figure 2-2:
The meaning of the status bar.

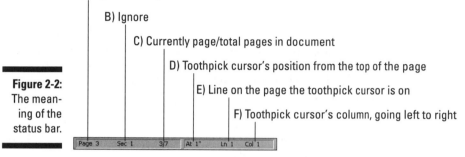

Page 3   Sec 1   3/7   At 1"   Ln 1   Col 1

That annoying line of dots

Occasionally, you see a row of dots stretching from one side of the screen to the other — like a line of ants in military school, marching straight across your screen. Don't spray 'em with bug killer!

···

That thing (shown above) marks the end of one page and the beginning of another. It's called a page break. The text you see above the ants, er, dots, is on the preceding page; text below the dots is on the next page.

To get a better idea of what the page break *really* looks like, switch from Normal view to Print Layout view: Choose View⇨Print Layout from the menu. Scroll your document up or down a few clicks to see the "real" page break. (Choose View⇨Normal to return to the normal — line-of-ants — view.)

✔ You cannot delete the line of dots. C'mon — what good would it even do? Think picnic: You sweep one trail of the little pests away and another trail instantaneously appears. It's insect magic!

✔ You can see how the line of dots works by looking at the scrambled statistics on the status bar. For example, when the toothpick cursor is above the dots, the status bar says Page 5 for page 5. When the cursor is below the dots, you see Page 6 for page 6.

✔ A row of dots close together — very friendly ants — marks a hard page break. The words Page Break even appear right in the middle of the line. This row of dots indicates a definite "I want a new page now" command given by the person who created the document. See Chapter 15, "Formatting Documents."

Spots between words!

There is no cause for alarm if you see spots — or dots — on-screen when you press the spacebar or Enter key — like this:

```
This•can•be•very•annoying.¶
```

What you see on your screen when your text looks like the preceding line are non-printing characters. These symbols represent spaces (produced by the spacebar), end-of-paragraph marks (the Enter key), and tabs (a tiny arrow, which isn't shown above).

The dots represent spaces (produced by the spacebar), the backwards *P* is an end-of-paragraph mark (made by the Enter key), and the tiny arrow at the beginning of the sentence is a tab symbol.

To turn the non-printing characters off, press the Ctrl+Shift+8 key combination. (Press it again to turn them on, if you're curious.) Use the 8 on the keyboard, not on the numeric keypad.

✔ The symbols show up on-screen but — fortunately — not in a printed document.

✔ Displaying the non-printing characters makes things such as rogue spaces and tabs easier to see and, therefore, delete.

✔ A good way to clean up rogue spaces in a document is to use the AutoFormat command. Refer to Chapter 18 for some automatic formatting tricks.

Red and green squiggly wigglies

If you make any typos or spelling mistakes in Word, you see them underlined with a wavy red line. That's Word's annoying real-time spell checker in action.

To "fix" the spelling error, right-click the offending word. A pop-up list of corrections or suggestions appears, from which you can choose the proper word. In Figure 2-3, I right-clicked on a poorly-spelled word and got a pop-up menu of proper choices. (Well, actually one choice, but you get the idea.)

Figure 2-3:
Right-click
misspelled
words to
correct
them.

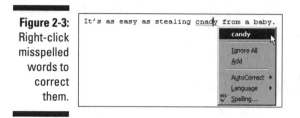

Another squiggly line alerting you to the fact that you're an adult and yet you still don't understand your native tongue, is the green squiggly line. That's more pesky than the red one. Green means a grammar mistake — at least according to Word it does.

I ignore the green squiggly lines. In fact, you can turn to Chapter 7 "Minding Your P's and Q's," to learn how to turn off or adjust grammar checking. (Unlike spell-checking, I think grammar checking is more of a suggestion than an absolute rule.)

Watch the dog (Office Assistant)!

As you type, the Office Assistant does various interesting things, which you may find amusing. In fact, if you wait too long while reading or composing your thoughts, you may notice the Office Assistant going to sleep (see the dog in the margin). That's a good clue that you should stop staring off into space and get back to work!

Oops! I made a boo-boo!

If you make a mistake, press the Backspace key to back up and erase. This key is named Backspace on your keyboard, or it may have a long, left-pointing arrow on it: ←.

Pressing and holding down the Backspace key puts you in Rapid Consumption mode — a whole lotta characters to the left of the blinking toothpick cursor are erased — until you release the backspace key.

The Delete key also gobbles characters, though it deletes the character to the *right* of the blinking toothpick cursor.

For even larger boo-boos *(el boo-boo grande),* Word has an Undo key. It doesn't erase text, but it helps you yank back text you accidentally erase. See Chapter 4, "Basic Editing," for more Undo information.

Formatting Your Document

Formatting is what makes your document look professional and not like it came from a vintage 1960 government mimeograph. There are several things you can format in your document:

- Characters
- Paragraphs
- Tabs
- The entire document
- Pages
- Columns
- Headers and Footers

Your primary duty in word processing is to get down the text. After that, you'll typically go back and format, changing the text style or adjusting the margins. This is all covered in Part II of this book.

- Word can format your document for you. I describe how in Chapter 18.

- Most folks format text as they type, adding italics or bold or whatever. You can also format paragraphs as you write, although some major formatting chores are best done *after* you write your text. (Examples of both techniques are shown in Part II.)

- Word also lets you format your document by adding drawings, pictures, lines, tables, columns or other elements that can really make things look snazzy. Parts IV and V cover those topics.

Getting Help from the Office Assistant

There's a reason you have a dog (or whatever) standing there in your document. The dog is there to help. And he never needs to be taken for a walk or fed dog food. Such a deal.

To get help from the dog, press the F1 key. A cartoon bubble appears over the dog's head, asking "What would you like to do?" Type in your question, as shown in Figure 2-4. Press the Enter key and the dog answers your question:

Bark! Woof! Woof! Woooooooff!

Figure 2-4:
Ask the dog
a question.

Seriously, a list of potential answers appears in the dog's cartoon bubble. For example, if you type "How do I save this document in WordPerfect format?" the dog shows you a list of possible answers, among which you may find "Convert between Word and WordPerfect." Clicking that answer tells you how to accomplish the task.

- ✔ If you don't see the dog — or any Office Assistant for that matter — choose Help⇨Show the Office Assistant from the menu.

- ✔ Hopefully you'll end up using this book more than you'll use the dog.

- ✔ Oh, and I know there are other Office Assistant characters. I'm just partial to the dog.

- ✔ If the dog doesn't know the answer, it says "I don't know what you mean. Please rephrase your question." That happens when you make unrealistic requests, like "fetch."

Save Your Stuff!

The computer is dumb. The computer is forgetful. And it loses things. To help the computer remember, you must tell it to save your stuff. Everything you create in Word should be saved to disk; stored there as a document.

 To save a document to disk, choose the File⇨Save command, Alt+F+S. (You can also click the Save button, which looks like a wee li'l disk, on the Standard toolbar.)

If you're saving your document for the first time, the Save As dialog box appears, as shown in Figure 2-5.

Save As

Save in:	My Documents

History

My Documents

Desktop

Favorites

Web Folders

Audio
Font Stowage
Graphics
Great American Novel
My Pictures
Personal
Temporary
Video
Work
Arlene is a creep
Alldone
beedy eyes
Delorian for sale
Envelope
Gross jokes

Letter
Letter to laywer
my trip
Nasty
Old Excel Documents
r
Test
Work

File name: Maxine goes to Plantax

Save as type: Word Document

Save

Cancel

Figure 2-5:
The Save As
dialog box.

Type a name for your document in the `File Name` area. The name `Maxine goes to Plantax` is shown in Figure 2-5. If you make a mistake typing, use the Backspace key to back up and erase.

Click the Save button to save your document.

✔ Chapter 8, "Basic Document Tricks," discusses saving your document in more detail.

✔ The filename is how you recognize the file later, when you want to edit or print it again.

✔ The fastest way to save a file is to use the keyboard. The Save file key combination is Ctrl+S. Press and hold the Ctrl (Control) key and press the S key. If you can pick up a basketball with one hand, you can also use the Shift+F12 key combo.

✔ When you save a document, watch the status bar — it temporarily displays a message telling you that Word is saving your document (or fast saving, for our Frequent Fliers).

✔ The dog tells you when you enter a forbidden filename. Click OK and try again, heeding the dog's advice.

✔ After the document is saved to disk, you see its name displayed on the window's title bar. This display is your clue that your document has been saved to disk.

✔ If you're not in a clever mood, you may decide to name your file with the name of a file already on disk. This decision is a boo-boo because the newer file overwrites the other file with the same name already on disk. For example, if you decide to save your new letter by using the LETTER filename and LETTER already exists on disk, the new file overwrites the old one. There is no way to get the original back, so use another, more clever name instead. The dog warns you with this message:

```
Do you want to replace the existing whatever?
```

Click the No button. Use another name.

Getting It Down on Paper (Printing)

The great authors didn't worry about printing. Tolstoy never had to save his document or use print preview. Hugo wrote *Les Misérables* on paper, so "printing" was what he did as he wrote. And Mark Twain, who wrote *The Adventures of Tom Sawyer* on that newfangled typewriter, thought he was pretty high tech. And you?

Printing is the end result of your word processing labors. Hercules? He had to retrieve some gal's girdle. You? You have to print your document. Everything looks nice and tidy on paper — almost professional.

First, preview your printing

 To see what your document will look like without wasting valuable paper, use the Print Preview command. Choose File⇨Print Preview or click the handy Print Preview button on the toolbar.

Figure 2-6 shows you what Print Preview mode looks like. Your document is shown exactly as it will print, including any pictures, headers or footers or other items that might not show up properly when you're editing.

Okay. It looks good. Click the Close button to return to your document for editing or printing.

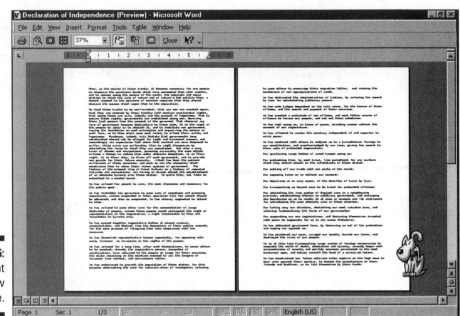

Figure 2-6:
Print
Preview
mode.

Time to print

To print your document in Word — the document you see on-screen, all of it —
do the following:

1. **Make sure that your printer is on and ready to print.**

   Refer to Chapter 9 for additional information about preparing the printer
   if you need to.

2. **Choose the File⇨Print command.**

   The Print dialog box opens. This is the place where printing and related
   activities happen.

3. **Click the OK button.**

   The document comes out of your printer.

   • You can also summon the Print dialog box by pressing Alt+F+P, or
     Ctrl+P. This method is more desirable if you have long fingers or do
     needlepoint or if the mouse is off eating the cheese again.

   • Chapter 9, "Getting It Down on Paper," provides detailed informa-
     tion about printing, including information about making sure that
     your printer is ready to print.

   • Notice that saving comes before printing. It doesn't have to, but I'm
     a stickler for saving, saving, saving your document.

Close 'er Up

To close a document when you're done, choose the File➪Close command (Ctrl+W). This step closes the document window and makes it vanish from the screen. Zzzipp! (Although you have to say "Zzipp!" when you do this; Word is strangely mute on the point.) This step is covered succinctly in Chapter 1, see the section "How to Quit What You're Doing Without Quitting Word" for all the details.

✔ Why close a document? Because you're done working on it! Maybe you want to work on something else or quit Word after closing. The choices are yours, and they're explained in the next section.

✔ If you try to close a document before it has been saved, Word displays a warning dialog box. Click the Yes button to save your document. If you want to continue editing, click the Cancel button and get back to work.

✔ If you are working on only one document and you close it, Word looks like it's vacated the premises; toolbars and menus disappear, as do scroll bars and other screen debris. Don't panic; you've just closed a document and Word has little else to do. Word sits patiently and waits for your next command.

✔ If you're done with Word, then quit. Otherwise, you can start working on another document. Refer to "Starting a New Document," earlier in this chapter.

You don't have to quit Word when you just want to start working on a new document.

Chapter 3

Basic Movement

• •

In This Chapter

▶ Moving the toothpick cursor

▶ Using key combinations to move up, down, top, bottom and you get the idea

▶ Using the Go To command

▶ Finding your place when you're lost

▶ Bookmarking memorable bits o' text

▶ Using the secret scroll bar buttons

• •

On the planet Jones, there lived a people without any bones. They did not talk nor make a sound, they were just puddles of pudding, rolling slowly around.

*W*riting means rewriting, which means there will be times when you're just perusing your document. If you need a mental image, picture a typewriter with only one long sheet of paper. To reread your document, you would have to rewind it back through the platen until you found the part you wanted. Ugh. What a chore!

Fortunately, Word has some basic toothpick cursor movement commands that let you scroll, read, or edit through your document much easier than cranking a knob. It's all about movement! Exercise! Be active, not like the roly-poly planet Jones people.

Moving Around Your Document

When you scribble on a pad of paper, it's hard to lose your place. And in the old typewriter days, a page of paper was only so big. But with Word, your documents can be downright humongous. Unfortunately, only a small part of that humongousness appears on your computer screen at a time. To get from one place to another, you need to do more than just press the arrow keys. You need to find out about Word's navigation keys and other special commands you can use to get around in your document.

Going hither, thither, and yon (basic arrow keys)

The most common way to move about in your document is to press the arrow keys, which are also called the *cursor-control keys* because they control the toothpick cursor on-screen. These keys can be used alone or with other keys on your keyboard to zippity-zap the toothpick cursor all over your document.

If you use the arrow keys on the numeric keypad, make sure that the Num Lock light is off. Do this by pressing the Num Lock key. If you don't do this, you see numbers in your text instead of the toothpick cursor dancing all over. Like444this.

The four basic arrow keys move the toothpick cursor up, down, right, and left:

Key	What It Does
↑	Moves the cursor up to the preceding line of text
↓	Moves the cursor down to the next line of text
→	Moves the cursor right to the next character
←	Moves the cursor left to the preceding character

If you press and hold the Ctrl (Control) key and then press an arrow key, the toothpick cursor jumps more than one character. This is cursor afterburner mode, used mostly by the desperately quick.

Press These Keys	To Do This
Ctrl+↑	Moves the cursor up to the start of the previous paragraph
Ctrl+↓	Moves the cursor down to the start of the next paragraph
Ctrl+→	Moves the cursor right to the start (first letter) of the previous word
Ctrl+←	Moves the cursor left to the start (first letter) of the next word

Use the Ctrl key with the arrow key in the same way that you use the Shift key with the *s* key to get a capital *S:* Press and hold the Ctrl key and then press an arrow key. Release both keys. You don't have to press hard.

✔ When the toothpick cursor is on the top line of the document window (the top line of text) and you try to move it up, your document scrolls to reveal the preceding line of text. If you're already at the top line of your document, the computer beeps at you, and the cursor stays in place and blinks with that special look it reserves for the numb-brained.

✔ When the cursor is on the last line of the screen and you press the down-arrow key, the document scrolls up to reveal the next line of text, if there is one. Otherwise, BEEP! This annoys the Office Assistant, so try not to do it.

✔ If the cursor has nowhere to go, Word bleeps at you. Annoyed? Turn to Chapter 29 to find out how to turn the sound off.

✔ Moving the cursor does not erase characters; using the Backspace and Delete keys erases characters (among other things discussed later in this chapter).

✔ The word "yon" was used in English as another form of the word "there." Here is here, there is there, and yon is like "there," but farther off. It's short for *yonder.*

Making that toothpick cursor skedaddle (moving by great leaps and bounds)

Not all your fingers are the same length. Look at them right now! See how some are shorter and some are longer? The short ones are probably that way because you press the arrow keys on your keyboard in an improper manner. So distasteful, because there's no reason to continually press the arrow keys. There are better ways to jump around a document.

Instead of woodpeckering your keyboard, try using some of the arrow key (and non–arrow key) combinations in the following sections to really make that toothpick cursor fly around your document.

Paging Mr. PgUp and Mr. PgDn!

PgUp is keyboard language for Page Up. And PgDn is keyboard language for Page Down. Your keyboard has both sets of keys: keyboard language PgUp and PgDn on the numeric keypad and Page Up and Page Down on the cursor area (to the left of the keypad). Isn't that nice?

One would think, logically, that the Page Up set of keys moves a document up one page and that the Page Down set of keys moves a document down. 'Tain't so, though. Rather than slide your document around a page at a time, these keys move things one *screen* at a time.

You'll get used to this illogic, if you're not already.

PgUp   The PgUp key moves the toothpick cursor up one screen. Or, if you're at the tippy-top of your document, this key moves you to the top of the screen.

PgDn   Moves the cursor down one screen or to the end of the document, if you happen to be there, or to the end of the document if you happen to be less than a screen away.

Ctrl+PgUp   Moves to the first line in the previous page. Note that pages of text are larger than one screen typically shows.

Ctrl+PgDn   Moves the toothpick cursor to the first line on the next page.

If you're just interested in moving to the top or bottom of the screen (the text displayed in Word's window), use these weirdoes:

Ctrl+Alt+PgUp   Moves the cursor to the top of the current screen

Ctrl+Alt+PgDn   Moves the cursor to the bottom of the current screen

There is no logic in the computer industry.

Beginnings and endings

Up/down, top/bottom, begin/end — sometimes you just need to get right there. These are the keys that do it — and they're named surprisingly well:

Key or Combination	Where It Puts Your Cursor
End	This key sends the toothpick cursor to the end of a line of text.
Home	This key sends the toothpick cursor to the start of a line of text.
Ctrl+End	This key combination whisks the toothpick cursor to the very, very end of your document.
Ctrl+Home	This key combination takes you to the very tippy-top of your document. Zoom!

Some keyboard thoughts for you to ruminate upon:

- ✔ There's no key like Home.

- ✔ You can use the Ctrl+End keyboard shortcut to get a feel for how big your document is. Press Ctrl+End and then look at the numbers on the status bar. You can see which page you're on, how far down the page you are, which line you're on, and which column you're in. Feel satisfied. Feel accomplished. Take a moment to gloat.

- ✔ Ctrl+End is an easy key combination to mistakenly press. It throws you — literally — to the end of your document. If you do this and feel that you have boo-booed, press Shift+F5, the Go Back keyboard shortcut, to return from whence you came (that is, back to your previous edit). Also see "Going Back," later in this chapter.

Other ways to move around

The mouse provides a quick and easy way to move the toothpick cursor: First, spy a new location for the cursor on-screen. Then move the mouse pointer to where you want the cursor to be and click. The cursor relocates there instantly.

You can also move about in your document by using the vertical scroll bar. You can scroll up and down, drag the elevator button, or click in funny places to view different parts of your document. But watch out! Scrolling the screen does not make the cursor flippity-jibbit all over. You must *click the mouse* in the text to actually move the cursor to a given spot.

- ✔ You must click the mouse to move the cursor to that spot. If you don't click the mouse, you're just messing with the computer's mind.

- ✔ If you click the elevator button in the scroll bar, you get a pop-up bubble in your document (as shown in Figure 3-1) telling you which page you'll land on if you release the mouse. If you're clever enough to use Word's heading styles, you also see the headings in your document.

- ✔ See Chapter 12, "Formatting Paragraphs," for more information on heading styles.

Figure 3-1:
An informa-
tive bubble.

Page: 6
The Shotgun Wedding

Wheeling around your document with the Intellimouse

If your PC sports one of the new "wheel" mice, such as the Microsoft Intellimouse, then you can scroll through your document using the center wheel button:

Roll the wheel up or down to scroll your document up or down.

If you press the wheel button down, you can drag the mouse up or down to smooth-scroll your document up or down. The farther you drag up or down, the faster the scrolling action.

Going Here or There with the Go To Command

Ah, one more time-saving tip: Suppose you need to get to page 14? Well, if you're on page one, you can: A) use the scroll bar's elevator button to find it, B) press Ctrl+PgDn to get there in 14 strokes, C) press the → key 14,000 times, or D) use the Go To command.

Yes, Go To fits the bill.

Go To, as in the Shakespearean "Getteth thee outta hereth," enables you to go directly to just about wherever in the document you want to be. The Go To command lets you find a specific page number, line, or what-have-you in your document.

To use the Go To command, choose Edit⇨Go To (or press Alt, E, G), and the Go To tab of the Find and Replace dialog box appeareth before thine eyes (see Figure 3-2).

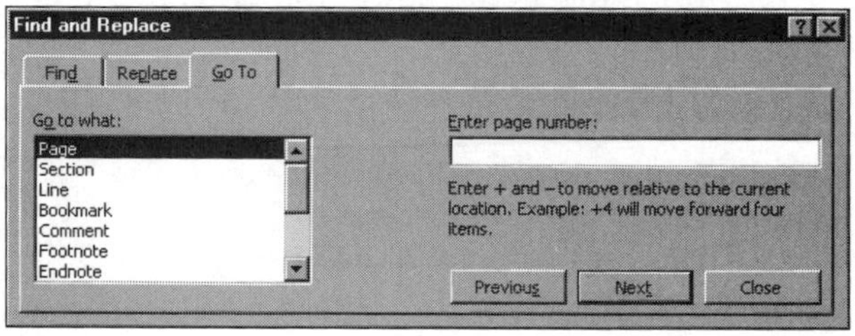

Figure 3-2:
The Go To part of the Find and Replace dialog box.

There are a lot of places you can go to, as the confusing items in the Go To What list in Figure 3-2 demonstrate. Usually, though, you'll want to go to a specific page number.

Type a page number into the Enter Page Number box.

For example, type **14** in the box and press Enter, and you go to page 14. That's supposing you have a page 14 to go to.

✔ You can also press the F5 key to open the Go To tab of the Find and Replace dialog box.

✔ Heck, you can also press the Ctrl+G keyboard shortcut. (Makes more sense than F5, anyway.)

✔ If you click twice on the page number on the status bar (muttering "Change, you idiot. Change, change," while you do this helps), the Go To dialog box appears like a genie out of a lamp.

✔ To be even more specific in your Go To commands, see "Bookmarking without Dog-Earing Your Monitor (The Bookmark Command)," later in this chapter.

Going Back

They say that once you commit, there's no going back. That is, unless you're running for office or using Word. If you go anywhere you don't want to be, press Shift+F5, and Word carries you back to where you started.

The Shift+F5 keyboard shortcut works only in Word; you can't use this command in real life.

Pressing Shift+F5 returns you to where you were before; pressing it again takes you back to where you were before that. This keyboard shortcut works about three times before it starts repeating itself. Repeating itself. Repeating itself.

Bookmarking without Dog-Earing Your Monitor (The Bookmark Command)

Do you ever encounter this situation: You're working away on great stuff, but you need to wander off elsewhere in your document for a sec? My brain works that way. I can't do one thing at a time. So I'm here. I'm there. And I have this itch on my back between my shoulder blades. What's a boy from El Cajon, California, to do?

Yes! It's the highly useful Bookmark command.

Setting a bookmark

To mark your place in your document, set a bookmark. Follow these steps:

1. **Put the toothpick cursor where you want to place a bookmark.**

2. **Choose the Insert⇨Bookmark command (or, if you have three hands, try Ctrl+Shift+F5).**

   The Bookmark dialog box opens, as shown in Figure 3-3.

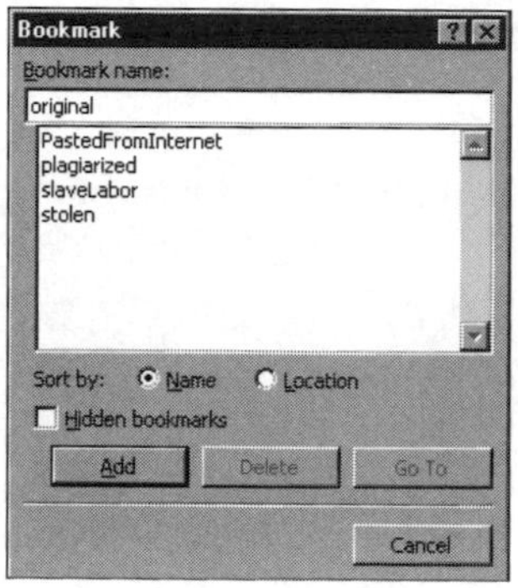

Figure 3-3:
The
Bookmark
dialog box.

3. **Type a name for the bookmark.**

   Be clever! The name reminds you of where you are in your document. So if you're creating a term paper, memorable flags for various parts of your document (and their original sources) would be proper.

   By the way, bookmark names cannot contain spaces. However, you can use unique capitalization if you like, as shown in Figure 3-3.

4. **Press Enter or click the Add button.**

Finding a bookmark and moving to that spot in your document

To return to a bookmark, use the Go To command, as covered in "Going Here or There with the Go To Command," earlier in this chapter. These steps keep you from turning the page and losing your train of thought:

1. **Press the F5 key.**

   The Find and Replace dialog box splats across your screen.

2. **Highlight Bookmark in the Go To What list.**

   Bookmark is the fourth item down.

   The Enter Page Number box changes to read Enter Bookmark Name. Your most recent bookmark appears in that space.

   If you don't see your bookmark, click the down-arrow and you see a long list of bookmarks in your document. Click the one you want.

3. **Click the Go To button.**

   You're there!

4. **Click the Close button to get rid of the Find and Replace dialog box and return to editing your document.**

Using Secret Scroll Bar Buttons to Navigate

Lurking at the bottom of the vertical scroll bar you find three buttons, as shown in the margin. These are the *browse* buttons, which allow you to scroll through your document in leaps and bounds of various sizes.

The top button is the *Browse Up* button.

The bottom button is the *Browse Down* button.

And the center button is the *What The Heck Am I Browsing For?* button.

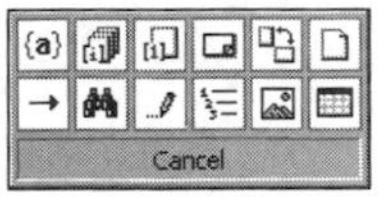

Figure 3-4:
Various
things to
browse for.

When you click the center button, a pop-up palette of things to browse for appears, as shown in Figure 3-4. Pointing the mouse at any one of the items displays text that explains the item in the bottom part of the palette.

Normally, the page item is selected (see margin). That means clicking the Browse Up or Browse Down buttons jumps you back or ahead in your document one page at time.

Choose another item to browse up or down to that item, though I'll admit that most of the items seem rather obscure:

If you're using heading styles (as described in Chapter 12, "Formatting Paragraphs"), you can click the Browse by Heading icon; click the tiny 1-2-3 picture. Clicking the up or down browse button then takes you to the preceding or next heading in your document.

The tiny pencil icon allows you to use the browse buttons to visit the various places you've been editing in your document. (My editor loves that one.) Click the up or down browse button to visit the spots where you've just made some changes.

The most useful way to put the Browse buttons to work is when you use the Find command (covered in Chapter 5, "Search for This, Replace it with That"). Clicking the Browse Down button finds the next occurrence of text in your document — which is handy if you're doing complex editing and need to move quickly without summoning the bothersome Find dialog box again.

The rest of these options are typically used by people who really know what they're doing. If you're just starting out, refer back here later.

Chapter 4

Basic Editing

● ●

In This Chapter

▶ Using Insert or Overtype modes

▶ Deleting text with Backspace and Deleting

▶ Deleting lines, sentences and paragraphs

▶ Undoing your mistakes

▶ Using Redo (un-undo) command

● ●

This chapter covers basic editing. Typing is only half the job of getting the words on paper (or phosphor or whatever is the word-processing equivalent). Beyond that you need to play with your text, retype, delete, and undo. Those are the basic editing tasks you'll find in the text that follows (which I typed, retyped, overtyped, and undid many times over).

To Insert or to Overtype: That Is the Question

Betcha didn't know that Word is usually in Insert mode. That means that any new text you type is inserted just before the blinking toothpick cursor. The new stuff pushes any existing text to the right and down as you type. This is Insert mode.

Insert mode's evil twin is Overtype mode. In Overtype mode, all the text you type overwrites the existing text on-screen, replacing it as you go.

To switch to Overtype mode, press the Insert key on your keyboard. Either the key labeled "Insert" or the Ins key on the numeric keypad (with Num Lock off) does the trick.

When you're in Overtype mode, the three letters OVR are highlighted on the status bar. In fact, you can double-click those letters to switch between Insert and Overtype mode.

Honestly, there is no reason to type in Overtype mode. Insert mode is fine by itself; you can use the various commands in this chapter to delete text at your whim.

✔ In Overtype mode, new text gobbles up text already on the screen. If you see this weirdness happen, double-click the OVR thing on the status bar to stop it, and then use the Ctrl+Z (Undo) keyboard shortcut to yank back any deleted text.

✔ So the answer to this section's title is that Insert mode is the answer.

Deleting Stuff

I knew a writer who was utterly afraid to delete *anything*. Instead of tossing out the random paragraph or two, he'd merely copy the paragraphs as *blocks* and move them to the end of the document for "safe keeping." Yeah. And if he eventually becomes the next Bill Shakespeare, then posterity will have all those discarded blocks of text to marvel over. Aren't we lucky?

The truth is, deleting text is a part of the editing process just like writing. Everyone edits and everyone deletes text. In fact, I'm fond of saying you can probably delete the opening paragraph of any first draft you do. If that's your urge, or if even deleting small stuff is in order, this part of the book is the right place to come.

The truth is, deleting text is as much a part of the editing process as writing is.

✔ It's said that Isaac Asimov never did second drafts of anything. That's not to say he didn't go back and self-edit, just that he was probably a lot better at writing than most folks I know.

✔ Moving blocks is covered in Chapter 6, "Working with Blocks of Text."

Your basic delete keys: Backspace and Delete

You can use two keys on the keyboard to delete single characters of text:

- ✔ Backspace key: Deletes the character to the left of the toothpick cursor.

- ✔ Delete key: Deletes the character to the right of the toothpick cursor.

```
Soon after, the Co|lonel put his finger in his ear and plucked
out the largest plum any of us had ever seen.
```

In the preceding line, the toothpick cursor is "flashing" (okay, it *would* be flashing on a computer screen) between the *o* and the *l* in "Colonel." Pressing the Backspace key deletes the *o* in "Colonel"; pressing the Delete key deletes the *l.*

- ✔ After deleting a character, any text to the right or below the character moves up to fill the void.

- ✔ If you're in Overtype mode, the Backspace key still pulls the rest of the text to the right.

- ✔ Backspace doesn't work like the Backspace key on a typewriter. The difference is that when you press Backspace in Word, the cursor backs up and *erases.* (The Word equivalent of the typewriter's Backspace key is the left-arrow key.)

- ✔ You can press and hold Backspace or Delete to continuously "machine-gun delete" characters. Release the key to stop your wanton destruction.

The backspace-blip phenomenon

One day, maybe not today, but soon, you will press the Backspace key and encounter an audible complaint from Word. *Blip!* That's Word's childlike reaction to something it doesn't like. You press Backspace and you get blip and not a deleted character. Whassup?

The blipping is Word's way of warning you. What you're trying to do is delete a special character or a secret code inserted into your document. Word is being nice by letting you know you're about to clobber something special. It's a good warning.

If you're really desperate to delete the character or secret code, press the ← key and then press the Delete key. No blip. Or you can press Shift+← (to select the forbidden character), then press Backspace.

And if you goof things up, remember you can press the Ctrl+Z key combination to undo your boo-boo.

Deleting a word

Word has two commands that gobble up an entire word:

- ✔ Ctrl+Backspace deletes the word that is in front (to the left) of the cursor.
- ✔ Ctrl+Delete deletes the word that is behind (to the right) of the cursor.

To delete a word by using Ctrl+Backspace, position the cursor at the last letter of the word. Press Ctrl+Backspace, and the word is gone! The cursor then sits at the end of the preceding word or the beginning of the line (if you deleted the first word in a paragraph).

To delete a word by using Ctrl+Delete, position the cursor at the first letter of the word. Press Ctrl+Delete, and the word is gone. The cursor then sits at the beginning of the next word or the end of the line (if you deleted the last word in a paragraph).

Unfortunately, if you're in the middle of the word, then these commands only delete from that middle point to the start or end of the word. Therefore, I bestow the following trick:

To delete a word, the whole word and nothing but the word, point the mouse at the offending critter and double-click the mouse button. This selects the entire word, highlighting it on the screen. Press the Delete key to zap the word away.

After deleting the text, Word neatly wraps up the remaining text, snuggling it together in a grammatically proper way.

- ✔ No mere pencil eraser can match Ctrl+Delete or Ctrl+Backspace for sheer speed and terror.
- ✔ If the cursor is positioned anywhere in the middle of a word, Ctrl+Backspace deletes everything from where the cursor is to the last letter of the preceding word.
- ✔ If the cursor is positioned anywhere in the middle of a word, the Ctrl+Delete command deletes everything from where the cursor is to the first letter of the next word.

Deleting lines, sentences, and paragraphs

In Word there is a difference between a line of text, a sentence, and a paragraph.

✔ A line of text is merely a line across the page (not really a grammatical thing at all). The Ln indicator in the status bar tells you which *line* of text you're on, as measured from the top of the page. For example, right now Word tells me I'm editing line 25. Whatever.

✔ A sentence is a sentence. You know: Start with a capital letter and end with a period, question mark, or exclamation point. You probably learned this in grammar school, which is why they call it *grammar* school anyway.

✔ A paragraph is a bunch of text ending with a press of the Enter key. So a paragraph can be one line of text, a sentence, or several sentences.

And just who cares? Well, this all comes into play when you want to delete various bits of text. There are different ways to delete lines, sentences, and paragraphs.

Deleting a line of text

Word has no single command for deleting a line of text from the keyboard. But with the mouse, deleting a line is only a matter of a click and a key press. Follow these steps:

1. **Move the mouse into the left margin of your document.**

   The cursor changes into an arrow pointing northeast rather than northwest. The winds of change are a-blowin'. . . .

2. **Point the mouse pointer arrow at the line of text you want to obliterate.**

3. **Click the left mouse button.**

   The line of text is highlighted, or selected.

4. **Press the Delete key to send that line into the void.**

When the mouse cursor is pointing northeast, you can drag it down the left margin and select as many lines of text as you care to. All the lines can then be deleted with one stroke of the Delete key.

Also see Chapter 6 on marking text as a block and then blowing it to Kingdom Come.

Deleting a sentence

Making a sentence go bye-bye is cinchy. Well, you could just press the Delete key once for each character in the sentence. But, as with everything in a computer, there's always a better, easier way:

1. **Place the toothpick cursor firmly in the midst of the offending sentence.**

   Click.

2. **Press the F8 key thrice.**

   Pressing the F8 key once turns on *extended selection mode,* which is covered in Chapter 6, "Working with Blocks of Text." Pressing F8 twice selects a word, and pressing it thrice selects a sentence.

3. **Press the Delete key.**

   Oomph! It's gone.

Pressing the F8 key three times highlights (selects) a sentence.

If you change your mind, press the Esc key. That cancels extended selection mode. Press any arrow key or click the mouse in your text to unhighlight.

Deleting a paragraph

There are two, nay, *three* ways to mark a paragraph for destruction:

- ✔ **The triple-click method.** Click the mouse three times on the paragraph. Click-click-click. Be quick about the triple click. That highlights the paragraph, and a deft press of the Delete key mooches it off the page.

- ✔ **The F8, F8, F8, F8 method.** You can also select and delete a paragraph by placing the toothpick cursor in the paragraph and pressing the F8 key fourice, er, four times. Press the Delete key and — presto! — vaporized text!

- ✔ **The northeast cursor/double-click method.** If you're fond of the northeast-pointing mouse, move the mouse pointer into the left column on the page (where it turns into the northeast pointer) and then double-click. The paragraph to the right of the mouse cursor is selected and primed for deletion with a quick tap of the Delete key.

Deleting odd shapes with blocks

Word can delete characters, words, and lines with nifty, specific commands. To delete anything else, you have to mark it as a block of text and then delete the block.

Refer to Chapter 6, "Working with Blocks of Text" for more information on marking a block of text. After any block is marked in your document, pressing the Delete key removes it. (If only getting rid of warts were so easy....)

Erase Your Mistakes with Undo Haste

Now mark me how I will undo myself. —Richard II, William Shakespeare

Be bold! Why not? Word has a handy Undo command. The Undo command remembers the last several things you added or deleted and quite easily unravels any mistakes you made. Furthermore, there's a Redo command, which is essentially Undo-Undo, though that's a double-negative, and it hurts my brain to think about it.

The blessed Undo command

To undelete any text you just accidentally zapped, do any of the following:

- Press Ctrl+Z.
- Choose Edit⇔Undo with the mouse.
- Click the Undo tool on the toolbar.

 These are all methods of grasping for the Undo command, though the quickest way to undo something is to press the Ctrl+Z key combination.

- When you choose Edit⇔Undo, the last action you did is undone; if you choose Edit⇔Undo again, you undo whatever you did before that.
- Unlike other programs, using the Undo command in Word twice doesn't undo your last undo. (Does that makes sense?)
- The Undo item in the Edit menu changes to pertain to whatever needs undoing: Undo Bold, Undo Typing, Undo Boo-boo, and so on.
- If you're annoyed by the sound the Undo command makes (and I ponder how strange that seems . . . but anyway), refer to Chapter 29, "Modifying Word's Appearance," to discover how to turn the darn sound off.
- To undo an Undo, choose Redo. See the section "Redo, or take two" a couple of sections from now.

Undoing stuff you did a while back

Because the Undo command remembers several things you just did, you can select any one of them individually for undoing. You do this by clicking the down-arrow next to the Undo button on the standard toolbar. There you find a brief and terse list of actions that Word remembers and can undo. Select any one of them for undoing, but keep in mind that they're out of sequence. To undo everything up to a point, select the action that you want as well as everything above it. Or just keep whacking Ctrl+Z until something looks familiar to you.

Can't Undo? Here's why . . .

Sometimes it eats you alive that Word can't undo an action. On the menu bar, you even see the message `Can't Undo`. What gives?

Essentially, whatever action you just did, Word can't undo it. This result can be true for a number of reasons: There is nothing to undo; not enough memory is available to undo; Word can't undo because what you did was too complex; Word just forgot; Word hates you; and so on.

I know that it's frustrating, but everyone has to live with it.

Redo, or take two

If you undo something and — whoops! — you didn't mean to, you must use the Redo command to set things back. To undelete any text you just accidentally zapped, do any of the following:

- ✔ Press Ctrl+Y.
- ✔ Choose Edit⇨Redo with the mouse.
- ✔ Click the Redo tool on the toolbar (if it's there).

How does would this work? Well, pretend that Earl stops by your office to bug you and sits his big old butt on your keyboard. He chats for a while and then leaves. You notice that his butt did some typing you don't like. So you use the Undo keyboard shortcut a few times:

Ctrl+Z

Ctrl+Z

Ctrl+Z

But — whoops! — you pressed one Ctrl+Z too many times. In that case, use the Edit⇨Redo command (or Ctrl+Y) to yank back the stuff you just undid.

- ✔ Honestly, no one uses the Redo command that much. If you do, you'll find it can be very frustrating because it tends to redo things you really wanted undone in the first place. (You'll understand this if you ever use Redo several times in a row.)
- ✔ The Redo button on the toolbar may not be visible. I urge you to rearrange your toolbars, which I cover in Chapter 29, "Modifying Word's Appearance."

✔ Like the Undo command, the Redo command has a button on the Standard toolbar. Next to the button is a down-arrow, which you can click to review the last few things you just undid. Or re-did. Or katydid. Oy.

✔ If there's nothing to redo, the Redo command becomes the Repeat command. See the section "The Repeat Key," covered in Chapter 10, "Tips from a Word Guru."

Chapter 5

Search for This, Replace It with That

Dear computer on my desk, find my brother (the little pest). Then change him, PC, into something I can use: A car. A tool. Or some new basketball shoes.

Ah! The miracle of search and replace. Well, actually, in Word it's called *find* and replace. That's because the word *find* starts with an F and Ctrl+F activates the Find (Search) command. (That still doesn't explain why Ctrl+V means Paste, but I digress. . . .)

Touted as a glorious feature in the mid-1980s, Search and Replace is one of the handiest tools your word processor offers. Imagine: Little Bo Peep could instantly find her sheep and replace them with jackhammers. (But her neighbors would never get any sleep, so they'd put Bo Peep in the slammer.)

Look What I Found!

Word can quickly locate any tidbit of text anywhere in your document, from a bombastic oratory down to the tiniest iota of plot. The command used to find text is called, surprisingly enough, the Find command. It dwells in the Edit menu. Follow these steps to use the Find command and locate text lurking in your document:

1. **Think of some text you want to find.**

   Uncle Cedric's will runs 20 pages. You want to quickly check to see whether Cousin Julia is mentioned. The Find command can locate her name instantly.

2. **Choose the Edit⇨Find command.**

   You see the Find and Replace dialog box, shown in Figure 5-1. Notice that this dialog box is also used for Replacing text and the Go To command, as indicated by the tabs. But you want to find text, so the Find tab is up front. Good.

Figure 5-1:
The Find
and
Replace
dialog box.

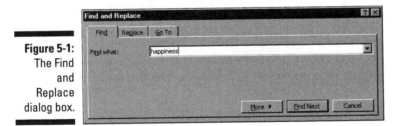

3. **Type the text you want to find.**

   Enter the text in the Find What box. For example, **Julia**. Type it in exactly as you want to find it.

   If you're not sure whether the text is typed in uppercase or lowercase, use lowercase letters.

4. **Click the Find Next button to start the search.**

   Or you can press Enter.

If any text is found, it's highlighted on-screen. The Find and Replace dialog box does not go away until you click the Cancel button or press the Escape key. (The dialog box remains so that you can keep searching for more text, if you're so inclined.)

- ✔ The quick shortcut key for finding text is to press Ctrl+F (the F stands for Find in this case).

- ✔ Type the text you want to find exactly. Do not end the text with a period unless you want to find the period also.

- ✔ If the text isn't found, the dog (or the Office Assistant of your choice) asks if you want to search again from the beginning. Click Yes or No, accordingly. Or if the text isn't found, the dog (Office Assistant) lets you know. (If you sent the dog outside, then the message is displayed in a dialog box.)

- ✔ If the text isn't found and you're *certain* it's in there, try again. Check your typing first, though.

- ✔ Drat! I was certain Julia wasn't in the will! And I so wanted the macramé owl!

- ✔ If you're working on more than one document at a time, be aware that Word finds text only in the current document (the one you see on the screen). To find text in another document, click that document's button on the taskbar and try again.

- ✔ To find an additional occurrence of the text, click the Find Next button.

- ✔ You can also use the Browse Up or Browse Down buttons to find the next occurrence of text — even if the Find and Replace dialog box is no longer visible on the screen. So if you've already searched for and found "Julia," clicking the Browse Down button finds her name again.

- ✔ After you close the Find and Replace dialog box, you can use the handy Shift+F4 key to repeat finding the next matching bit of text in your document. Just like the Browse Down button, pressing Shift+F4 finds the next bit of matching text ("Julia") in your document.

- ✔ Your Office Assistant may grow a lightbulb over its head after you close the Find and Replace dialog box. Clicking the lightbulb displays additional information about the Find command, most of which is summarized in the preceding bullet points.

Finding more stuff

The basic finders-keepers dialog box (refer to Figure 5-1) is okay for quickly finding tidbits of text. But sometimes you may want to find more detailed stuff, or stuff you can't readily type from the keyboard (like a new paragraph's Enter keystroke). Or you may want to find text that specifically matches "Dweeb" instead of plain old "dweeb." In those cases, you need to use the more robust Find and Replace dialog box.

To activate more options in the Find and Replace dialog box, press Ctrl+F. Click the More button. The Find and Replace dialog box gets taller, with a bunch of options and doodads at the bottom, as illustrated in Figure 5-2.

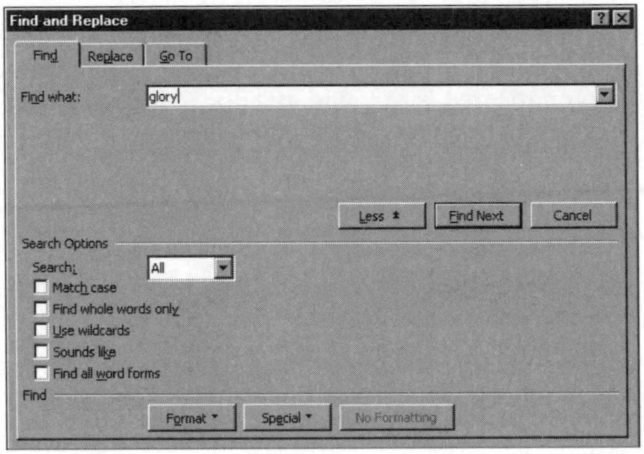

Figure 5-2:
The more
detailed
Find and
Replace
dialog box.

The following sections tell you why you may want to mess with some of those doodads.

- ✔ The following sections address the options available when you select the More button in the Find and Replace dialog box.

- ✔ Choosing some options disables other options. This only makes sense; if you select the Find All Word Forms option, then also selecting the Match Case option would work against you.

- ✔ The More button changes to the Less button after you press it. Click the Less button to restore the Find and Replace dialog box to its former, diminutive size.

Finding an exact bit of text

There is a difference between *Sandy* and *sandy*. One is a name and the other is something composed of sand. To use the Find command to find one and not the other, select the Match Case option under Search Options. That way *Sandy* matches only words that start with an uppercase *S* and have lowercase "andy" in them.

Finding a whole word

The Find Whole Words Only option allows you to look for words such as "right" and "set" without finding words like "alright" and "upset."

Finding text that you know only a small part of (using wildcards)

Here's a can-o-worms for you. It's possible to use wildcards to find words you know only a part of, or a group of words with similar letters. This is a highly technical thing, so I advise you not to drive or operate heavy machinery when reading the following.

The two basic wildcard characters are ? and *, where ? represents any single letter and * represents a group of letters. So, suppose you type the following in the Find what box:

```
w?n
```

If you select the Use Wildcards option, Word searches for any three-letter word that starts with a W and ends with an N. Any letter can be in the middle. So you may find *win* or *won* or *wan* and so on.

```
w*s
```

The asterisk finds a group of characters, so the above wildcard locates any word starting with W and ending with S. There are a lot of them.

There are a bunch of other wildcard characters you can use to find text in a number of interesting and strange ways. For example:

```
adverti[sz]e
```

The above bracket-and-wildcard nonsense actually finds the word "advertise" or "advertize" depending on how you prefer to spell it.

Word has many more variations of wildcards available, although * and ? are the most popular and should get you by. To see the rest of the wildcards available, click the question mark button in the upper-right corner of the Find and Replace dialog box, then select the Use Wildcards option.

Finding text that sounds like something else

The Sounds Like option allows you to search for homonyms, or words that sound the same as the search word. You know: their and there, or deer and dear, or hear and here. How this is useful, I'll never know.

Oh! This is not a rhyming search command. If you try to use it to find, for example, everything that rhymes with "Doris," for example, it will not find Boris, chorus, pylorus, or anything of the like.

Finding variations of a word

No, no, no! Superman doesn't walk anywhere! He flies! Change this! So off you go into Word, searching for every variation of the word *walk*: walking, walked, and so on. Word can do it. Just type **walk** into the Find What box and click the Find All Word Forms option.

Word may need to install the Find All Word Forms feature from your Microsoft Office CD-ROM. This needs to be done only once, so if the dog says "Hey! Get the CD-ROM" (or something like that), you need to do it.

Searching up, down, left, and right

The Find command is not Janus, the Roman god of beginnings and endings, who had two faces looking two directions. The Find command looks only one way, usually toward the end of your document, when you go hunting for text.

As soon as you reach the end of your document, Word (or the dog) asks if you want to search again from the beginning. You do, so you click Yes. Eventually the Find command stops looking when it returns to where the toothpick cursor was when you first cast the Find command spell.

Of course, you don't have to look "down" all the time. You can tell the Find command to look from the toothpick cursor to the *start* of your document. That's looking "up." Or you can look through the entire document. You do all this in the More part of the Find and Replace dialog box.

Locate the Search drop-down box (see Figure 5-2) and click the down-arrow. There you find three options:

- **Down:** Searches from the toothpick cursor to the end of the document.

- **Up:** Searches from the toothpick cursor to the beginning of the document.

- **All:** Fie on the toothpick cursor — Word searches the entire document.

I was just kidding about searching left and right in this section's title. Left is actually "up," or before the toothpick cursor; right is "down," or after the toothpick cursor. And starboard is right and port is left, if you happen to be using Word on a laptop somewhere in the ocean.

Finding stuff you just can't type in

No, this isn't a censorship issue. Some characters you just can't properly type in the Find and Replace dialog box — unprintable, unmentionable stuff.

For example, try finding a Tab character: You can't! Press the Tab key in the Find and Replace dialog box and — whoops! — nothing happens. That result is because the Tab character, plus a few others, are special, and you must force-feed them to the Find and Replace dialog box.

To find a special, unprintable character, click the More button to see the expanded Find and Replace dialog box, and then click the Special button (see Figure 5-2). Up pops a list of various characters Word can search for but that you would have a dickens of a time typing (see Figure 5-3).

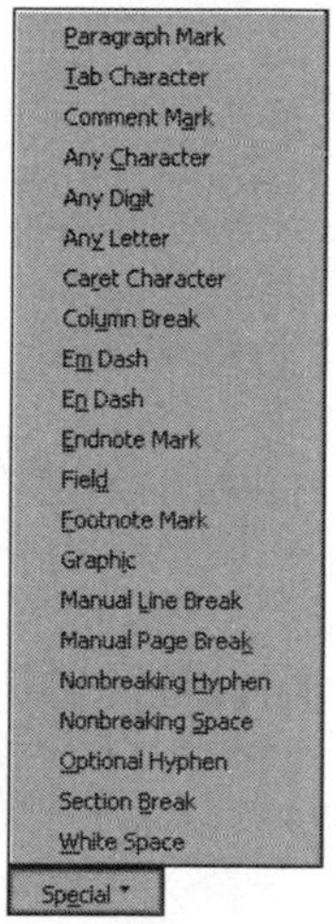

Figure 5-3:
Some special stuff to find.

Paragraph Mark
Tab Character
Comment Mark
Any Character
Any Digit
Any Letter
Caret Character
Column Break
Em Dash
En Dash
Endnote Mark
Field
Footnote Mark
Graphic
Manual Line Break
Manual Page Break
Nonbreaking Hyphen
Nonbreaking Space
Optional Hyphen
Section Break
White Space

Special ▼

Choose one of the items in the list to search for that special character. When you do, a special, funky shorthand representation for that character appears in the Find what box (such as ^t for Tab). Click the Find Next button to find that character.

Here are some of the most useful special characters available when you click the Special button in the Find dialog box:

- ✔ **Any Character, Any Digit, and Any Letter** are special characters that represent, well, just about anything. These buttons are used as wildcards for matching lots of stuff.

- ✔ **Caret Character** allows you to search for a caret (^) symbol, which is a special character. If you just type the caret symbol itself (^), Word thinks you're trying to type in another special character.

- ✔ **Paragraph Mark** (¶) is a special character that's the same as the Enter character — what you press to end a paragraph.

➤ **Tab Character** is the character that moves the cursor to the next tab mark.

➤ **White Space** is any blank character: a space, a tab, and so on. (I can see room here for a "white space" joke, but I'm feeling subdued today.)

Yes, you can mix and match the special characters with other text you want to find. So if you want to find a Tab character followed by "Hunter," you use the Special button to insert the Tab Character (^t on the screen), and then you just type in **Hunter** using your fingers. It looks like this:

```
^tHunter
```

Now does anyone remember who Tab Hunter is?

Finding formatting

The final and most insane thing the Find command can do for you is to find formatting codes laced throughout your document. For example, if you want to find only those instances of the word "coward" in boldface type, you can do that.

A lot of the formatting searches require that you know a bit about how Word formats text, characters, and documents. So I highly recommend that you familiarize yourself with the chapters in Part II of this book if you haven't yet done so.

To find formatting stuff in a document, use the More part of the Find and Replace dialog box (refer to Figure 5-2). Click the Format button to see a pop-up list of formatting options in Word, as shown in Figure 5-4.

Figure 5-4:
Various
formatting
options
you can
search for.

Each one of the menu items displays a dialog box that lets you choose which formatting options to search for. (Again, it helps if you know the options in the dialog boxes.) The Font and Paragraph items display two popular dialog boxes most Word users are familiar with.

As an example, suppose you want to find the bold-faced *coward* in your document. Follow these steps:

1. **Summon the Find and Replace dialog box.**

   Pressing Ctrl+F is the only sane way to do this.

   Optionally, delete any previously searched for text in the Find What text box. (The last text you searched for always hangs around, just in case you forget what you last found.)

2. **Click the More button to display the bottom part of the Find and Replace dialog box.**

   This step isn't necessary if the bottom part is already showing. (And we all know how embarrassing that can be.)

3. **Click the Format button.**

   Up pops the Format list.

   Use the Font dialog box to apply bold to your text.

4. **Click the Font button.**

   The Font dialog box appears, as shown in Figure 5-5. This can be strange territory, but this is a tutorial so relax. What you're looking for is the Bold item, which appears in the Font Style list near the top center of the Font dialog box.

5. **Click the Bold button.**

6. **Click OK.**

   The Font dialog box goes away, and you're returned to the Find and Replace dialog box.

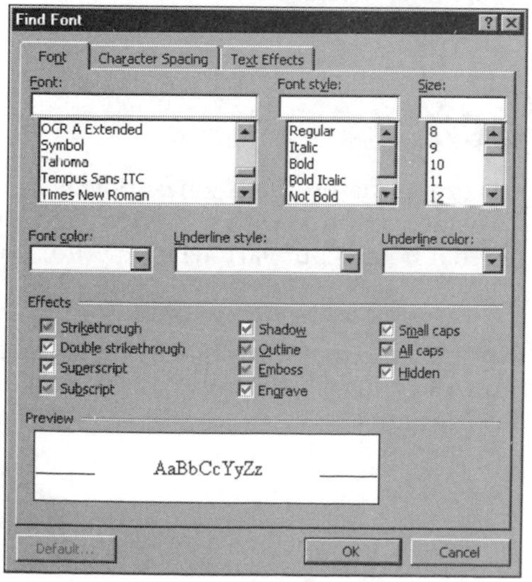

Figure 5-5: The Font dialog box, borrowed for use by the Find command.

Notice the text just beneath the Find What box? It says `Format: Font: Bold`. That's telling you that Word is now geared up to find only bold text.

If you were to click the Find Next button now, Word would simply locate the next occurrence of bold text in your document. However, if you want to find a specific example of bold text, you need to fill in the Find What box.

7. **Type** coward **in the Find What box.**

8. **Click the Find Next button to find your formatted text.**

Word locates the text you formatted — however you formatted it.

WARNING!

Word remembers your formatting options! When you go to search for non-formatted text, you need to click the No Formatting button. Doing so removes the formatting options and allows you to search for plain text again. You'll forget this a few times and it will really heat you up that Word cannot find your text. Do not forget to click the No Formatting button to return Word to normal text finding mode.

✔ You can use this technique to look for specific occurrences of a font, such as Courier or Times New Roman, by selecting the font from the selection list. Scroll through the font menu to see what you can choose.

✔ You can look for a particular size of type (24-point, for example) by selecting it from the Size list. See Chapter 11, "Formatting Characters," for information about character formatting.

✔ You can also search for paragraph formatting by choosing Paragraph rather than Font from the Format menu in the Find and Replace dialog box. See Chapter 12 for information about paragraph formatting.

✔ The remaining options in the Format pop-up list are fairly obscure, although if you become fluent with Word know that you can search for text formatting with those, well, whatever-they-ares.

Finding and Replacing

By itself, the Find command is really handy. But its true power lies in its ability to not only find text but replace that text with something else. It's one of the word-processor features that helped put various typewriter companies out of business.

If you've mastered the Find command, then your black belt in the Replace command is only a paragraph away. In fact, the only trouble you'll have with the Replace command is its shortcut key.

No, it's not R — The Ctrl+R shortcut command is used to right-align text in a paragraph. (Nice try, though.) Apparently Microsoft thought there would be more folks out there desperate to right-align paragraphs than there would be those who desire to search and Replace.

Okay, just give up now. Every other word you can think of for replace (oust, relieve, substitute, zap) has a shortcut key of its own. So the shortcut key for the Replace command is . . . Ctrl+H!

Enough dallying. As an example, suppose you want to replace the word "use" with "utilize." Both mean the same thing, but the suits who run the store think "utilize" is more important-sounding and earns them a bigger paycheck. Since they sign the checks, you go for it by using, nay, *utilizing* the Replace command:

1. **Choose Edit⇨Replace.**

   Or if you can remember what the Heck H stands for, type Ctrl+H. (I believe I'm the only Word user in my state who knows the Ctrl+H keyboard shortcut off the top of my head.)

   The Find and Replace dialog box, shown in Figure 5-6, appears on-screen. This tab is actually another panel in the Find and Replace dialog box — which makes sense because finding is a big part of find and replace.

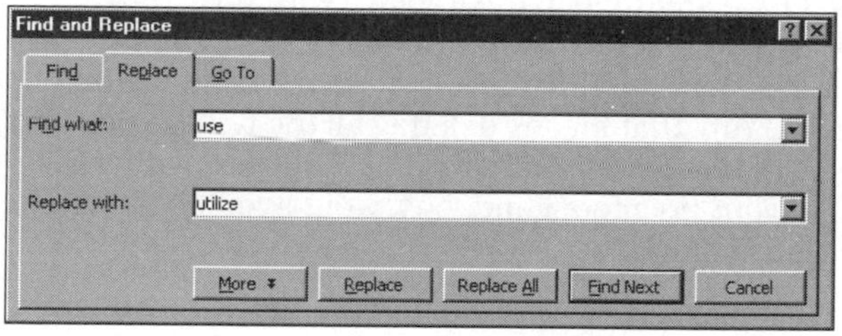

Figure 5-6:
The Find
and
Replace
dialog box.

   The Find and Replace dialog box also has a More button. If you see the More options, click the Less button to make your screen look like Figure 5-6. Also see the section "Finding more stuff" earlier in this chapter.

2. **In the Find What box, type the text you want to find.**

   This is the text you want to replace with something else.

   Press the Tab key when you're done typing.

3. **In the Replace With box, type the text that you want to use to replace the original text.**

4. **Ask yourself, "Do I want a chance to change my mind before replacing each bit of found text?"**

   If so, click the Find Next button (taking this action is usually a good idea). If not, you can click the Replace All button; text is found and replaced automatically, giving you no chance to change your mind.

5. **If you click Find Next, Word pauses at each occurrence of the text.**

   The found text is highlighted on-screen just like in the regular Find task. When this highlighting happens, you can click the Replace button to replace it or click Find Next to skip it and find the next matching bit of text. Click the Cancel button or press the Escape key when you tire of this process.

   Word may find your text, such as "use," in the middle of another word, such as "causes." Oops! Click that More button and select the Find Whole Words Only option to prevent that from happening.

If there's nothing to replace, then the dog says:

```
Word has completed its search of the document and has made 9
replacements.
```

Of course, the number of replacements depends on what you were searching for.

- ✔ If you don't type anything in the Replace with box . . . oops! Forgetting to type replacement text does not turn the Replace command into the Find command. No, Word just assumes you want to find the text and replace it with nothing. Yup, that means deleting all the text found. This process can be a scary thing, so be sure to click Find Next. Otherwise, you may zap parts of your document and, boy, would you be bummed (until you used the Undo command).

- ✔ My advice is to click Find Next most of the time. Only if you're absolutely certain (a rare occurrence, at least in my travels) should you click Replace All.

- ✔ The Undo command restores your document to its previous condition if you foul up the Replace operation.

- ✔ The *American Heritage Dictionary* has this to say about replacing *use* with *utilize*: "A number of critics have remarked that *utilize* is an unnecessary substitute for *use*. It is true that many occurrences of *utilize* could be replaced by *use* with no loss to anything but pretentiousness." (Ha!) However, *utilize* does have a slight tendency to mean "using in a way that is profitable," that makes it edge out the word *use* in a few (mark me, **a few**) instances.

Chapter 6

Working with Blocks of Text

· ·

· ·

*W*hat would writing be without blocks? No, I'm not talking about writer's block. That's the brain lock some people claim to have when they can't find the right word or when the opening paragraph of a chapter seems to elude them. It's a myth, in my opinion; writer's block is a catchy phrase and easier to blame than the fact your fingers just aren't doing what your brain wants.

In Word, though, a *block* is a piece of text. Word lets you rope off a chunk of text — words, sentences, paragraphs, or the whole document — and then do fun and interesting things with that block of text. This chapter is all about those blocky things. Hey! It's time to play with blocks boys and girls!

Marking Blocks of Text

A seasoned and famous writer once told me to triple-space everything, to type on thick, 20-pound paper, and to keep scissors and rubber cement handy to help me rearrange and edit. After all, he boasted, cutting and pasting your text beats typing it over and over again. His advice may have been true in 1978, but it's completely moot today.

Word lets you do numerous things with blocks of text. And you don't have to worry about triple-spacing, typing on 20-pound paper, or even spending $1.29 for the industrial-sized jar of rubber cement. Instead, you need to know how to mark the block. As usual, Word offers you several trillion ways to do this. I describe some of those methods below, each of which is well-suited for marking different-sized chunks of text.

A Shifty way to mark tiny bits of text

To quickly mark a small chunk of text — a word, line, or paragraph — you can use the Shift key in combination with any of the arrow keys (also known as cursor-movement keys). This technique is best-suited to marking a small slab of text on-screen. Let Table 6-1 be your beacon.

Table 6-1	Shifty Selection Wizardry
To Do This . . .	*Press This . . .*
Select a character at a time to the right of the toothpick cursor	Shift+→
Select a character at a time to the left of the toothpick cursor	Shift+←
Select a block of text from the toothpick cursor to the end of the line	Shift+End
Select a block of text from the toothpick cursor to the beginning of the line	Shift+Home
Select a block of text from the toothpick cursor to a line above	Shift+↑
Select a block of text from the toothpick cursor to a line below	Shift+↓

Random Shift key ruminations:

- ✔ You can use the Shift key with the other cursor-movement key combinations, however there are better ways of marking blocks larger than a line or two.

- ✔ Refer to Chapter 3 for more information about cursor movement keys.

- ✔ I use the left Shift key and then work the arrow keys on the right side of the keyboard. If you can train yourself to work that way also, you'll find you can get quite deft at these Shift-arrow key selection methods.

✔ If you use the Shift key to mark to the end of a paragraph, note that the Enter key press (marking the end of the paragraph) is also selected. That means if you delete or reformat the block, it might also change the formatting of the next paragraph. To avoid that, press Shift+→ to back up and not select the Enter key press at the end of the paragraph.

✔ No, you don't have to use the left Shift key. Either Shift key works.

Marking a block with your mouse

The mouse was born to select text. Well, Mickey, he's different. He was born to rule a kingdom. But most computer mice work best in a word processor as text selectors. Table 6-2 tells you how to put your little rodent to work for you in selecting stuff.

Table 6-2	Mouse Selection Arcana
To Accomplish This . . .	*Perform This Bit of Mouse Magic*
Select a word	Point at the word with your mouse and double-click.
Select a line	Move the mouse into the left margin beside the line you want to select. The mouse pointer changes to a northeasterly-pointing arrow. Click the mouse to select a line of text, or drag the mouse to select several lines.
Select a sentence	Point the mouse at the sentence and Ctrl+click; press the Ctrl key and click the mouse. The sentence is selected.
Select a paragraph	Point the mouse somewhere in the paragraph's midst and triple-click.

You can select a chunk of text of any size with a mouse. However, my advice is to select only as much text as you can see on the screen at one time. If you try to select text beyond what you see on the screen, then you have to select and scroll — which can be unwieldy. To select a block of text with your mouse, follow these rodent-like steps:

1. **Position the mouse pointer where you want the block to start.**

2. **Hold down the left mouse button and drag the mouse over your text.**

   As you drag, the text becomes highlighted, or selected, as shown in Figure 6-1. Drag the mouse from the beginning to the end of the text that you want to mark as a block.

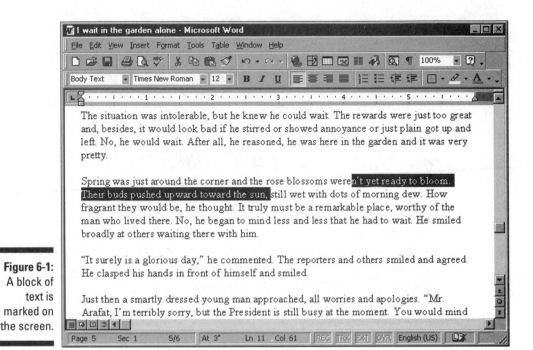

File   Edit   View   Insert   Format   Tools   Table   Window   Help

Body Text ▾   Times New Roman ▾   12 ▾   **B** *I* U

The situation was intolerable, but he knew he could wait. The rewards were just too great and, besides, it would look bad if he stirred or showed annoyance or just plain got up and left. No, he would wait. After all, he reasoned, he was here in the garden and it was very pretty.

Spring was just around the corner and the rose blossoms weren't yet ready to bloom. Their buds pushed upward toward the sun, still wet with dots of morning dew. How fragrant they would be, he thought. It truly must be a remarkable place, worthy of the man who lived there. No, he began to mind less and less that he had to wait. He smiled broadly at others waiting there with him.

"It surely is a glorious day," he commented. The reporters and others smiled and agreed. He clasped his hands in front of himself and smiled.

Just then a smartly dressed young man approached, all worries and apologies. "Mr. Arafat, I'm terribly sorry, but the President is still busy at the moment. You would mind

Page 5   Sec 1   5/6   At 3"   Ln 11   Col 61   REC TRK EXT OVR   English (US)

Figure 6-1:
A block of
text is
marked on
the screen.

Notice how Word automatically selects whole words when you drag over them with your mouse. To tell Word not to select whole words, choose Tools⇨Options from the menu. In the Edit panel, deselect the When Selecting, Automatically Select Entire Word check box by clicking in the check box to remove the check. Click the OK button to save your change.

3. Release the mouse — stop the dragging — to mark your block's end.

Using the miraculous F8 key to mark a block

Who in their right mind would assign the F8 key to mean "select text?" Probably the same gang of Talking Rain-swilling, Volvo-driving, stock option-obsessed people at Microsoft who brought you the F4 key. Remember that F4 is the Repeat key. F8 should mean select text, natch.

Never mind! If you can find room in your skull to remember the F8 key, you can put it to good use. F8 selects text in unique chunks, unavailable with other commands. What follows is a small sampling of what it does best.

Select a word. Pressing the F8 key twice selects a word. But honestly, if you're going to point at the word to move the toothpick cursor there anyway, you may as well go ahead and double-click the word.

Select a sentence. Position the toothpick cursor in a sentence and then press the F8 key three times to select the sentence.

Select a paragraph. Position the toothpick cursor in a paragraph and then press the F8 key four times to select the whole paragraph.

Select your document. Pressing the F8 key five times selects your entire document, but there's a better way to do that as well, which is covered in the section, "Marking the whole dang-doodle document," later in this document.

Oh! And pressing the F8 key only one time? Does that order you a new cup of coffee? Turn on WebTV? Activate Voice mode? Nope! Keep reading in the next section to learn the awful secret.

Dropping anchor with the F8 key

What the F8 key does is place Word into the handy (but potentially annoying) Extended Selection mode. In this mode, the F8 key "drops anchor" on one end of a block. You can then use the cursor keys, the mouse, or a letter key to continue marking the block. However — and this is important — the entire time you're in Extended Selection mode you cannot use Word for anything other than selecting a block.

Don't let this annoy you! Sure, it may confuse you at times, but using the F8 key in Extended Selection mode is the best way to select a chunk of text spanning more than one screen.

Heed these steps to use the Extended Selection mode:

1. **Position the toothpick cursor at the start of the block of text you want to mark.**

2. **Press the F8 key.**

   The F8 key drops anchor, marking one end of the block.

   Notice the three letters EXT become highlighted on the status bar. This is an important hint. You're now in Extended Selection mode and the keys on your keyboard serve to select text, not to write anything. Beware!

3. **Select the block of text.**

   You can select the block of text using the arrow keys or any of the cursor navigation keys discussed in Chapter 3.

You can also press a letter key to select text up to and including that letter. So if you press N, you'll select all text up to and including the next N in your document. Nice. Nifty. Bitchen.

Word highlights text from the point where you dropped anchor with F8 to wherever you move the toothpick cursor (refer to Figure 6-1). Text appears in white-on-black.

4. **After the block is marked, you're ready to do something with it.**

5. **Do something with the selected block of text.**

This is the annoying part. After you mark a block, you *must* perform some block command. See the status bar? The EXT is still highlighted. You're still marking a block! So unless you copy, cut, paste, spell check, or do something else, you're still in block-marking mode.

If you want to cancel the Extended Selection, press the Esc key. Or you can double-click the EXT in the status bar (which forces you to pay attention to EXT so it doesn't frustrate you later).

✔ You can use the mouse and the F8 key to get real fancy. Position the cursor at either end of the block you want to mark and press the F8 key. Then position the mouse cursor at the other end of the block and press the left mouse button. Everything from there to there is marked.

✔ No matter how many times you press F8, be aware that it always drops anchor. If you press it twice or thrice (see the previous section), F8 marks a chunk of text — but you're still in Extended Selection mode. Do something with the block or press Esc to cancel that mode.

✔ Get used to using the keyboard commands to block your text, and you will be much happier, believe me.

Marking the whole dang-doodle document

To mark everything in your document as a block, choose <u>E</u>dit⇨Select A<u>l</u>l. The Windows key equivalent for the Select All command is Ctrl+A.

In Word you can also use the obscure Ctrl+5 (the 5 on the numeric keypad) key combo, or you can whack the F8 key five times.

Naaaa: Just press Ctrl+A to mark the whole thing.

Deselecting a Block

Now that you have a block marked, uh, what were you going to do with it? And how do you go back to normal mode, getting rid of the highlighted block so you can actually type something? Frustrated? Be no more!

Here are some handy ways to deselect that pesky block of highlighted text:

✔ **Press the → key.** This unhighlights the block and returns the toothpick cursor to the point where the block started, or to the top of your document if you selected the whole document. This works for stuff you've selected with the mouse or with the Shift key.

✔ **Click the mouse.** This method deselects the block and puts the toothpick cursor wherever you click. This method works for selections made with the mouse or with the Shift key.

✔ **Press the Esc key and then the → key.** This method works when you're using the Extended Selection command (the F8 key, or the EXT button on the status bar, remember?).

✔ **Don't forget the Shift+F5 command!** Pressing this not only deselects the block (whether you selected it with the mouse, the Shift key, or with the F8 key) but it also returns you to the text you were editing before making the selection. Nifty!

The super-duper Copy, Cut, and Paste commands!

Word uses the Windows standard Copy, Cut and Paste commands to help you copy and move blocks of text. These are actually Windows commands, but they come in handy when you're using Word.

✔ Ctrl+C is the Copy command, copying a selected block of text.

✔ Ctrl+X is the Cut command, cutting a selected block of text (for moving a block).

✔ Ctrl+V is the Paste command, which pastes a previously copied or cut block of text back into your document.

Please don't try to make sense of these commands. I mean, "C" for Copy is okay. And "X" for Cut works because Xing is also crossing and you cross stuff out and X even looks like a pair of scissors. But "V" for paste? What? Vomit? I just don't get it.

Copying and Pasting a Block

After a block is marked, you can copy and paste it into another part of your document. The original block remains untouched by this operation. Follow these steps to copy a block of text from one place to another:

1. **Mark the block.**

   Detailed instructions about doing this task are offered in the first part of this chapter.

2. **Conjure up Edit⇨Copy.**

    Or, if you're adept at such things, press Ctrl+C for the Copy shortcut, or click the Copy tool.

   Word places a copy of the marked block in the Windows Clipboard — a storage area for text or graphics that you cut or copy and are about to paste back into your document.

3. **Move the cursor to the position you want the block copied.**

   Don't worry if there isn't any room there; Word inserts the block into your text just as though you had typed it there manually.

4. **Choose Edit⇨Paste.**

   Pressing Ctrl+V is the Paste shortcut (or you can click the Paste tool).

   You now have two copies of the block in your document.

✔ After you copy a block, you can paste it into your document a second time. I cover this subject in "Pasting a Previously Cut or Copied Block," later in this chapter.

✔ You can even paste the block into another document you're working on, or into another application. (This is a Windows trick, which most good books on Windows discuss.)

Cutting and Pasting a Block

Cutting and pasting a block is essentially moving a block. The block was here, now the block is there. This is especially useful for those times when you're writing a novel, and you have Old Uncle Cedric playing with the grandkids and then realize that you killed him off two chapters ago. You can easily move the passage back to when Cedric was alive by cutting and pasting.

Cutting a block of text works like copying a block except that you use the Ctrl+X (or Edit⇨Cut) command instead of Ctrl+C.

Don't be alarmed when the block disappears; it reappears when you use the Ctrl+V (or Edit⇨Paste) command. Whew!

- ✔ You can use the Cut tool on the toolbar to move a block of text.

- ✔ Instead of using Ctrl+V you can paste the block using the Paste tool.

- ✔ Additional information about marking a block is in the first two sections of this chapter.

- ✔ The Ctrl+Z Undo shortcut undoes a block move.

- ✔ After you cut and move a block, you can paste it into your document a second time. This subject is covered in the next section, "Pasting a Previously Cut or Copied Block."

Copying or Moving a Block with the Mouse

If you have to move a block only a short distance you can use the mouse to drag-move or drag-copy the block. This is handy, but usually works best if you're moving or copying between two locations you can see right on the screen. Otherwise, you're scrolling your document with the mouse, which is like trying to grab a snake.

To move any selected block of text with the mouse, just point and drag the block: Position the mouse cursor anywhere in the blocked text and hold down the mouse while you drag the bar-looking cursor to the location where the block is to be moved. Then release the mouse. Notice how the mouse grows a box (see the margin)? That means you're dragging and copying text.

Copying a block with the mouse works just like moving the block, though you press the Ctrl key as you drag. When you do that, a plus appears in the mouse's pointer (see the margin). That's your sign that the block is being copied and not just moved.

- ✔ When you drag a block of text with the mouse you're not copying it to the clipboard. You cannot use the Paste (Ctrl+V) command to paste in the block again.

- ✔ A *linked copy* is created by dragging a selected block of text with the mouse and holding down *both* the Shift and Ctrl keys. When you release the mouse button, the copied block plops down into your document, but with a gray shading behind it. From that point on, any time you edit the original text, the copy is edited and updated as well. Strange, but Word can do it, and I'd be chastised if I didn't write about this capability somewhere in this book.

Pasting a Previously Cut or Copied Block

Whenever a block of text is cut or copied, Word remembers it. You can yank that block into your document again at any time — sort of like pasting text again after it's already been pasted in. You use Ctrl+V, the Paste shortcut.

Yes, Ctrl+V works whether the original block was copied or cut. It doesn't matter. Pasting text again simply pastes down a second copy of the block, spit-spot (as Mary Poppins would say).

Copying Multiple Blocks (Collect and Paste)

In its normal, timid state, Windows lets you copy only one thing at a time. Copy some text, okay. Paste away! But copy another bit of text and the original text you copied is replaced. Not so with Word's multicopy feature, "collect and paste."

For example, you can collect bits and pieces of text all over a document, across several documents or from other Microsoft Office programs like Excel or PowerPoint. The secret is to keep using the Copy command. Copy. Copy. Copy.

When you use the Copy command (Ctrl+C or the Copy tool) two or more times in a row, a special Clipboard window appears, as shown in Figure 6-2. Word stores everything copied in a special Clipboard window, up to 12 items. When you copy the unlucky thirteenth item, the Office Assistant displays the message shown in Figure 6-3.

Figure 6-2:
The
Clipboard
stores the
last several
items
copied.

Figure 6-3:
The Office
Assistant
warns you
that the
multi-
Clipboard is
full up.

 To paste in the items all at once, click the Paste All button. The items are pasted back into your document in the order they were copied, one after the other.

 Or you can click on individual "scraps" in the window to paste those items in particular order. Pointing the mouse at a scrap icon displays information about what's stored in the scrap.

 Click the Clear Clipboard button to remove everything from the multi-Clipboard. Or you can just close the Clipboard window and return to editing your document to clear.

> ✔ You can copy up to 12 things in a row with Collect and Paste. You must use two or more Copy commands in a row or it doesn't work.

> ✔ The Clipboard window can be displayed at any time: Choose <u>V</u>iew↭ <u>T</u>oolbars↭Clipboard. You can then use the Copy button in the window to copy items to the multi-Clipboard.

More than Pasting, It's Special Pasting!

 When Word pastes text into your document, it does so by pasting it in fully formatted and with all the bells and whistles. Sometimes I don't like that. For example, if I'm updating an older document, I may *not* want all the formatting codes pasted. All I want is text! To get it, I use the <u>E</u>dit↭Paste <u>S</u>pecial command.

The <u>E</u>dit↭Paste <u>S</u>pecial command may not be readily visible on the Edit menu. To see it, click the down-arrows at the bottom of the Edit menu. This displays the full menu, complete with lots of options you'll probably never use. Among them you'll find Paste Special.

Choosing the Paste Special command displays the Paste Special dialog box, as seen in Figure 6-4. There are lots of serious options for pasting in the text.

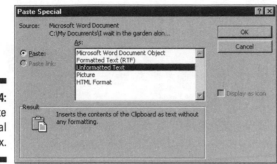

Figure 6-4:
The Paste
Special
dialog box.

When I want to paste in text without formatting, I choose the Unformatted Text option. To discover what the other special pasting options do, select each one and read the description in the Result area of the dialog box.

Click OK to paste in the text in a special manner. Click Cancel not to paste.

By the way, this dialog box is how Word pastes in links to other Office applications, such as an Excel spreadsheet or information from Access.

Other Things to Do with Your Blocks

There are hat blocks, engine blocks, building blocks, mental blocks, nerve blocks, down-blocks, and finally blocks of text. I don't know about the other things, but when you have a block of text you can do any of a number of things to it. The command you use affects only the text within that block.

Aside from using the Copy, Cut, and Paste commands, you can do the following with a block of text in Word:

✔ Format the block (see Part II).

✔ Use the Replace command to find and replace only in the block of text (see Chapter 5).

✔ Print the block (see Chapter 9).

✔ Delete the block with the Delete or Backspace keys.

Chapter 7

Minding Your Ps and Qs

. . . .

In This Chapter

▶ Understanding on-the-fly spell-checking

▶ Letting Word automatically correct your spelling

▶ Allowing Word to do the typing for you with AutoText

▶ Correcting your grammatical boo-boos

▶ Proofing your document all at once

▶ Using the thesaurus

▶ Counting your words

. . . .

Before the spelling-book came with its arbitrary forms, men
unconsciously revealed shades of their characters and also added enlighten-
ing shades of expression to what they wrote by their spelling,
and so it is possible that the spelling-book has been a doubtful benevolence
to us.

—Mark Twain

*T*here's nothing wrong with English spelling that fewer vowels can't fix. Seriously, spelling English properly has been an issue for less than 200 years. And no matter what old Ms. Lattimore says, there are no real rules. (Twain called them "arbitrary.") So that leaves you with two choices: Don't write anything, just talk. Or use Word's spelling and grammar checking abilities to ensure that your English is perfect — or at least as close to that as possible.

Impruv Yor Spelling wit Werd

My first version of Word was for DOS way back in 1985. It was remarkable back then because it was the only DOS word processor to show *italics* on the screen. That surely was something. But Word was slow. I could easily out-type it, and if I didn't wait for Word to catch up, it would forget what I typed. That didn't impress me.

Welcome to the year 2000 version of Word! Your word processor lives on one of the fastest computers ever designed. (It has to if you're running Windows 98, but that's another story.) Basically, you can never out-type Word. In fact, Word has so much time on its hands, waiting for you to pitifully type your document, that it can proof what you type *while* you're typing it. This is known as on-the-fly spell-checking.

Let's turn this on (or off)

To ensure that Word automatically checks your typing, choose Tools⇨ Options from the menu. Click the Spelling & Grammar tab, which is shown in Figure 7-1.

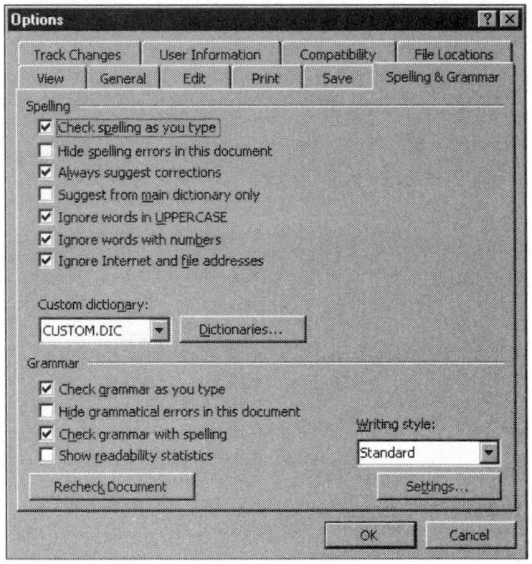

Figure 7-1:
Select
various
spell-check
and proofing
options
here.

Look up top for the Check Spelling as You Type option, and click in the check box to select it. That starts automatic spell-checking.

If you detest automatic spell-checking, then you can click in the box to remove the check mark. Word no longer annoys you with wiggly-underline text, though you can still use the Tools⇨Spelling and Grammar command to check your document at any time.

TECHNICAL STUFF

Automatic spell-checking doesn't work!

There are a few instances when automatic spell-checking doesn't seem to work. If that happens to you, try these things:

First, check to ensure that on-the-fly spell-checking is activated. See the section, "Let's turn this on (or off)."

Second, go visit the Options dialog box: Choose Tools⊅Options. Click the Spelling & Grammar tab. If there is a check mark by the Hide spelling errors in this document item, click to remove it. Click OK.

Third, your document may be formatted with "no proofing" language. To solve that problem, select your entire document by pressing Ctrl+A. Then choose Tools⊅Language⊅Set Language. (You may have to click the down-arrows at the bottom of the Tools menu to see the Language menu item.) In the Language dialog box, choose English (US) (for the United States), and click OK. This should reactivate the on-the-fly spell-checking.

The automatic spell-checker in action

Word automatically checks everything you type as you type it. Make a boo-boo, and Word lets you know. The second you press the spacebar or type some punctuation character, Word examines what you typed and immediately flags it as wrong, wrong, wrong. It does this by underlining the word using a red zigzag pattern. See Figure 7-2 for a sampling.

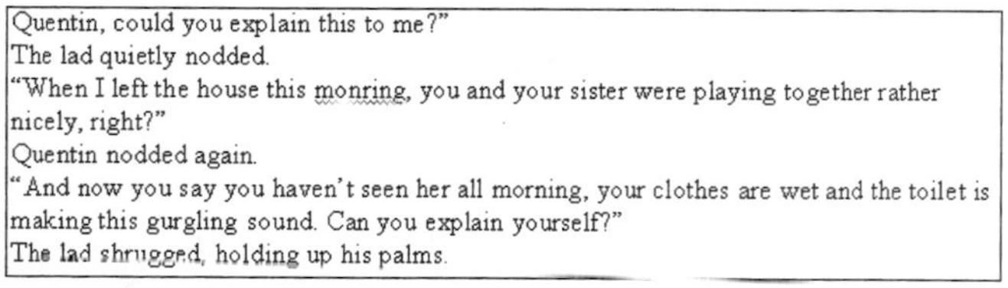

Figure 7-2:
The word "monring" is flagged as misspelled.

Quentin, could you explain this to me?"
The lad quietly nodded.
"When I left the house this monring, you and your sister were playing together rather nicely, right?"
Quentin nodded again.
"And now you say you haven't seen her all morning, your clothes are wet and the toilet is making this gurgling sound. Can you explain yourself?"
The lad shrugged, holding up his palms.

My advice: keep typing. Don't let the "red weave" tweak you. It's more important to get your thoughts up on the screen than to stop and fuss over inevitable typos. (Besides, I show you a trick in the next section to automatically correct your boo-boos.)

When you're ready, go back and fix your spelling errors. I do this every two or three paragraphs:

1. **Find the misspelled word.**

   Look for the red underline.

2. **Right-click on the misspelled word.**

   This pops-up a shortcut menu, similar to the one shown in Figure 7-3.

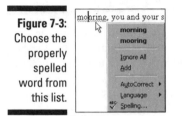

Figure 7-3:
Choose the
properly
spelled
word from
this list.

3. **Choose the word you intended to type from the list.**

   In Figure 7-3, the word "morning" fits the bill. Click that word and it's automatically inserted into your document, replacing the bogus word.

4. **Continue with the next misspelled word.**

   You can scan the page for the next word, but it's better to double-click the spelling thing on the status bar (see the margin). Double-clicking that, uh, "book," takes you instantly to the next misspelled word (or grammatical error).

If the word you intended to type isn't in the list, don't fret. Word isn't *that* smart. You may have to use a real dictionary, or take another stab at spelling the word phonetically and correct it again.

Select the Ignore All item from the list if the word is properly spelled and you don't want Word to keep flagging it as misspelled. For example, if I'm writing a short story about a guy named *Nordnick,* I have Word "Ignore All" occurrences of the word: Even though Word thinks it's wrong, it's okay by me.

The Add item is used to add commonly-used words to Word's dictionary. For example, my last name is Gookin, which Word thinks is a misspelling of the word "Goofing." No, no, no. So I click the Add menu item to insert the word "Gookin" into Word's internal dictionary.

The Ignore All command ignores spelling mistakes for a certain word only in the document you're editing. If you want to ignore the word forevermore, choose the Add command to add the word to the Word's this-is-spelled-okay list.

The Joys of AutoCorrect

There are some words you'll never learn to spell. For me, it's "achieve." My mom still types "vacume" though I tell her over and over it's "vacuum." And then there are the typos: ehre for here and teh for the. Oh, I could go mad! But I remain sane and collected, because I use Word's AutoCorrect option.

Using AutoCorrect

When you stumble upon a word you misspell over and over, you should throw that word into the AutoCorrect bin. Once there, Word automatically corrects the typo or misspelling as it happens. Think about it: You type "recieve" and on the screen Word magically changes it to "receive." Wow.

To throw a commonly misspelled word into the AutoCorrect bin, right-click on the word and choose AutoCorrect from the pop-up menu, as shown in Figure 7-4. Choose the properly spelled word from the sub-menu that appears.

Figure 7-4:
Auto
Correcting
a word.

Any word you add to AutoCorrect's repertoire is automatically fixed right after you type it.

If possible, try to add only lowercase words with AutoCorrect. For example, Figure 7-4 shows the word "source" being added. AutoCorrect will fix all variations of that word, upper/and lowercase, from "srouce" to "source." However, if you add "Source" (big S), then AutoCorrect will not correct "srcoue" (little s). Always add words in lowercase.

Undoing AutoCorrect's correction

If AutoCorrect makes a change you don't like, you can undo it. Usually pressing the Ctrl+Z shortcut for the Undo command right after you see the automatically corrected text does the trick. Sometimes pressing the Backspace key also works.

Other AutoCorrect tricks

Try typing the following in Word:

```
Copyright (C) 1999, WonderBlorb Corp.
```

When you type the (C), Word automatically converts it into the © copyright symbol. That's also a function of AutoCorrect in action.

Try this one too:

```
Please turn the page here -->
```

The --> turns into a right-pointing arrow.

And then there's the ever-popular:

```
Bill, I want to break up with you now, okay? :-)
```

See how the :-) turns into a ☺. It really lightens the tone of the message, don't you think?

How about some AutoText tricks?

Another Word trick that works like AutoCorrect is AutoText. Unlike AutoCorrect, which rewrites text you may misspell, AutoText *finishes* writing words you start to spell.

As an example, try to type the following in Word:

```
Ladies and Gentlemen:
```

When you get to about the *i* in "Ladies" a box of text appears above the toothpick cursor, as shown in Figure 7-5. That's AutoText in action.

Getting AutoText to Work

If AutoText doesn't seem to work as described in the "How about some AutoText tricks?" section nearby, then you need to turn it on. Choose Tools⇨AutoCorrect. In the AutoCorrect dialog box, click the AutoText tab. Select the Show AutoComplete Tip for AutoText and Dates check box by clicking in it. Then click OK.

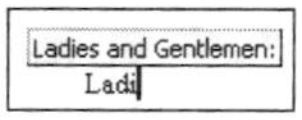

Figure 7-5:
AutoText
makes a
suggestion
for finishing
a word.

Ladies and Gentlemen:|
Lad

To accept the word(s), press the Enter key. Word types them in for you automatically.

AutoText keeps a repertoire of commonly-used words, plus you can add your own. The next section explains how.

Reviewing your AutoCorrect and AutoText settings

You can check out AutoCorrect and AutoText's vocabularies, either because you're curious, or because you want to remove or add words or phrases. To do this you must summon the AutoCorrect dialog box.

From the menu, choose Tools⇨AutoCorrect. (You may have to click the down-arrows on the menu to find the AutoCorrect menu item.) Make sure the AutoCorrect tab is selected, as shown in Figure 7-6.

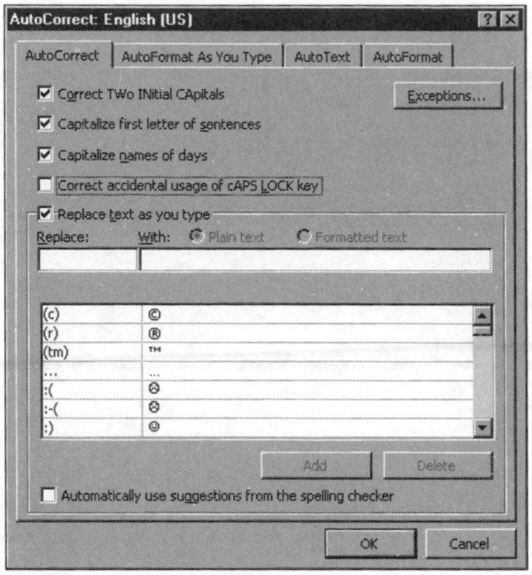

AutoCorrect: English [US]

| AutoCorrect | AutoFormat As You Type | AutoText | AutoFormat |

☑ Correct TWo INitial CApitals   Exceptions...

☑ Capitalize first letter of sentences

☑ Capitalize names of days

☐ Correct accidental usage of cAPS LOCK key

☑ Replace text as you type

Replace: With: ⦿ Plain text   ○ Formatted text

(c)	©
(r)	®
(tm)	™
...	...
:(	☹
:-(	☹
:)	☺

Add   Delete

☐ Automatically use suggestions from the spelling checker

OK   Cancel

Figure 7-6:
The
AutoCorrect
dialog box.

You can have AutoCorrect fix several common boo-boos for you by using the options at the top of the dialog box: Two capital letters at the start of a sentence (for you fast typists); the first letter of a sentence; names of days, and a fix for the times when you accidentally have the Caps Lock key on.

The fifth item down, which is the Replace Text as You Type check box, turns on AutoCorrect. Make sure it's selected.

The following sections assume the AutoCorrect dialog box is open and ready for business.

Manually adding an AutoCorrect entry

In the AutoCorrect tab of the AutoCorrect dialog box, you can manually create your own entries by using the Replace and With boxes.

✔ Typos and misspellings go in the Replace box.

✔ The correct word goes into the With box. (Choose "Plain text" to ensure your formatting stays okay.)

✔ Click the Add button to add an entry.

✔ Click OK to close the AutoCorrect dialog box when you're done.

Being cruel with AutoCorrect is entirely possible. For example, inserting a meanie like "thier" for "their" would drive some people nuts. Remember, AutoCorrect is subtle. If you type looking at the keyboard rather than the screen, you never know what it's up to.

Removing unwanted AutoCorrect entries

To remove an item from AutoCorrect, locate it in the list. For example, AutoCorrect lists "hda" as a correction for "had," but you're working on a project named HDA and you don't want it corrected to "had" every time you type it.

When you find the offending spelling in the list, position the mouse pointer over it and click to select it and then click the Delete button. It's gone.

Click OK to close the AutoCorrect dialog box when your destructive urges have been quenched.

Adding a new AutoText entry

To add a new AutoText entry, click the AutoText tab in the AutoCorrect dialog box. This displays information about AutoText, as shown in Figure 7-7.

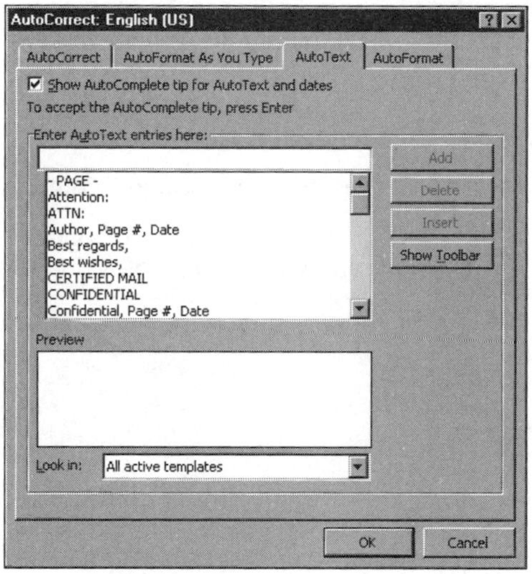

Figure 7-7: The AutoText dialog box.

There are no shortcuts with AutoText. Basically you're adding a word or phrase that you want Word to finish typing for you, such as your address. For example, the following address could be typed into the Enter AutoText Entries Here box:

```
5701 Repecho Drive
```

Clicking the Add button places that item in AutoText's bin. Now whenever you type **5701** in a document, AutoText takes over and displays the rest of the address. Press Enter to insert it.

Click the OK button to close the AutoCorrect dialog box.

As an alternative to typing the text in the AutoText dialog box, you can select text in your document, then choose Tools⇨AutoCorrect. Click the AutoText tab and the text you selected appears in the dialog box. Click Add, then click OK and you're done.

Removing an AutoText entry

Don't let it spook you that your name is in the AutoText list. Go ahead — open the AutoCorrect dialog box, click the AutoText tab and scroll down to find your name.

Well, maybe you won't find your name, maybe you will. Remember that you entered your name when you first installed Microsoft Office or Word. Or if someone else did it for you, then their name might appear instead.

✔ The most common name is "Preferred Customer," which is who Word thinks you are if you didn't fill in anything else.

✔ To remove an entry, locate it in the list. Click it once to highlight it. Click the Delete button.

✔ Click OK to exit the AutoCorrect dialog box after you've zapped enough entries.

Grammar Be Good

If spelling is arbitrary, then grammar is a myth. Oh, I could rant on this for hours. Suffice it to say, no matter what the grammarians think, English is not Latin. It can't be. In Latin there is usually one, very proper way to say something. In English, there are many ways and many words with which to express the same thought. That's why English is so poetic.

Regardless of what I think, Word does come with a grammar checker and it will, at times, underline suspicious words or phrases in an ugly green zigzag. That's your clue that you've somehow offended Word's sense of grammatical justice. Figure 7-8 shows an example. Right-clicking on the green-underlined text displays a pop-up menu, similar to the spell-checker's menu.

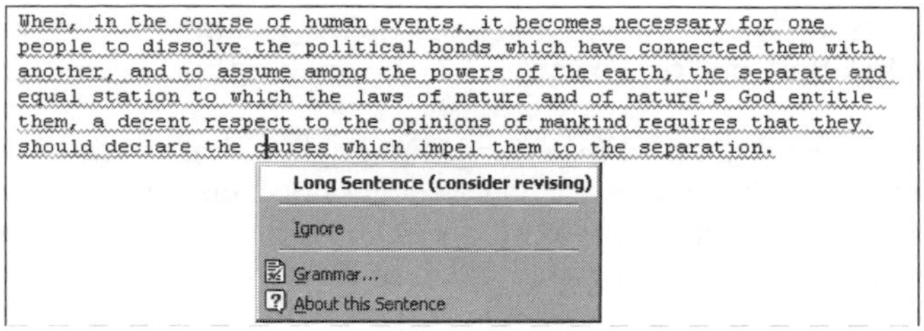

> When, in the course of human events, it becomes necessary for one
> people to dissolve the political bonds which have connected them with
> another, and to assume among the powers of the earth, the separate and
> equal station to which the laws of nature and of nature's God entitle
> them, a decent respect to the opinions of mankind requires that they
> should declare the causes which impel them to the separation.
>
> **Long Sentence (consider revising)**
>
> Ignore
> ─────────────────────
> 📝 Grammar...
> ❓ About this Sentence

Figure 7-8:
Radical
politics or
just bad
English?

Of course, I could drag all of classic literature through the grammar checker
and we'd both be slapping our thighs with laughter. My point is: most of the
grammar checker's suggestions can be ignored: Select Ignore from the menu
and the green zigzag goes away.

Where the grammar checker really comes in handy is checking commonly
misused words like "its" and "it's" and "there" and "their" and even "they're."
It's also good at finding mistakes like the following:

> This just doesn't adds up.

The grammar checker underlines "adds" as potentially wrong. Right-clicking
on the word displays "add" as a suggested replacement.

If you select About This Sentence from the pop-up menu, the Office Assistant
dog explains which part of the English Language Book of Rules you offended.
(Well, more or less. Sometimes the dog is way off in his explanation.)

✔ Sometimes the grammar checker seems to be wrong. But don't give up!
  Always check your entire sentence for a potential error. For example, it
  may suggest "had" instead of "have." Chances are "have" is correct but
  some other word in the sentence may have an unwanted "s."

✔ If you detest on-the-fly grammar checking, you can turn it off. Choose
  Tools➪Options from the menu. Click the Spelling & Grammar tab. Near
  the bottom of the dialog box, in the Grammar area, you'll find the Check
  Grammar as You Type check box. Click in the check box to deselect the
  option and click OK. Grammar is off.

Proofing Your Document All at Once

If you turn on-the-fly spelling or grammar checking off, then you might prefer
to do the proofing when you're done writing your document. Or maybe you
just want Word to quickly review your document, just in case in the flame of
passion you neglected to go back and find all the red and green zigzags.

To proof your entire document, choose Tools⇨Spelling and Grammar. You can also click the Spell tool or press F7, the Spelling and Grammar shortcut.

Word scans your document for offenses to English that would de-bun your seventh-grade English teacher's hair. When a boo-boo is encountered, the proper dialog box is displayed on the screen. You see either a spelling or a grammar dialog box; both look similar (see Figures 7-9 and 7-10).

Figure 7-9:
A misspelled word is caught.

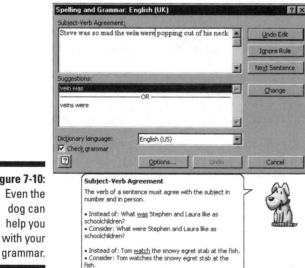

Figure 7-10:
Even the dog can help you with your grammar.

Instructions on how to handle each of these dialog boxes are given in the check mark list that follows the next paragraph. Basically, if you find a suggestion or correction that appeals to you, click the Change button. Otherwise, click the Ignore button until the entire operation is over.

Word continues checking your document until it says it's all done. Or, if you started checking in the middle somewhere, Word asks if you want to continue checking at the start of the document; click OK.

✔ If the correction you want isn't in the list at the bottom of the dialog box, you can make up your own. Just edit the text that appears in the top part of the dialog box, making the change you feel is necessary. Then click the Change button. Word continues checking your sentence and the rest of your document.

✔ If the misspelled word is really a word, consider adding it to Word's dictionary by clicking the Add button.

✔ If you don't want to be bothered with the same mistake over and over, click the Ignore All button.

✔ If you want to change every instance of a misspelled word to whatever is in the Change box, click Change All.

✔ If you have the annoying habit of typing "breif" rather than "brief," for example, you can click AutoCorrect and Word fixes that problem right after you type it.

✔ Undo undoes your corrections, most of the time. This option is great for those sleepy nighttime checks when you quickly select the wrong replacement word. Just click Undo and check out the last word again. (Undo may not work all the time; don't count on it.)

✔ The Word dictionary is not a substitute for a real dictionary. Only in a real dictionary can you look up the meaning of a word, which tells you whether you're using the proper word in the proper context. No computer writer works with an electronic dictionary alone; a good, thick Webster's is usually sitting within arm's reach.

✔ If two identical words are found in a row, Word highlights them as a `Repeated Word`. Error, error! Click the Ignore button to tell Word to forget about the double word or click the Delete button to blow the second word away.

✔ My, but this is a long list of check marks.

✔ The Spelling and Grammar command also locates words with weird capitalization. For example, gONer. You're given an opportunity to correct the word to proper capitalization just as though it were misspelled.

✔ The word *spell* here refers to creating words by using the accepted pattern of letters. Spelling has nothing to do with magic. Many people assume that a spell check instantly makes their document better. Wrong! You have to read what you write and then edit, look, and read again. Spell checking doesn't fix things other than finding rotten words and offering suggested replacements.

✔ *They spell it 'da Vinci' and pronounce it 'da Vinchy.' Foreigners always spell better than they pronounce.* —Mark Twain

Word's Silly Thesaurus

If you think that I'm smart enough to use all the big words in this chapter, you're grievously mistaken. Witness *grievously*. That's just another word for badly. Behold! It's Word's thesaurus in action. An amazing tool, astounding utensil, or marvelous implement. You get the idea. The thesaurus helps look up synonyms or other words that have the same meaning but carry more weight or offer more precision.

Here's how to instantly become a master of big, clunky words in English:

1. **Place the toothpick cursor within a simple word, such as big.**

   Adjectives are best for the thesaurus, although the Word Statistical Department tells me that the thesaurus contains more than 120,000 words.

2. **Do the Thesaurus command.**

   Choose Tools⇨Language⇨Thesaurus or press the Thesaurus shortcut, Shift+F7. Instantly, the Thesaurus dialog box opens (see Figure 7-11). Word displays several alternatives for the word. They're grouped into categories by meanings on the left and synonyms on the right.

Figure 7-11: The thesaurus displays other terms for big.

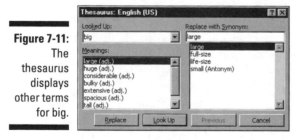

3. **To replace the word in your document, highlight your choice and click the Replace button.**

   After selecting a word, you return to your document. If you don't find a word, click the Cancel button to return to your document.

   ✔ A thesaurus is not a colossal, prehistoric beast.

   ✔ If one of the words in the left column is close but not exactly what you want, select it and click the Look Up button. The new word's synonyms appear in the right column.

A quick way to get a synonym

A thesaurus is a book of synonyms. A synonym is one word that carries the same or similar meaning to another. Like "giant" and "big" or "wee" and "small." English is full of these and Word's Shift+F7 Thesaurus command shows you a lot of them.

A handy way to get some quirky and commonly used synonyms for any word in your document is to right-click on the word and choose Synonym from the pop-up menu. For example, the figure nearby shows a pop-up list of syn-

onyms for the word "Prudence." Included among the list is even an antonym — a word that means the opposite of the original word.

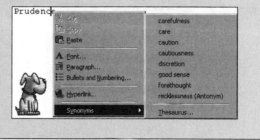

- ✔ If the word you select has no synonym, the thesaurus displays an alphabetical list of words. Type a new, similar word, or click the Cancel button to get back to your document.

- ✔ After inserting a new word, you may have to do a bit of editing: Add "ed" or "ing" to the word or maybe replace "a" with "an" in front of it. A bit of editing is usually required whenever you replace one word with another.

Pulling a Word Count

One of the silliest writing assignments you probably ever got in school was the "I want you to write a five-page dissertation on why ketchup isn't green" type of project — five pages! Are they nuts? Didn't Strunk and White stress brevity and clarity of thought over ghastly verbiage? I mean, if you can't offer a lucid argument in a single seven-word sentence, why do it?

But I digress.

Then there are those of us who get paid by the word. "Dan, write a 1,000-word article on Windows Registration Editor." I need to know when to stop writing. Also, curiosity generally gets the best of any writer, and you want to get a good feel for how many words you have in your document. To sate your scrivening curiosity, choose Tools⇨Word Count.

The Word Count dialog box displays a summary of your document's pages, words, characters, paragraphs, and lines. Figure 7-12 shows the stats for this document (before my editor got his blue ink-stained hands on it). How impressive. Okay. Click the Close button to get back to work.

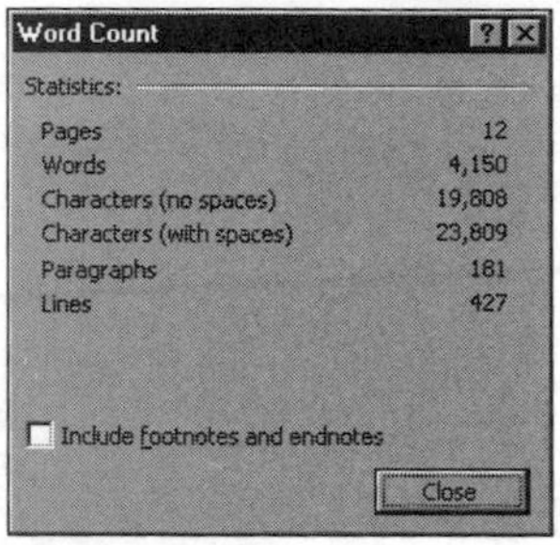

Figure 7-12:
Gonna
count me up
some
words.

The Word Count command is far more accurate than a page count. Pages can be fudged. Larger fonts and narrower margins have saved many a student from the perils of turning in a paper that was too short.

Chapter 8

Basic Document Tricks

*R*ight after you type the smallest modicum of text, you should save your document. There, on the disk, your document becomes a file, a permanent record you can open again for editing or printing or review just as if you typed it all in today. As long as you save your work to disk — even the most seemingly insignificant stuff — you'll have it forever. And don't worry about it taking up too much space. Word processing documents are space-savers on disk. Keep the lot of 'em!

This chapter shows you how to save a document to disk and how to open a document you created that's already been saved to disk. And just because it's a sunny day outside, I'll also tell you how to open one document *inside* another. Such a deal.

✔ What you save to disk is a *document* — all the text and stuff you've created in Word. Some people refer to a document saved on disk as a *file*. Same thing.

✔ Relatively speaking, a word processing document takes up little space on a hard drive. Each chapter in this book is 5 to 10 pages long, and the document files on disk for each chapter average about 42K in size, compared with 100K or more for a simple picture file.

✔ By the way, if you *are* writing a book in Word, save each chapter as its own document. While Word can handle large documents (the absolute size is unlimited), smaller documents are easier to deal with in the long run.

Saving a Document to Disk (The First Time)

Don't think you have to wait until you finish a document to save it to disk. In fact, saving should be done almost immediately — as soon as you have a few sentences or paragraphs. Save! Save! Save!

To save a document that hasn't already been saved to disk, follow these steps:

1. **Summon the Save command.**

    Just click the Save button on the toolbar. The Save As dialog box enlightens you with its presence, as shown in Figure 8-1.

Figure 8-1:
The Save As dialog box.

   If you don't see the Save As dialog box, it means that you already saved your document once. So, this time you're merely saving it again. That's fine.

2. **Type a name for your document.**

   Word automatically selects the first line or first several words of your document as a filename and puts it in the Save dialog box. If that's okay, you can move on to Step 3.

   If you want to give your document a name other than the one listed in the Save As dialog box, type in the new name. You can use letters, numbers, spaces, and a smattering of symbols. Though the filename can be tediously long, my advice is to keep it short, simple, and descriptive (which prevents most lawyers from effectively naming files).

3. **Click the Save button.**

   If everything goes right, your disk drive churns for a few seconds, and the file is saved.

   Your clue that the file has been successfully saved is that the filename now appears in the document's title bar, near the top of the screen.

If a problem arises, you'll likely see one of two error messages:

```
The file [whatever] already exists. Do you want to replace
        the existing file?
```

Press N for No. Word (or the Office Assistant) is telling you that there is already a file on disk with the name you've chosen. Skip back up to Step 2 and type another name. (If you press Y, your file replaces the other file on disk, which is probably not what you want.)

The second problem message reads something like this:

```
The file name, location, or format '[whatever]' is not
        valid. Type the filename and location in the cor-
        rect format, such as c:\location\filename.
```

Whatever. Basically you used a boo-boo character to name the file. To be safe, stick to letters, numbers, and spaces. Going beyond that means you may offend Word's sense of what a filename is or isn't. Check the sidebar, "Complicated — but important — information about filenames." Then click OK and try again.

- ✔ Another message may appear if you try to save a file using the name of another file you're editing. This, too, is wrong, and Word (or the Office Assistant) will let you know.

- ✔ You can also choose File➪Save to save your document. And for the keyboard wacky: there's the Ctrl+S shortcut; or use the forgetful Shift+F12 key.

- ✔ Always save your document, even after you've typed only a few lines of text.

- ✔ You should also organize your files by storing them in their own special folders on your disk.

Complicated — but important — information about filenames

You must name your file according to the loving, yet firm, Windows filenaming rules. This task isn't as tough as memorizing stuff for a DMV test, and it's not as horrid as things were in the ancient days of DOS — but it's darn close:

✔ A filename can be up to 255 characters long; even so, try to keep your filenames short and descriptive.

✔ A filename can include letters, numbers, and spaces and can start with a letter or a number.

✔ A filename can contain periods, commas, and hyphens.

✔ A filename cannot contain any of the following characters:

   \ / : * ? " < > |

✔ Don't bother typing a three-letter extension — .DOC — on the end of any of your Word files. (This is for anyone who used an older version of Word where the .DOC at the end of the name was required. It's not anymore.)

Saving a document (after it's already been saved once)

Just because you save your document to disk once doesn't mean you're all done. Every so often, you should save your document again. That way any changes you've made since the last time you saved are remembered. This doesn't mean you have to be obsessive about saving. For example, I save once every few pages of text I write, or whenever the phone rings or I need to get up and stretch my legs.

To save a document after saving it the first time (described in the previous section), press Ctrl+S or click the Save button on the toolbar. You see the status bar change oh-so-quickly as the document is saved.

Saving a document to disk with a new name

With a word processor, there is no such thing as a "draft." You know: rough draft, first draft, third draft, and so on. Well, in a way, whenever you print the document, you're printing a draft. But the "draft" concept isn't necessary because you just keep saving the same document to disk after you fix it up.

If you do want to save drafts, or you want to save any document to disk with a new name, choose File➪Save As. This displays the Save As dialog box (refer to Figure 8-1), in which you can type in a new name for the file, such as **Invasion Plans, 2nd Draft**.

You must choose File➪Save As to save a file under a new name. Choosing File➪Save, clicking the Save button on the toolbar, and pressing the Ctrl+S shortcut, not the same things.

Automatic recovery (in case you forget to save)

You should press Ctrl+S every so often to save your document. The justification here is fear: You're afraid that something nasty will happen to the computer and you'll lose everything you typed. (That's happened to me enough, let me tell you.)

Pressing Ctrl+S does save your stuff to disk, but as a backup to that strategy, Word also has the AutoRecover feature.

What AutoRecover does is to secretly save information about your document every few minutes or so. That way, if there's a power outage or other mishap and you forgot to press Ctrl+S, you can get some of your document back. This is a handy feature everyone should use.

To turn on AutoRecover, follow these steps:

1. **Choose Tools➪Options.**

   You may have to click the down-arrows at the bottom of the menu to find the Options menu item.

2. **Click the Save tab.**

   The Options dialog box has lots of tabs. Locate the Save tab and click it to display information about saving your document.

3. **Ensure that the Save AutoRecover check box is selected.**

   It's the last check box, near the middle of the left side of the dialog box. If you don't see a check mark in the Save AutoRecover check box, click in the box to select it. Doing so activates automatic recovery.

4. **Enter the backup interval in the Minutes text box.**

   For example, the number 10 directs Word to back up your documents every ten minutes. If the power is unstable at your home or office, enter 5, 3, 2, or even 1 minute as the backup interval. (Though the smaller the interval, the more often Word may interrupt your work to do the backup.)

Don't bother with Fast Save

Fast Save is one of those ideas that sounds real good . . . until you use it. The idea is to avoid having to save everything in your document every time you use the Save command. I suppose the logic is, "Why not just save the changes?" If you have Fast Save on, Word only saves the new stuff you typed to disk, which is faster than saving the whole document. Unfortunately, it can lead to problems.

For example, if Word saves only your changes to disk, what's someone else going to make of such a file? What if Tolstoy only changed a character's name in Chapter 43? He would have turned in a disk to his publisher with a Chapter 43 file that contained only the single word Ludmilla. That just doesn't work.

To ensure that Fast Save is disabled, choose Tools⇨Options. Then click the Save tab. If the Allow Fast Saves box is selected, click that option to deselect it. Click OK to return to your document. Saving is something the computer can take time with, as far as I'm concerned.

5. Press Enter to return to your document.

Even though Word has the AutoRecovery option, don't get sloppy! It's still best to save with Ctrl+S or the Save button on the toolbar as often as you can.

Saving when you're done

You're done for the day. Your fingers are sore, your eyes glaze over, "I don't want to type no more!" Everywhere you look, you see a mouse pointer. You blink and rub your eyes and stretch out your back. But before you slap your buddies on the back and walk into the sunset in a beer commercial, you need to save your document and quit for the day. You have two choices:

✔ **Choose File⇨Close.** This closes the document you're working on without actually quitting Word. That allows you to stick around, start a new document, open an old document or just play with the dog.

✔ **Choose File⇨Exit.** This closes Word and lets you return to Windows for fun and folly.

Either way, when you close the document you're working on, Word may ask you if you need to save. Click Yes. The document is saved to disk one final time.

If the document you're working on has yet to be saved, then you'll see the Save As dialog box (refer to Figure 8-1), in which case you need to give the file a name and save it that way.

The point is, Word won't let you quit or close any document that isn't saved to disk.

If you choose File➪Close or File➪Exit and if Word doesn't ask you to save, then the document has already been saved to disk. No need to fret. Everything's okay.

 ✔ The shortcut key for the File➪Close command is Ctrl+W.

 ✔ The shortcut key to close Word is — are you ready? — Alt+F4.

 ✔ There is no reason to quit Word and start it again to begin working with a blank slate.

 ✔ Always quit Word properly. Never turn off your PC or reset when Word or Windows is still on-screen. Only turn off your PC when Windows tells you that it's safe to do so. If you don't, your computer starts running slower and Windows may crash (more frequently).

Opening a Document on Disk

To fetch a document from disk, you use the Open command. This command retrieves a document you saved to disk, opening it in a window where you can read, edit, print, or do whatever to it all over again.

To grab a file from disk — to open it — follow these steps:

1. Summon the Open command.

Choose File➪Open to display the Open dialog box, as shown in Figure 8-2.

Figure 8-2:
The Open
dialog box.

The shortcut key for the Open command is Ctrl+O, and there's also a quick shortcut button on the toolbar, as shown in the margin.

2. Click the document's name.

The Open dialog box — vast and wild as it is — contains a list of documents previously saved to disk, as you can see in Figure 8-2. Your job is to find the one you want to open.

Sometimes you may have to open a folder icon to locate your document. For example, the Great American Novel folder, in Figure 8-2, contains chapters from my next book.

When you find the file, click once on its name. This highlights the file.

3. Click the Open button.

Word opens the file, carefully lifting it from your disk drive and slapping it down on the screen where you can edit it, print it, read it, or just look at it in glowing admiration.

✔ Opening a document does not erase it from your disk drive.

✔ Opening a document is one of the first things you can do when you start your Word day.

✔ Word may complain that it can't open a document because a certain conversion feature is unavailable. If so, click Yes to load that feature. (You may need to obtain the Word or Office CD to complete the operation.)

✔ If you can't find your document, refer to Chapter 28, "Working with Documents."

✔ If you want to edit a file you recently had open, pull down the File menu and look at the list on the bottom of the menu to see whether the file is listed. Word "remembers" the last few documents you worked on. If you see what you want there, click the file's name to open it.

Chapter 9

Getting it Down on Paper

● ●

In This Chapter

▶ Getting the printer ready to print

▶ Previewing your document before printing

▶ Printing a document the quick and easy way

▶ Printing on another printer (if you have more than one)

▶ Printing specific parts of a document

▶ Printing several documents

▶ Printing multiple copies of a document

▶ Canceling the Print command

● ●

*A*re you old enough to remember carefully advancing the paper in a type-writer so you could erase something with a pencil eraser? Or how about swapping in the "erase cartridge" so you could back up and erase? And who can forget whiffing Wite-Out fluid, or holding a page up to the light to see how often Wite-Out was used. Thanks to your word processor, computer, and printer, those days are long gone.

This chapter is about the final step you take after creating your masterpiece, getting it down on paper. It sounds easy: coax your document out of the computer and into the printer, where it prints just like you want it to. Of course, there may be some problems and issues, which this chapter addresses. After all, no single device in your entire computer system deserves a good flogging like the printer.

Of course, you may have some problems or questions, which this chapter addresses.

Preparing the Printer (Do This First!)

Before printing, you must make sure that your printer is ready to print. Check these few items:

1. **Make sure your printer is plugged in and properly connected to your computer.**

   A cable connects the computer and your printer. The cable should be firmly plugged in at both ends. (This cable needs to be checked only if you're having printer problems.)

   Never plug a printer cable into a printer or computer that is on and running. Always turn your printer and computer off whenever you plug anything into them. If you don't, you may damage the internal electronic components.

2. **Make sure that your printer has enough toner and ink, or a decent ribbon.**

   Laser printers should have a good toner cartridge installed. If the laser printer's "toner low" indicator is on, replace the toner at once.

   Most ink printers let you know when they're out of ink, or you'll notice the image appears fuzzy or is missing information. Replace the ink cartridge at once.

   Frayed ribbons in older printers produce faint text and are bad for the printing mechanism.

3. **Check the printer for paper.**

   The paper can feed from the back, come out of a paper tray, or be manually fed one sheet at a time. However your printer eats paper, make sure that you have it set up properly before you print.

4. **Your printer must be *online* or *selected* before you can print anything.**

   Somewhere on your printer is a button labeled *Online* or *Select* and, usually, a corresponding light or display. Press that button to turn on the option (and the light). Although your printer is plugged in, the power switch is on, and the machine is doing its warm-up stretching exercises, the printer doesn't print unless it's online or selected.

   ✔ If you're printing to a network printer — and the thought makes me shudder — someone else is in charge of the printer. The network printer should be set up and ready to print. If not, someone to whom you can complain is usually handy.

   ✔ The printer you use affects the way Word displays and prints your document, so before you do a lot of formatting, check to be sure that you selected the correct printer. Refer to the section "Choosing Another Printer (If You Have More Than One to Choose From)" later in this chapter.

Preview Before You Print

Before the Print Preview command, people often printed out documents to see how they looked — even when the screen pretty much showed them what was going on. For some reason, seeing it "on paper" was a big deal. And they'd print and print, making small adjustments each time, and eventually they printed so much paper that all the forests were gone and Mr. Bunny had no where left to live.

Save Mr. Bunny!

 To sneak a preview of how your printed document will look, choose File⇨Print Preview or click the handy Print Preview button on the Standard toolbar. Doing so displays your document in a rather standoffish view, as shown in Figure 9-1.

Take note of how your text looks on the page. Look at the margins. If you're using footnotes, headers, or footers, look at how they lay out. The idea here is to spot something dreadfully wrong *before* you print.

When you're done gawking, click the Close button to return to your document.

Figure 9-1:
A document is being previewed before printing, saving most of the Amazon rain forest.

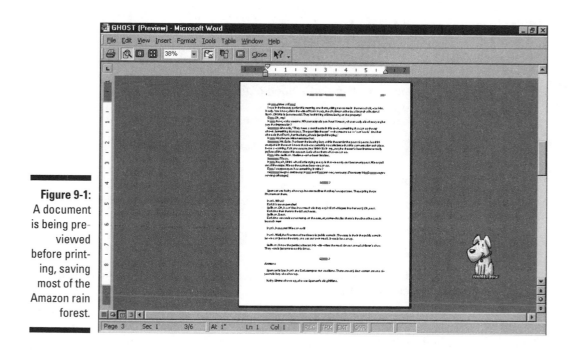

Or if everything looks hunky and dory, click the little Print button and your document prints instantly.

✔ Use the scroll bars to see more of your document.

✔ If you have a wheel mouse like the Microsoft Intellimouse, you can roll the wheel up or down to scroll one page up or down in your document.

✔ If your mouse is wheel-less, you can use the Page Up and Page Down buttons to peruse various pages of your document.

 ✔ To get a closer look at your document in Print Preview mode, click the Magnifier button. The mouse pointer changes to a magnifying glass. Click the mouse on any part of your document to zoom in for a closer look. Click the mouse again to zoom back out.

✔ You can, kind of, sort of, edit in Print Preview mode. You can click the mouse in the document and get a toothpick cursor for typing and what-not. Even so, I don't recommend it. Instead, if you want to edit, click the Close button to return to proper editing mode.

✔ I don't really use Print Preview mode much. However, if I'm really formatting something heavily — with footnotes, strange columns, and stuff like that — Print Preview can be a godsend.

Printing a Whole Document

If you think that your work is worthy of being smeared on a sheet of paper, follow these steps. To print your entire document, from top to bottom, gavel to gavel, head to toe, from *once upon a time* to *happily every after:*

1. **Make sure that the printer is online and ready to print.**

   See the first section in this Chapter, "Preparing the Printer (Do This First!)"

2. **Save your document.**

   Ha! Surprised you. Saving before you print is always a good idea. Click the little Save tool for a quickie save, and if you need any extra help, refer to Chapter 8 on saving your stuff to disk.

3. **Print your document.**

   The quickest way to do this is to click the Print tool. Click it and your document starts to print.

   If you choose File⇨Print or press Ctrl+P instead of using the Print tool on the toolbar, the Print dialog box appears (see Figure 9-2). You need to then click OK or press the Enter key to print your document.

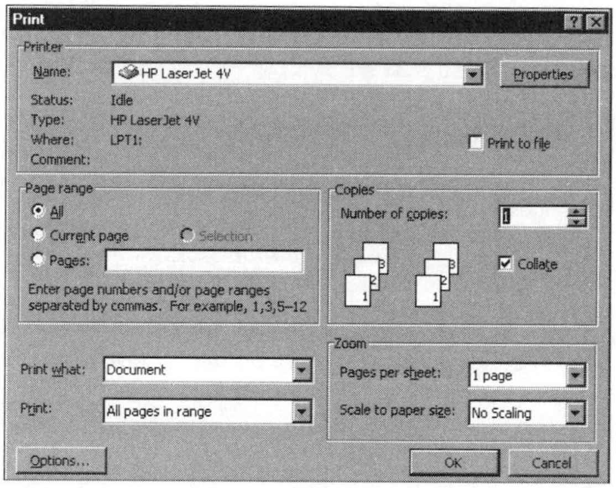

Print

Printer

Name: HP LaserJet 4V ▾ Properties

Status: Idle
Type: HP LaserJet 4V
Where: LPT1: ☐ Print to file
Comment:

Page range
◉ All
○ Current page ○ Selection
○ Pages:
Enter page numbers and/or page ranges
separated by commas. For example, 1,3,5–12

Copies
Number of copies: 1
☑ Collate

Print what: Document
Print: All pages in range

Zoom
Pages per sheet: 1 page
Scale to paper size: No Scaling

Options... OK Cancel

Figure 9-2:
The Print
dialog box.

Printing may take some time — really. A long time. Fortunately, Word lets you continue working while it prints in the *background*. To ensure that Word works this way, refer to the techie sidebar, "Printing and getting on with your life."

✔ If nothing prints, don't hit the Print command again! There's probably nothing awry; the computer is still thinking or sending (downloading) text to the printer. If you don't get an error message, everything will probably print, eventually.

✔ The computer prints one copy of your document for every Print command you incant. So if the printer is just being slow and you impatiently click the Print button ten times, you get ten copies of your document. (See the section "Canceling a Print Job" later in this chapter.)

✔ If you have a manual-feed printer, the printer itself begs for paper. Your printer says, "Beep, feed me!" You must stand by, line up paper, and then shove it into the printer's gaping maw until your document is done printing. Refer to "Printing Envelopes," later in this chapter, to figure this one out.

✔ Aside from saving your document, you may consider proofreading it before you print. See Chapter 7.

✔ Windows actually does the printing. Word simply acts as a messenger. Because of this fact, you see the li'l printer guy appear by the current time on the taskbar whenever something is printing in Word. This display isn't very important.

Printing and getting on with your life

Word has the capability to print while you do something else. If this background printing capability isn't coddled to life, you may wait a dreadfully long time while your documents print. To ensure that the background printing option is on, click the Options button in the Print dialog box (press Ctrl+P and then Alt+O to get at the Options button). A special dialog box appears.

In the upper part of the dialog box, you find the Printing Options corral. The top item in the right column is the Background Printing check box, which should have a checkmark in it. If not, click in the check box or press Alt+B to put one there. Click the OK button to close that dialog box, and then click the Close button to banish the Print dialog box. Now you're all set with background printing.

Choosing Another Printer (If You Have More Than One to Choose From)

After someone properly sets up your computer to recognize and work with multiple printers, you can direct Word to use one or more of them at any time. Don't think this is absurd either: Any PC can easily handle two printers. But in most cases, the extra printers are often found on a network.

To choose a different printer, such as an old dot matrix for a draft, a color printer for a new brochure, or a network printer because, honestly, the boss has the best printer and it's in her office, follow these steps:

1. **Choose File⇨Print.**

   Or, better yet, press Ctrl+P, the Print shortcut. Do not use the Print button on the toolbar for this because you need to see the Print dialog box and the toolbar button doesn't give you that option.

   The Print dialog box appears (see Figure 9-2). Notice the top area, which describes your current printer.

2. **Click the down-arrow on the Name list box.**

   When you click the down-arrow, a list of the printers your PC knows about is displayed, as shown in Figure 9-3.

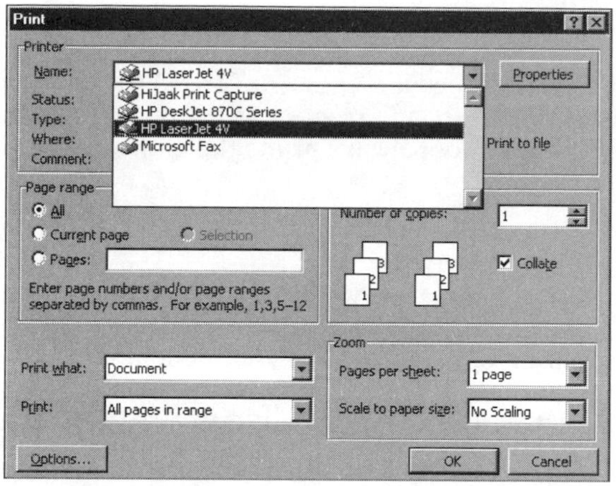

Figure 9-3:
Other print-
ers you can
choose.

3. **Select the printer that you want to use.**

   Click once on the printer's name.

4. **Click Close.**

   Clicking the Close button confirms that you've changed the printer, but does not tell Word to print. If you want to print as well as change the printer, click the OK button.

Instantly, Word is alerted to your new printer. You're done. That's it.

✔ Word remembers which printer you last chose and continues to use that printer until you tell it to change. This happens whether you use the Print button on the toolbar or the Print dialog box. Always remember which printer you're using.

✔ You're automatically switched back to your computer's favorite (or "default") printer when you quit and restart Word. Of course, you can always switch back by repeating the above steps and choosing the other printer.

✔ Information on setting up multiple printers in Windows can be found in *PCs For Dummies*, 6th Edition, from IDG Books Worldwide, Inc.

Printing Bits and Pieces

You don't have to print your entire document every time you want some hard copy. No, Word lets you print a single page, a range of pages, or a selected block of text. This is all done in the Page range area of the Print dialog box (in the middle, on the left).

The following sections assume your printer is on and ready to print.

Also, note that you must choose File➪Print (or Ctrl+P) to summon the Print dialog box. You cannot print bits and pieces of a document using the Print tool on the toolbar; the Print tool always prints the entire document, no matter what.

Printing a specific page

Follow these steps to print only one page of your document:

1. **Move the toothpick cursor so that it's sitting somewhere in the page you want to print.**

   Check the Page counter in the lower-left corner of the screen (on the Status bar) to ensure that you're on the right page.

   You can use the Go To command (the F5 key) to go to any specific page in your document. See Chapter 3.

2. **Choose File➪Print, or press Ctrl+P.**

3. **Select the Current Page option in the Print Range panel.**

   Refer to Figure 9-2.

4. **Click OK.**

   The dialog box closes and that one page prints. (It may take some time to print as Word organizes its thoughts.)

The single page prints with all the formatting you applied even though it's only a single page that prints. For example, if you have a document with headers, footers and a page number, then all that information is included on the one page you print — just as though you had printed the complete document.

Printing a single page in this manner is great for when you (or the printer) goof up one page in a document and you need to reprint only that page. This saves trees over reprinting the whole document just to fix one boo-boo. And it keeps Mr. Bunny happy.

Printing a range of pages

Word enables you to print a single page, a range of pages, or even some hodgepodge combination of random pages from within your document. To print a range or group of pages, follow these steps:

1. **Conjure up the File⇨Print command.**

2. **Click the Pages button in the Page Range area of the Print dialog box.**

   The Pages button is on the left side of the dialog box, near the middle.

3. **Type the page numbers and range of page numbers.**

   To print pages 3 through 5, type **3-5**.

   To print pages 1 through 7, type **1-7**.

   To print pages 2 and 6, type **2,6**.

4. **Click OK.**

   The pages you specify — and only those pages — print.

You can get very specific with the page ranges. For example, to print page 3, pages 5 through 9, pages 15 through 17, and page 19 (boy, that coffee went everywhere, didn't it?), you type **3**, **5-9**, **15-17**, **19**.

Printing a block

After you mark a block of text on-screen, you can beg the Print command to print only that block. Here's how:

1. **Mark the block of text that you want to print.**

   See Chapter 6 for all the block-marking instructions in the world.

2. **Choose File⇨Print.**

   You can also press Ctrl+P, or qualify for the Finger Gymnastics event at the next Olympics by pressing Ctrl+Shift+F12.

3. **Tickle the button by the word** Selection.

   The Selection item in the Print dialog box is available only when you have a block selected. Press the Alt+S key or click the button by the word Selection. (Selection is located in the Page range area of the Print dialog box.) This step tells Word that you want to print only your highlighted block.

4. **Click the OK button.**

   In a few moments, you see the hard copy sputtering out of your printer. The page selection prints in the same position and with the same headers and footers (if any) as it would had you printed the entire document.

Printing Several Documents

You may think that the best way to print several documents at a time is to open each one and print them one at a time. A better way exists, however, and it's hidden in the Open dialog box, the same one you use to open any old document on disk.

To print several files at a time, follow these steps:

1. **Make sure that the printer is on, selected, and rarin' to print.**

2. **Choose File➪Open.**

   Or you can press Ctrl+O or click the Open tool. Any way you choose, the Open dialog box appears in all its glory.

3. **Select the documents you want to print.**

   To select a document, Ctrl+click it with the mouse: Press and hold the Ctrl key and click the file. This highlights that document.

   Keep Ctrl+clicking documents until you highlight all those you want to print.

4. **Click the Tools button at the top of the Open dialog box.**

   A list of commands appears in a pop-up menu (see Figure 9-4). The one you want is the Print command.

Figure 9-4: Choosing the Print command in the Open dialog box.

5. **Choose the Print command.**

   Word happily prints all the documents you selected.

- When you print a gang of documents, they just all print. No Print dialog box or no warning asks you if the printer has enough paper or if you're really spiritually prepared to print all those documents at once.

- Yes, as with printing a single document, printing multiple documents takes a while.

Printing More Than One Copy of Something

Every year I concoct a family Christmas letter and bring joy to the hearts of dozens of friends and relatives by sending them a copy. Rather than drive off to Kinko's and pay the exorbitant fee of six cents per copy, I instead opt to do my own printing and direct Word to have the printer spew out the several dozen copies I need. This approach is real cinchy, providing you have enough paper, and you know which part of the Print dialog box to tweak.

To print several copies of a document, heed these steps:

1. **Prepare everything.**

   Ensure that the document is up to snuff (use Print Preview for that, as discussed earlier in this chapter) and make sure the computer is stocked with the proper, festive paper.

2. **Choose File⇨Print.**

   Or press Ctrl+P. As with other printing variations, you cannot use the Print button on the toolbar to print multiple copies (unless you just want to click it twice to get two quick copies.)

3. **Enter the number of copies in the Number of Copies box.**

   The Copies area is in the middle on the right side of the Print dialog box (refer to Figure 9-2). In the box, type the number of copies you want Word to spew out. For three copies of a memo, type **3**.

4. **Click OK to print your copies.**

Under normal circumstances, Word prints each copy of the document one after the other. This process is known as "collating." However, if you're printing seven copies of something and you want Word to print seven page 1s and then seven page 2s (and so on), click in the Collate check box to *remove* the check mark. (Normally you leave the check mark there.)

Canceling a Print Job (Omigosh!)

Since you probably need to quickly cancel your printing, here goes:

 1. Double-click the li'l printer dude by the current time on the taskbar.

This step opens up your printer's window (see Figure 9-5) and displays a list of documents waiting to be printed.

Figure 9-5:
Documents
waiting in
your
printer's
queue.

Mongo				
Printer Document View Help				
Document Name	Status	Owner	Progress	Started At
Microsoft Word - 07.doc	Printing	ed	4 of 13 pages	6:02:22 PM 11/3/99
Microsoft Word - 08.doc		ed	9 page(s)	6:02:22 PM 11/3/99
Microsoft Word - Too much S...		ed	6 page(s)	6:04:03 PM 11/3/99
3 jobs in queue				

2. Click the name of your Word document "job" in the Print Manager list.

3. Choose Document⇨Cancel Printing.

4. Click OK to terminate the job.

If you're using a network printer, you may not be able to cancel the document. Oh well.

5. Cancel more print jobs if you're in an especially vicious mood.

Repeat Steps 3 and 4 for each job you want to sack.

6. Close your printer's window after you're done.

Choose Printer⇨Close to make the window run away from the desktop. You're zapped back to Word, ready for more editing action.

Obviously, canceling a print job is the act of a desperate person. In its efforts to make life easy for computer users, Windows tries hard to help us change our minds. Canceling something that's printing may or may not work as planned. My advice is just to be careful with the Print command in the first place.

✔ The little printer icon appears only when Windows is sending something to the printer. Depending on how much you're printing and how fast your printer is, you may not even see it at all. If you don't, you're out of luck and you may as well quit right now and eat some ice cream.

✔ Documents appear in the printer's window from top to bottom in the order they were sent to the printer. The top document in the list is currently printing; other documents are waiting in the queue (which is the way the British say "line").

Chapter 10

Tips from a Word Guru

· ·

· ·

*F*or the past 10 years or so, I've been using Microsoft Word as my main word processor. That makes me an expert, or at least enough of an experienced user that I have oodles and oodles of tips stored away, which I'd like to pass on to you. In this chapter are suggestions and random thoughts that relate to other topics in this part of the book, but I put them all here for easy reference. These tips and tricks are ones I wish *I'd* known about when I first started using Word — some of these tips surprise even long-time Word users.

It may be a good idea to flag this chapter for later reference. Or, if you're a new Word user, make a mental note to return here for review after you've been working with Word a while.

The Office Assistant Has Thought of Something!

Here's one reason to turn the Office Assistant on: The lightbulb! After you do certain common tasks in Word, the Office Assistant grows a halo of sorts, shaped like the lightbulb pictured in the margin. That means the Office Assistant has a suggestion that may make your task easier.

To see the suggestion, click the lightbulb. A cartoon bubble with helpful or insightful information is displayed, as shown in Figure 10-1. Click OK when you're done reading.

Figure 10-1:
The Office
Assistant
says
something
useful.

It would have been a really great idea to buy Microsoft stock back in 1986.

OK

TIP

To see the Office Assistant, choose Help➪Show the Office Assistant from the menu.

Finding Your Place Quickly

At the start of the day, you open your document and then what? You scroll down, reading and editing until you think you get to where you were last editing yesterday. Needless to say, this can be a tedious waste of time.

Alas, the Shift+F5 shortcut ("Go Back") doesn't remember where you were when you open a document (unless you never quit Word). So a trick I use is to insert two ampersands (&&) into the document where I was last editing. For example:

```
"So," Desmond continued, "It wasn't Uncle Jared who killed
father after all. No! The night nurse really did call in sick,
and the power company said there was no outage on the street
that night. That means that only &&
```

Above, the two ampersands mark the spot where I was writing last. To find that spot after opening a document, I press Ctrl+F to display the Find and Replace dialog box, then search for &&. I close the Find and Replace dialog box; then get on with my work.

You don't have to use the && symbols (which is Shift+7 twice, if you've been mentally geared by Word to think that way). You can use any symbols to mark your place. Just remember what they are.

Taking Advantage of the Repeat Key

The F4 key in Word is known as the Repeat key, and it can be a real time-saver. If you press a Word command, cursor key, or character, and then press the F4 key, that command, cursor key, or character is repeated. (You can also choose Edit⇨Repeat Typing or press Ctrl+Y.)

For example, type the following lines in Word:

```
Knock. knock.
Who's there?
Knock.
Knock who?
```

Now press the F4 key. Word repeats the last few things you typed. (If you had to press the Backspace key to back up and erase, then F4 repeats only from that point on.)

Another handy F4/repeat deal: Type a bunch of underlines on-screen, like blank lines in a form. Then press Enter. Press the F4 key a few times, and the page is soon filled with blank lines. Hey! Create your own ruled paper!

Previewing Documents Before You Open Them

You can name a file the most descriptive and useful name you can think of, then ten days later forget what's in it. Or maybe you're working on a book and need to double-check the real name you gave Chapter 8. Naturally, you say (because you're with-it), I can just open that document for a sneak-peek.

Oh! But there's a better way. You can use the Open dialog box to preview any document *before* you open it, saving valuable time and effort. Here's how:

1. **Choose File⇨Open.**

   Or you can click the Open button on the toolbar or use Ctrl+O. Whatever. The Open dialog box appears.

2. **Click the down-arrow by the Views button.**

The Views button is located in the top left part of the dialog box. (It's similar to the Views button in Windows 98.) Clicking the down-arrow by that button drops down a menu.

3. Choose Preview from the menu.

The look of the Open dialog box changes to reveal the Preview mode. Any file you choose on the left side of the Open dialog box is previewed on the right side, as shown in Figure 10-2.

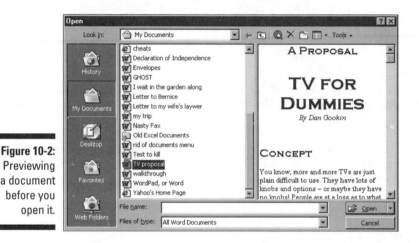

Figure 10-2: Previewing a document before you open it.

You can scroll the Word document down to read more of it if you like.

Choose another file to preview by clicking its name.

4. To open the file, just click the Open button. Or if you're done looking, click Cancel.

The Open dialog box stays in Preview mode until you choose another mode from the Views button drop-down list. (Normally Word uses "List" view, which is the top item in the Views menu.)

✔ If you choose All files from the Files of Type list, then you can use the Open dialog box's preview window to preview other types of files: graphics files, text documents, even Excel documents.

✔ Previewing some types of documents may prompt Word to display a File Conversion dialog box. Click OK if you want to open the file; otherwise — if you're just poking around — click Cancel.

✔ If you attempt to preview a Web page document that you saved to disk, Windows may attempt to connect to the Internet to update the information on the document. (Just a warning in case something like that tends to bug you.)

✓ If the file is of a mysterious type that Word cannot display you get the message, `Preview not available`. Oh well.

✓ See Chapter 8 for more general information on opening documents.

✓ See Chapter 28, "Working with Documents," for information on other things you can do with files in the Open dialog box.

Counting Individual Words with Find and Replace

A nifty thing about the Replace command is that it tells you how many words it found and replaced when it's done. You can take advantage of that in a sneaky way to see how many times you use a certain word in your document.

As an example, suppose you know that you use the word "actually" way too much. One or two actuallies are okay, but more than that and you're being obsessive.

To discover how many "actually" words (or any words) are in your document, summon the Find and Replace command and enter the word in *both* the Find what and Replace with boxes. The same word. Two times. Click Replace All and Word dutifully counts the instances of that word in your document.

Nothing is replaced with this trick because you're searching for a word and replacing it with the same word. (Believe it or not, this does not confuse the Office Assistant.)

Multiple Document Mania

Word lets you work on up to a zillion documents at once. Well, actually, you can work on several documents at once. Any time you open a new document or choose File⇨New to start a new document from scratch, Word opens another document window.

All the document windows appear as buttons on the taskbar, as shown in Figure 10-3. To switch from one document to another, click its button on the taskbar.

Figure 10-3:
Word's
document
buttons on
the taskbar.

✔ Yes, in a way having all those buttons means that you do have more than one copy of the Word program running at a time. There isn't anything wrong with that. In fact, I encourage you to open as many document windows as you need.

✔ A quick way to switch from one document window to another is to press the Alt+Tab key combination.

✔ Another way to switch documents is to use the Window menu. Alas, the Window menu displays only the first nine documents you have open (which is a lot). For any more than nine windows, you see a More Windows menu item that displays the entire list of all the documents/windows you're working on in Word.

✔ The goings-on in one document are independent of any other: Printing, spell checking, and formatting affect only the document you can see on-screen.

✔ You can copy a block from one document to the other. Just mark the block in the first document, copy it (Ctrl+C), open the second document, and paste it in (Ctrl+V). Refer to Chapter 6 for detailed block action.

Closing your documents

When you're working with several open document/windows at a time, you can close the documents by clicking the X "close" button in the window's upper-right corner. However, when you get to the last open document, do not click the X button unless you want to quit Word as well as close the document.

Seeing more than one document

You can arrange all your documents on-screen by choosing Window⇨Arrange All. (You may need to click the down-arrows at the bottom of the menu to see this command displayed.) The Arrange All command arranges each document window in a tiled pattern on the screen, allowing you to view more than one document at a time.

Of course, choosing Window⇨Arrange All works best with two documents. Three or more documents arranged on the screen and, well, see Figure 10-4 for the ugly result.

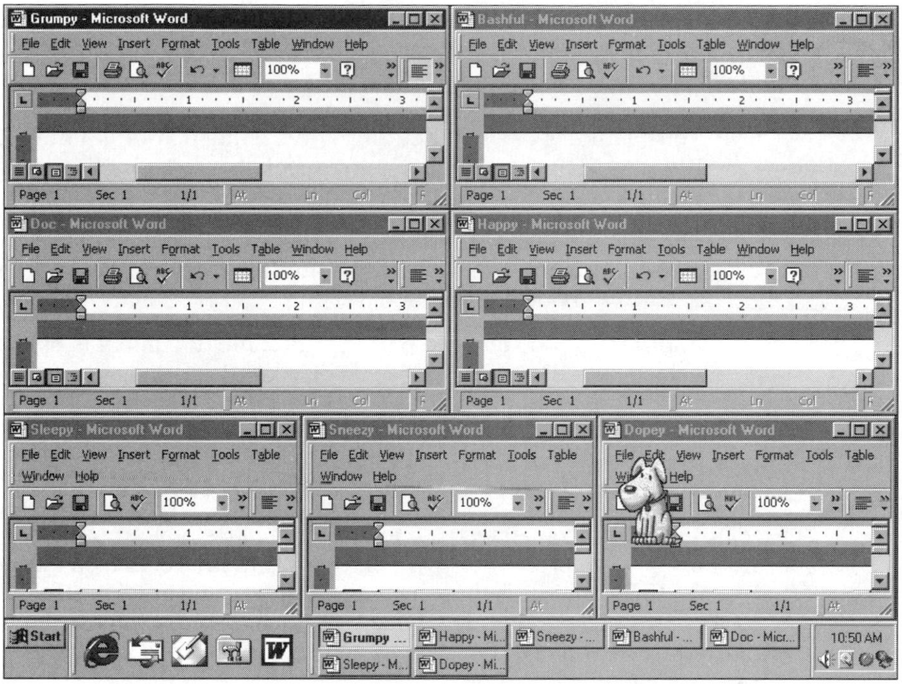

Figure 10-4:
Too many
documents
arranged in
a puzzle-like
pattern.

✔ Although you can see more than one document at a time, you can *work* on only one at a time: The document with the highlighted title bar.

✔ After the windows are arranged, you can manipulate their size and change their positions with the mouse.

✔ Clicking a window's Maximize button restores the document to its normal, full-screen view.

Working on one document in two windows

It's possible in Word to show one document in two windows. This allows you to view two or more different parts of the same document in a large window.

To set up a second window for your document, choose the Window⇨New Window command. (You may need to click the down-arrows at the bottom of the menu to see the New Window command.) The second window opens, as does a second button for that window on the taskbar.

Even though there are two windows open, you're still working on only one document. The changes you make in one of the copies are immediately included in the other. (If you want to make a copy of the document, use Windows to copy the document file.)

When you're done with the second window, click the X button to close it. This closes the window without closing your document; the first window stays open.

✔ This feature is useful for cutting and pasting text or graphics between sections of the same document, especially when you have a very long document.

✔ The title bar tells you which copy of your document you're looking at by displaying a colon and a number after the filename. For example, `Boring Stuff:1` in one window and `Boring Stuff:2` in the second window.

✔ Another way to view two parts of the same document is by using the old split-screen trick. This feature is discussed . . . why, it's right here.

Using the old split-screen trick

Splitting the screen allows you to view two parts of your document in one window. No need to bother with extra windows here. In fact, I prefer to use Word with as little junk on-screen as possible. So when I need to view two parts of the same document, I just split the screen — Moses-like — and then undo the rift when I'm done. You can accomplish the same splitting-screen feat by following these steps:

1. **Place the mouse cursor on the little gray thing located just above the up-arrow button on the vertical scroll bar (on the upper-right side of your document).**

   Oh, brother. Just refer to Figure 10-5 to see what I'm talking about.

Figure 10-5:
The little gray thing you use to split a window.

The little gray thing

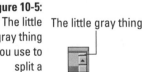

When you find the sweet spot, the mouse pointer changes shape and looks like a pair of horizontal lines with arrows pointing down and up.

2. **Hold down the left mouse button and drag the pointer down.**

   As you drag, a line drags with you and slices the document window in half. That marks the spot where the screen splits.

3. **Release the mouse button.**

   Your screen looks something like Figure 10-6.

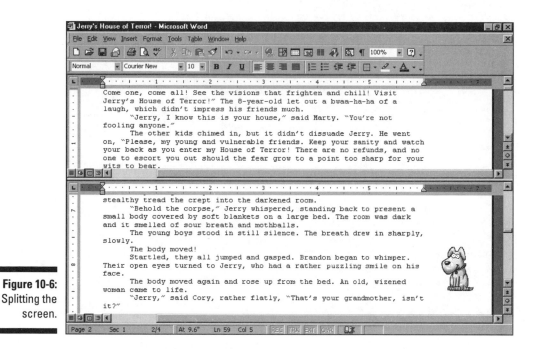

Figure 10-6:
Splitting the
screen.

✔ Each section of the screen can be manipulated separately and scrolled up or down. But the windows still represent the same document; changes that you make in one of the copies are immediately included in the others.

✔ This feature is useful for cutting and pasting text or graphics between parts of the same document.

✔ The fastest way to split a window is to point the mouse at the little gray area and double-click. It's also the fasted way to undo a split screen: Put the mouse pointer on the little gray area and double-click.

✔ You can also choose <u>W</u>indow⇨<u>S</u>plit to split your screen and <u>W</u>indow⇨ Remove S<u>p</u>lit to undo it. (The Remove Split command can be seen if you click the down-arrow at the bottom of the Window menu.)

Part II

Letting Word Do the Formatting Work

The 5th Wave   By Rich Tennant

Software Obsolescence Syndrome—The need to own only the latest version of any program.

In this part . . .

Formatting is the art of making your document look less ugly. It's the second part of word processing, coming right after the writing part, yet often consuming far more time. After all, text is text. You have a gift for it or you don't. And if you don't, Word is capable of taking plain, boring text and making it look pretty. (It may still read bad, but it *looks* pretty.) Ah, let me tell you, nothing makes you swell with pride like a well-formatted document.

This part of the book tells you how to format your document. You can format text, characters, paragraphs, sentences and entire documents. I also tell you about styles and templates plus automatic formatting tips and tricks to sate the desires of documents most demanding.

Chapter 11

Formatting Characters, Fonts, and Text

● ●

In This Chapter

▶ Changing the font

▶ Formatting text with **bold,** *italics,* and <u>underline</u>

▶ Using text attributes

▶ Changing text size

▶ Making superscript and subscript text

▶ Undoing text formatting

▶ Doing the Font dialog box

▶ Changing to upper- and lowercase

● ●

*T*he most basic thing you can format in a document is a character. Characters include letters, words, and all the text in a paragraph. They do not include anything painted on a mug or T-shirt in the Warner Bros. Store.

You can format characters to be bold, underlined, italicized, little, big, in different fonts or colors — or even animated if you're building a Web page. Word gives you a magnificent amount of control over the appearance of your text. This chapter contains all the details.

How to Format Your Text

There are two ways to change your text formatting:

    ✔ Choose a text formatting command, then type the text. All the text you
      type has the format you chose.

> ✔ Type the text, and then select the text as a block and apply the format-
> ting. This works best when you're busy with a thought and need to return
> and format the text later.

You'll use both methods as you compose text in your document. Sometimes
it's easier to use a formatting command and type the text in that format. And
other times you'll be reviewing your document and selecting text to apply
formatting to that block. Either way works.

See Chapter 6 for more information on marking blocks of text.

Changing the Font

One of the fun things about Word is its capability to use lots of different fonts.
Sure, you can make text be bold, italic, underlined, big, little, and on and on,
but adjusting the font to match your mood takes expression to an entirely
new level.

To switch to a different font, follow these steps:

1. Drop down the Fonts list.

Click the down-arrow by the Font dialog box to display a drop-down list
of fonts, similar to the one shown in Figure 11-1.

Figure 11-1:
The Font
list.

2. Scroll to the font you want.

The fonts are listed by name in alphabetical order, and the font typestyle
is displayed in the menu (see Figure 11-1).

3. Click to select a font.

Everything you type after choosing a new font appears on-screen in that font.
The text should print and look the same as well. If you select a block of text,
then all the text in that block switches over to the new font.

✔ The Fonts drop-down list displays whichever font you're currently using. Normally that's the Times New Roman font. When you switch to another font, its name appears in the font drop-down list.

✔ If you know the name of the font you want, you can save time by typing it into the box on the toolbar. But beware: Word is not lenient on font name spelling mistakes.

✔ Oddball shortcut key for this one? Try Ctrl+Shift+F. Then press the ↓ key to scroll through the font list and press Enter to choose your font. (Tiring, isn't it?)

✔ Fonts are the responsibility of Windows, not Word. New fonts are installed in the Control Panel's Fonts folder (the procedure is really no big deal). Thousands of fonts are available for Windows, and they work in all Windows applications. See your favorite Windows book for more information.

✔ The Fonts list appears on the Formatting toolbar. To see more about that toolbar, refer to Chapter 29, "Modifying Word's Appearance." (Also refer there if you can't find the Fonts list.)

Basic Character Formatting

After picking out a font, the most basic way to format your text is to make it **bold,** *italic,* or underlined. Easy-to-use keyboard shortcuts and buttons on the formatting toolbar make these the handiest text formatting tools.

Quickly reusing fonts

Any font you've recently chosen from the Fonts list appears in the top of the list, as shown below. If you want to reuse any font for a document, just scroll to the top of the list and pluck out the font.

For example, the image below shows the fonts Monotype Corsiva, Arial Black, and Times New Roman as being recently selected. Since they now appear at the top of the list, choosing them again is handy.

To make text bold, press Ctrl+B or use the Bold button on the toolbar.

Use **bold** to make text stand out on a page — for titles and captions, for example — or to emphasize text that carries a great deal of weight, speaks its mind at public meetings, wears a cowboy hat; you know the type.

I To make text italic, press Ctrl+I or use the Italic tool on the toolbar.

Italics are replacing underlining as the preferred text-emphasis format; it looks so much better than shabby underlined text. Italics are light and wispy, poetic, and free. Underlining is what the Department of Motor Vehicles does when it feels creative.

U Underline text by pressing Ctrl+U or use the Underline tool on the toolbar.

Unless you're writing a paper on <u>War and Peace</u> for that stodgy professor who thinks that all modern influence is of the devil, you'll most likely use italics instead of underlining.

✔ Basic character formatting affects only selected text or any new text you type.

✔ To turn off a text attribute, use the command again. For example, press Ctrl+I to type something in *italics*. Then press Ctrl+I again to return to normal text.

✔ You can mix and match character formats; text can be bold and underlined or bold and italicized. Yes, you may have to type several Word character-formatting commands before typing your text: Ctrl+B, Ctrl+I, and Ctrl+U for bold, italicized, and underlined text all at once, for example. Then you'll have to type each of those commands again to switch the text back to normal.

✔ To apply text formatting to a single word, put the toothpick cursor in that word and then give the formatting command. For example, putting the toothpick cursor in the word *incredulous* and pressing Ctrl+I (or choosing the Italic button from the toolbar) makes the word italicized.

✔ The Bold, Italic, and Underline tools on the toolbar can show you which formatting attributes are applied to your text. For example, when the toothpick cursor is in a bold word, the B on the toolbar appears depressed. (Don't try to cheer it up, it's just doing its job.)

The boring difference between a bold font and bold text

In Windows, you can have bold fonts, such as Arial Rounded MT Bold, as well as the Bold text command. This concept sounds weird, but keep in mind that you're using a *computer,* and it's not supposed to be logical.

The difference between a bold font and the Bold command is that a bold font is designed to be bold. It looks better on the screen and when printed. Making text bold with the Bold command merely tells Windows to redraw the current font, making it look fatter. Although this approach works, the Bold command doesn't display or print the font as nicely as a font that's born to be bold.

Obviously, using the Bold command is easier than switching to a bold font in the middle of a paragraph. But if you can, consider using a bold font for long expanses of text, titles, headings, or captions wherever possible. The Bold command is okay for making text bold in the middle of a sentence. But bold fonts always look better.

An example: Making italic text

To italicize your text, follow these steps:

1. **Press the Ctrl+I key combination.**

   Italics mode is on! (You can also click the Italic button.)

2. **Type away to your heart's content!**

   Watch your delightfully right-leaning text march across the screen.

3. **Press Ctrl+I after you're done.**

   Italic formatting is turned off. (Or you can click the Italic tool again.)

✔ You can use any text formatting command (or toolbar button) instead of italics above: Ctrl+B for bold or Ctrl+U for underline.

✔ If the text you want to italicize is already on-screen, you must mark it as a block and then change the character format to italics. Mark the text as a block, following the instructions detailed in Chapter 6, and then press the Ctrl+I key combination or use the leaning I Italic tool.

Text-attribute effects roundup

Bold, italics, and underlining are the most common ways to dress up a character. Beyond that, Word has a whole bucketful of character attributes you can apply to your text. Table 11-1 shows the lot of them, including the basic bold, italics, and underline commands.

Table 11-1	Text-Format Samples and Commands	
Key Combination	*Toolbar Button*	*Applies This Format*
Ctrl+Shift+A		ALL CAPS
Ctrl+B		**Bold**
Ctrl+Shift+D		Double underline
Ctrl+Shift+H	Hidden	Hidden text (it doesn't print — shhh!)
Ctrl+I		*Italics*
Ctrl+Shift+K		SMALL CAPS
Ctrl+U		Continuous underline
Ctrl+Shift+W		Word underline
Ctrl+=		subscript
Ctrl+Shift + =		superscript

Applying one of the weird text formats shown in Table 11-1 is cinchy. Just follow the instructions in the preceding section, "An example: Making italic text," and substitute the proper shortcut from Table 11-1.

  ✔ Some of the toolbar buttons you see listed in Table 11-1 are not on the toolbar. You can add them, if you like (if you plan on using that text attribute quite a bit). *Everything* in Word 2000 is customizable. See Chapter 29, "Modifying Word's Appearance," for the details.

  ✔ Pay special attention to word underline and continuous underline. Some people like one and despise the other. If you prefer to underline only words, remember to use Ctrl+Shift+W and not Ctrl+U.

✔ Hidden text — what good is that? It's good for you, the writer, to put down some thoughts and then hide them when the document prints. Of course, you don't see the text on-screen either. To find hidden text, you must use the Find command (covered in Chapter 5) to locate the special hidden-text attribute. You have to click the Format button, choose Font, and then click the Hidden box. (This information really should have been hidden to begin with.)

Big Text, Little Text: Text Size Effects

Attributes — bold, italics, underline, and so on — are only half the available character formats. The other half deal with the text size. By using these text formatting commands, you can make your text teensy or humongous.

Before getting into this subject, you must become one with the official type-setting term for text size: It's point. That's what Word uses: point instead of text size. It's not point, as in "point your finger" or the "point on top of your head." It's point, which is a measurement of size. One point is equal to ½ inch. Typesetters. . . .

✔ The bigger the point size, the larger the text.

✔ Most text is either 10 or 12 points in size.

✔ Headings are typically 14 to 24 points in size.

✔ Most fonts can be sized from 1 point to 1,638 points. Point sizes smaller than 6 are generally too small for the average person to read.

✔ Seventy-two points is equal to one inch-high letters.

✔ The author is 5,112 points tall.

Setting your text size

Text size is set in the Font Size box on the toolbar (it's just to the right of the Font box). Clicking the down-arrow displays a list of font sizes for your text, as shown in Figure 11-2.

Figure 11-2:
Choose a
font size
from here.

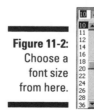

The new text size affects any marked block on the screen. If a block of text isn't marked, then any new text you type appears in the new size.

Here are some things to remember about setting the font size:

- ✔ You can type a specific text size into the box (though I rarely do this).
- ✔ The weirdo keyboard shortcut for getting to the Font size box is Ctrl+Shift+P. (Sounds like a disposable undergarment to me.)
- ✔ Bigger numbers mean bigger text; smaller numbers mean smaller text.

Making text bigger or smaller

You can use a couple of quickie shortcut keys to instantly shrink or grow text in a marked block. The two most popular ones are:

Ctrl+Shift+>   Makes the font larger in the next "look good" size

Ctrl+Shift+<   Makes the font smaller in the next "look good" size

These are easy to remember because > is the "greater than" and < is the "less than" symbol. Just think, "I'm making my text greater than its current size" when you press Ctrl+Shift+> or "I'm making my text less than its current size" when you press Ctrl+Shift+<.

If you want to increase or decrease the font size by smaller increments, use the following shortcut keys:

Ctrl+]   Makes text one point size larger

Ctrl+[Makes text one point size smaller

These commands (all four of them) affect a selected block of text on the screen. Otherwise, the command affects only the word the toothpick cursor is in.

Hey! I did this whole section without a Viagra joke!

Making superscript or subscript text

Superscript text is above the line (for example, the 10 in 2^{10}). Subscript text is below the line (for example, the 2 in H_2O). Here are the two shortcut keys you need to use:

Ctrl+Shift+EQUAL turns on superscripted text

Ctrl+EQUAL turns on subscripted text

EQUAL means the = (equal) key on your keyboard. (It looks gross for me to put "Ctrl+Shift+=" here.)

Now you can use these commands as you type to create superscript or subscript text. However, I recommend that you type your text, then go back and select the superscript or subscript text as a block and *then* use these commands. The reason is that the text you modify tends to be rather teensy and hard to edit. Better to write it first, then format.

Undoing All This Text-Formatting Nonsense

The character formatting command comparable to the eraser end of a pencil is Reset Character Formatting. This command removes all text attributes and returns your text to the unadulterated font and text size. Here's the secret:

Press Ctrl+spacebar, the Reset Character shortcut.

So if you have too many text formats going at once and just want to end them all, press Ctrl+spacebar and they're gone. This works as you type or on any block of text you selected.

✔ Before you make an offering to the Word gods, a warning: Ctrl+spacebar returns the text to the font, size, and attributes specified in your document's *style*. So, for example, pressing Ctrl+spacebar may return your text to Times New Roman, 10-point size — even though you formatted it to another font and size. Don't let this upset you. Instead, turn to Chapter 16, "Working with Styles" for more information on Word's styles.

✔ Another key combination for Ctrl+spacebar is Ctrl+Shift+Z. Remember, Ctrl+Z is the Undo command. To undo formatting all you're doing is adding the Shift key, which may make sense — well, heck, if any of this makes sense.

Doing the Font Dialog Box

There is a place in Word where all your Font formatting delights are kept in a neatly organized fashion. It's the Font dialog box, as shown in Figure 11-3.

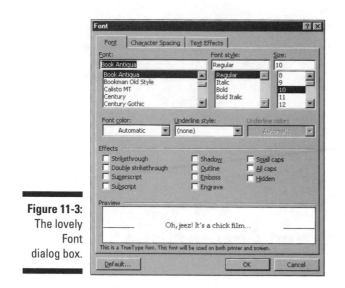

Figure 11-3:
The lovely
Font
dialog box.

To summon the Font dialog box, choose Format⇨Font from the menu. The handy keyboard shortcut is Ctrl+D.

This dialog box is definitely not for the timid — just like Fantasy Island. All sorts of exciting and exotic things happen here, most of which this chapter shows you how to do in other ways. But when you want it all done at once, this is the spot. You can change font, size, text attributes, everything.

Changes you make in the Font dialog box affect any marked block on the screen, or any new text you type after you click OK.

Click OK when you're done setting the font information. Or click Cancel if you're just visiting.

✔ The best benefit of the Font dialog box is the Preview window at the bottom. That window shows you exactly how your choices affect text in your document.

✔ Note that the Underline attribute is selected from the Underline Style drop down list. There are actually several different types of underlining Word can do.

✔ Check out Emboss and Engrave! But, from everyone who plans on reading your stuff — don't do a whole document that way. Save the festive fonts for titles and headings.

> ✔ The Character Spacing tab displays advanced options for changing the size and position of text on a line. This is okay for messing with special text, such as a title, but don't make it a regular stop.
>
> ✔ The Text Effects panel is kind of fun to play in, though most of the effects shown there appear only on Web page documents you create. (Unless you plan on training actual ants to march around on your paper.)

Changing the CASE of Your Text

Upper- and lowercase effects aren't considered part of a font, character attribute, or format. But still, the Word geniuses at Microsoft found room in their bustling bag o' tricks for a two-fingered command that lets you mix around the case of your text.

Press Shift+F3 to change the case of your text.

The Shift+F3 command works on a block of select text or on any single word the toothpick cursor is in (or next to).

Press Shift+F3 once to change a lowercase word to an initial cap (or all words to initial cap). Press it again to change the words to ALL CAPS. Press Shift+F3 again to change the text to lowercase. And pressing Shift+F3 again starts the process all over again.

Chapter 12

Formatting Paragraphs

. . . .

In This Chapter

▶ Justifying paragraphs (centering, justifying, and flushing)

▶ Changing line spacing

▶ Making room between paragraphs

▶ Indenting a paragraph

▶ Making a hanging indent

▶ Double-indenting a paragraph

▶ Paragraph-formatting survival guide

▶ Using the Ruler

. . . .

*P*aragraph formatting is the second formatting step, after formatting your words. It's really easy because you can do only so much with a paragraph of text. As usual, Word takes care of all the details, centering things for you, aligning tab stops, even adding an extra puff of air between your paragraphs. And, as usual, Word does things in the strangest manner possible. This chapter does its best to cushion the blow.

Paragraph Formatting Techniques

Formatting paragraphs works like formatting text or characters (or anything, really). There are two modes of operation:

✔ Use the formatting command in a single paragraph to format that paragraph. (Place the toothpick cursor in that paragraph, then use the formatting command.)

✔ Use the formatting command on a block of selected paragraphs to format them all together.

Word's paragraph formatting commands work only on paragraphs, not on sentences or words. Of course, if your paragraph is only a single word or sentence, then that's okay.

✔ Refer to Chapter 6, "Working with Blocks of Text," for specific and entertaining block-marking instructions.

✔ To make a single word a paragraph, just type the word followed by a press of the Enter key.

✔ Remember, a paragraph is a chunk of text that ends when you press the Enter key.

✔ If you want to see the Enter key symbol (¶) at the end of each paragraph, choose Tools⇨Options. Click the View panel. In the second area down (Formatting Marks), select the Paragraph Marks option. Click OK. Now every time you press the Enter key, a ¶ symbol marks the end of the paragraph. (Many Word users prefer this mode of operation.)

Aligning Paragraphs

There may no longer be four food groups but there are still four ways to align paragraphs in Word: left (normal), center, right, and fully justified. Each alignment has its own keyboard shortcut and button on the toolbar. (Well, not all of them have toolbar buttons, but you can always add toolbar buttons.)

 To center a paragraph, press Ctrl+E or use the Center tool on the toolbar.

I'm sure the
artsy
poet types
will like centering
all
their text.
It's just so
symmetrical.
For everyone else,
centering
a single line or block of text
is usually done for document
titles
and
headings.

To flush your text along the right side of the page, press Ctrl+R or click the Align Right tool on the toolbar.

Flush right describes the way text aligns on-screen. (You soon discover that a great deal of flushing occurs in paragraph formatting.) Text is usually flush left, with everything lining up at the left margin. Flush-right text aligns at the right margin. In other words, all the text is slammed against the right side of the page — like picking up the paper and jerking it wildly until the text slides over.

 To give your paragraph full justification, press Ctrl+J or choose the Justify button on the toolbar.

Full justification gives your paragraphs even sides, both left and right. It's the way text is formatted in most newspapers and magazines.

 To left-align your text — normal — press Ctrl+L or choose the Align Left button on the toolbar.

When you tire of seeing your text centered, right-justified or fully justified, make it normal by aligning it on the left.

- ✔ You can best see the Align Right and Justify buttons if you arrange the Formatting and Standard toolbars on top of one another. Otherwise you have to click the down-arrow at the end of the Formatting toolbar to see those buttons.

- ✔ You can also center or left-justify a single word on a line by itself by using the center tab. This is covered in the next chapter, "Formatting Tabs and Margins."

- ✔ When you type a new flush-right paragraph, the characters push right, always staying flush with the right side of the document. It's like writing in Hebrew!

- ✔ Flush right is a design term that means the same thing as right align or right justification.

 ✔ Typographers use words other than justification. They occasionally use the word ragged to describe how the text fits. For example, left justification is ragged right; right justification is ragged left. A rag top is a convertible with a soft top, and a rag bottom is any child still in diapers.

- ✔ Word achieves full justification by inserting extra spaces and small pieces of wood (shims) between the words in a line of text.

 ✔ If you do manage to center your soul on the cosmic plane, you'll probably receive lots of respect and fame. If so, remember never to let your acolytes see you eat at Sizzler.

Adding Vertical Air to Your Paragraphs

You can space out your text in an up-and-down fashion in two ways. The first, traditional method is to change the line spacing, the second is to add space before or after your paragraphs.

Changing the line spacing merely inserts extra space between *all* lines of text in a paragraph (or all paragraphs in a block). I cover this in the next section "Changing line spacing."

Adding space between paragraphs is roughly equivalent to pressing the Enter key twice after a paragraph — but with Word the computer can do that work for you. See the section, "Adding Breathing Room Between Paragraphs."

Changing line spacing

There are three handy keyboard shortcuts for three types of line spacing: Single-spacing, 1½-line spacing, and double-spacing. Beyond these you have to use the Paragraph dialog box, as described in the next section.

> To single-space a paragraph (or all paragraphs in a block), press Ctrl+1.
>
> To double-space paragraph(s), press Ctrl+2.
>
> To use 1½-spaced lines, press Ctrl+5.

Line spacing is usually done to accommodate notes or rude comments to be penciled in later.

For example, double-spacing is often required by fussy editors who, without enough room in their precious 1-inch margins, want to write under, over, and between what you write. Not to mention that increasing your line spacing easily makes a 1-page paper fill out the full 3-page requirement the teacher gave.

- ✔ Ctrl+5 means 1½-line spacing, not 5-line spacing.

- ✔ For your Ctrl+5 key press, don't use the 5 key on the numeric keypad; that's the command to select all the text in your document. Instead, use the 5 key hovering over the R and T keys on your keyboard.

Adding Breathing Room Between Paragraphs

Some people, myself included, are in the double-Enter habit. That is, you press Enter, Enter to end a paragraph, when all Word really needs is a single Enter. It's a similar disorder to pressing Space, Space after a period — an utterly useless affliction in the age of modern word processing, kind of like writing down your stutter.

If you want your paragraphs to automatically have some padding around them — like the cushions of air in Dr. Scholl's insoles — you need only to tell Word to stick some padding down there. Here's how:

1. **Position the toothpick cursor in the paragraph you want more air around, or mark a block of paragraphs to affect them all.**

   The air can be either above or below the paragraph.

2. **Choose Format➪Paragraph.**

   This summons the Paragraph dialog box, as shown in Figure 12-1.

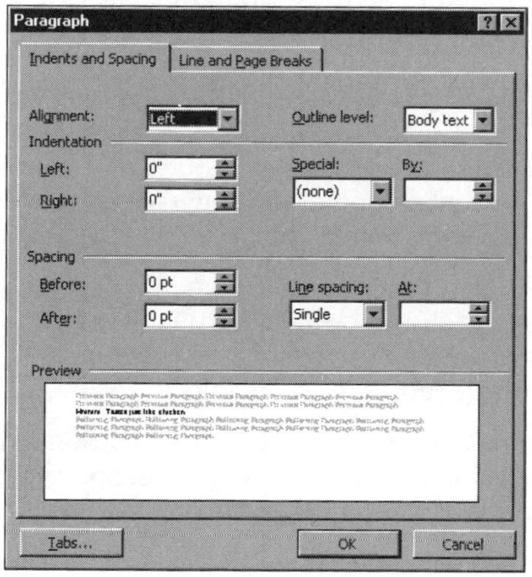

Figure 12-1:
The
Paragraph
dialog box.

Make sure the Indents and Spacing panel is forward, as shown in the figure. (Click that panel's tab or press Alt I, if it isn't forward already.)

You want to concentrate on the area that says Spacing.

3a. **To add space before a paragraph, enter 2 value in the Before box.**

3b. To add space after a paragraph, enter a value in the After box.

For example, to add space after every paragraph — just like pressing the Enter key twice — click twice on the up-arrow by that box. The value 12 pt means that there will be just about one blank line after the paragraph.

Even though you're adding space *below* a paragraph you need to click the up arrow to increase the value in the After box. This is weird, and you'll do it wrong occasionally because it's a bad mental model. (I've been reading Norman.)

Generally speaking, 6 pt (points) is about half a line of text. A value of 12 pts means one extra line. (The "pt" thing is explained in the sidebar, "The pt thing.")

Use the Preview window at the bottom of the Paragraph dialog box to see how the spacing before or after your paragraph affects things.

4. Click OK.

The paragraph(s) now have extra spacing. After you press the Enter key, you notice some extra room between that paragraph and the next.

✔ So which do you use, Before or After spacing? My advice is always to add the padding at the end of the paragraph, in the After box. I only use the Before spacing if I *really* want to separate something from the previous paragraph (which is rare).

✔ To make a blank line between your paragraphs, follow the above steps and select 12 pt in the After box.

✔ Adding space before or after a paragraph isn't the same as double spacing the text inside the paragraph. In fact, adding space around a paragraph does not change the paragraph's line spacing one iota.

✔ You can also use the Paragraph dialog box to change the paragraph(s) justification. The Alignment drop-down list in the top area contains Word's four paragraph alignment options. See the section "Aligning Paragraphs" earlier in this chapter for more information.

✔ The Paragraph dialog box can also be used to set traditional line spacing. The Line spacing drop-down list contains all sorts of spacing options.

✔ If you select Multiple from the Line Spacing drop-down list, you can enter exact values for your line spacing in the At box. For example, choose Multiple and then 3 from the At box to set triple spacing.

That pt thing

The amount of space Word sticks between paragraphs is measured in _points_ — which is a typesetter's measurement. There are 72 points to an inch. (It's the same size that fonts are measured in.) So if you use a 12-point font, a space of 12 points between paragraphs adds an extra line. Six points (6 pt) is half a line of text.

The boxes where you input point values in the Paragraph dialog box have "spinners" on them.

If you click the up or down arrows on the spinners, you increase or decrease the spacing between lines in 6 point increments. If you need more specific values, you can type them in directly (though I've only used 6, 12, and maybe 18 in my short life).

Changing a Paragraph's Indentation

Word can indent your paragraphs for you just as easily as a shopping cart can indent your car door.

Right now I'll bet you're indenting each of your new paragraphs by pressing the Tab key. While I won't sneer at that, there is a better way: Let Word do the indenting for you. Automatically!

The following sections discuss several indenting options.

Automatically indenting the first line of a paragraph

Word can automatically indent the first line of any paragraph you create. You tell it to do this by selecting your whole document and then following these commands, or just go through these steps at the start of a document (before you start writing) to affect the whole thing:

1. **Choose the Format⇨Paragraph command.**

   The Paragraph dialog box appears. Make sure that the Indents and Spacing panel is up front (like in Figure 12-1).

2. **Locate the Special drop-down list.**

   You find this in the Indentation area of the dialog box, off to the right.

3. **Select First Line from the list.**

4. **Enter the length you want the first lines indented in the By box.**

   Unless you've messed with things, the box should automatically say 0.5", meaning Word automatically indents the first line of every paragraph a half inch. Type another value if you want your indents to be more or less outrageous. (Things are measured here in inches, not points.)

5. **Click OK.**

   The selected block, or the current paragraph (and remaining paragraphs you type), all automatically have an indented first line.

To remove the first-line indent from a paragraph, repeat the steps, but select (none) from the drop-down list in Step 3. Then click the OK button.

When you tell Word to automatically indent your paragraphs you no longer need to start each one with the Tab key. See? Word is saving you valuable typing energy molecules.

Making a hanging indent

A hanging indent has committed no felonious crime. Instead, it's a paragraph in which the first line sticks out to the left and the rest of the paragraph is indented. Like this:

Fake Dog Doo. $13.00/quart. Amaze your friends and annoy your neighbors. Just like the real thing. The classic prank! Non-edible, though bio-degradable. Discounts for bulk orders. Item #869.

To create such a beast for whatever fabulous reasons, follow these steps:

1. **Move the toothpick cursor into the paragraph you want to hang and indent.**

   Or you can position the cursor to where you want to type a new, hanging-indent paragraph. Or you can select a block.

2. **Press Ctrl+T, the Hanging Indent shortcut.**

   The Ctrl+T in Word moves the paragraph over to the first tab stop but keeps the first line in place.

You can also accomplish this task in the Paragraph dialog box. Choose First Line from the Special drop-down list and enter the indent (usually half an inch) in the By box. Click OK! See the previous section, which follows similar steps for hanging an indent.

✔ If you want to indent the paragraph even more, press the Ctrl+T key more than once.

✔ It's stupid that they have a shortcut key for a hanging indent but not for indenting the first line of a paragraph, which I feel more people do more often than this hanging nonsense.

✔ To undo a hanging indent, press Ctrl+Shift+T. That's the unhang key combination, and your paragraph's neck will be put back in shape.

Indenting the whole paragraph

Indenting a paragraph means that you indent, or nest, the entire paragraph by aligning its left edge against a tab stop. Here's how you do it:

1. **Move the toothpick cursor anywhere in the paragraph.**

   The paragraph can be already on-screen, or you can be poised to type a new paragraph. Or you can try this command on a selected block of text.

2. **Press Ctrl+M, the indent shortcut.**

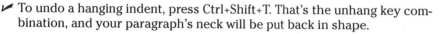

   Ummm — indent! Ummm — indent! Say it over and over. It kinda works. (You can also click the Increase Indent button on the Formatting toolbar.)

3. **Type your paragraph if you haven't already.**

   If you selected the paragraph as a block, it is indented to the next tab stop.

✔ To indent the paragraph to the next tab stop, press Ctrl+M again.

✔ To return the original margin, press Ctrl+Shift+M. You can also click the Decrease Indent tool. (You may have to click the down-arrow at the end of the Formatting toolbar to see the Decrease Indent tool.)

✔ Although the Ctrl+M and Ctrl+Shift+M shortcuts aren't mnemonic, their only difference is a Shift key. So once you get used to using them (hopefully before the afterlife), they're easy to remember.

Double-indenting a paragraph

Sometimes an indent on the left just isn't enough. There are those days when you need to suck a paragraph in twice: once on the left and once on the right (for example, when you lift a quote from another paper but don't want to be accused of plagiarism). I do this to Abe Lincoln all the time. When I quote his stuff (and he doesn't mind), I follow these steps:

1. **Pick your paragraph.**

   If the paragraph hasn't been written yet, move the cursor to where you want to write the new text. Or put the toothpick cursor into the paragraph or just select multiple paragraphs as a block.

2. **Choose the Format⇨Paragraph command.**

   The Paragraph dialog box appears (refer to Figure 12-1). Locate the Indentation area.

3. **Enter the amount of left indentation.**

   For example, type **.5** to indent half an inch, or you can use the up-or-down arrows to increase or decrease the left indentation.

4. **Enter the amount of right indentation.**

   Type the same value as you did in the Left box.

   Check the Preview part of the Paragraph dialog box to ensure your paragraph is indented as you prefer.

5. **Click OK.**

To un-indent the paragraph, you need to repeat the above steps, but enter zero in both the Left and Right boxes.

Watch out when you try to mix Left and Right indenting with a First line or Hanging indent. It could drive you nuts, until you select (none) from the Special drop-down list.

Who Died and Made This Thing Ruler?

Word's main throwback to the typewriter era is the Ruler, which is the final strip/bar information on Word's screen (refer to Figure 1-3). The Ruler can be used for on-the-fly indention changes in a paragraph, as well as for setting tabs. (Tabs are covered in Chapter 13.)

If you don't see the Ruler on-screen, choose the View⇨Ruler command. (You may have to click the down-arrows at the bottom of the View menu.)

Figure 12-2 shows the typical Word Ruler. Note the three parts of the Ruler that deal with indenting a paragraph (or a group of selected paragraphs).

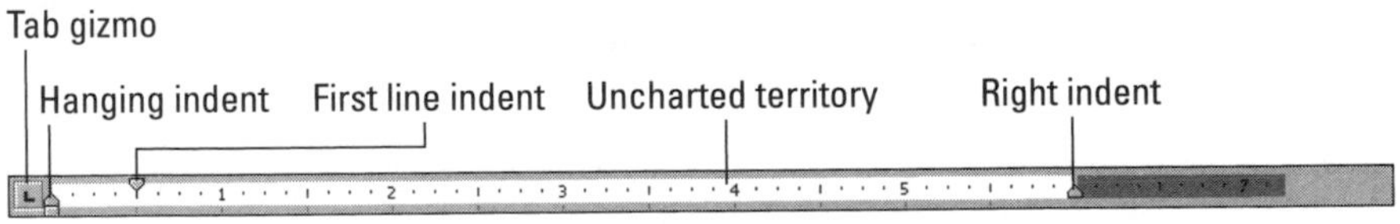

Figure 12-2:
The typical
Word ruler.

Tab gizmo

Hanging indent   First line indent   Uncharted territory   Right indent

The following actions affect the paragraph the toothpick cursor is in or a group of paragraphs selected as a block:

◊ To adjust the indent for the right side of a paragraph, grab the Right Indent guy on the Ruler and drag him right or left.

▢ To adjust the indent for the left side of a paragraph, grab the Left Indent box. Note that moving this box moves both the First Line Indent and Hanging Indent triangles.

◊ To adjust the left indent without moving the first line indent, grab the Hanging Indent thing and drag it left or right.

▽ To adjust the first line indent, grab the First Line Indent doojobbie with the mouse and drag it up or down, er, left or right.

✔ The Ruler is a mouse gizmo; you use the mouse to make changes on it. Even so, just about everything you can do to a paragraph with the Ruler can also be done in the Format Paragraph dialog box.

✔ You can select different types of tabs with the Tab gizmo. See Chapter 13.

✔ The Ruler is fine for visually setting indents, but if you need to be precise, you must use the Paragraph dialog box. Only there can you enter exact amounts for indents. Refer to the previous several sections in this chapter for detailed information on setting various paragraph indents.

✔ Setting the indents for a paragraph is not the same thing as setting margins. Margins are set at the page-formatting level. See Chapter 14, "Formatting Pages," for more information on setting margins.

Paragraph-formatting survival guide

This table contains all the paragraph-formatting commands you can summon by holding down the Ctrl key and pressing a letter or number. By no means should you memorize this list.

Key Combo	Does This
Ctrl+E	Centers paragraphs
Ctrl+J	Fully justifies paragraphs
Ctrl+L	Left aligns (flush left)
Ctrl+R	Right aligns (flush right)
Ctrl+M	Indents text
Ctrl+Shift+M	Unindents text
Ctrl+T	Makes a hanging indent
Ctrl+Shift+T	Unhangs the indent
Ctrl+1	Single-spaces lines
Ctrl+2	Double-spaces lines
Ctrl+5	Makes 1½-space lines

Chapter 13

Formatting Tabs

●●

●●

*W*ord's tabs are strange. Not *Twilight Zone* strange: The tab stops harbor no native intelligence nor are they out to eat the human race. No, it's more of a new food strangeness. You know: like sushi looks like raw fish until you taste it and discover that it's rather yummy. Then it's not so strange to *you* anymore, but if you tell someone you're craving monk fish liver paté, well, then, *that's* strange.

Tabs in Word are confusing because the tab stops you set are more than just tab stops. They can be used to line up or arrange text in useful ways. In fact, knowing the proper tab to set can save you oodles of time. The problem is that tabs in Word are just not logical. That's why I wrote this chapter.

The Story of Tab

Once upon a time, a giant cola company searched for a diet beverage.

Whoops! Wrong Tab story.

A tab is like a big space. When you press the Tab key, Word zooms the tooth-pick cursor over to the next *tab stop*. You can use tabs to line up columns of information or to indent paragraphs or lines of text. They're handy. This you should know. This chapter tries dutifully to explain the rest of the tab mystery.

✔ Pressing the Tab key inserts a tab "character" in your document. That character moves the toothpick cursor, and any text you type, over to the next tab stop.

✔ Pressing the Tab key does not insert spaces. When you use Backspace or Delete to remove a tab, you delete one character — the tab character.

✔ Word can display the Tab character for you if you like. It looks like a tiny arrow pointing right. To display this character, choose Tools➪Options. Click the View tab. Choose Tab characters from the Formatting marks area. Click OK.

✔ Tab stops are set at ½-inch intervals on each line of text — unless you specify otherwise.

✔ It helps if you have the Ruler visible when you work with tabs. Choose View➪Ruler from the menu if the Ruler is not visible. You may have to click the down-arrows on the menu to see the Ruler command. (See Figure 1-3 for the location of the Ruler on Word's screen.)

The Tab Stops Here

Just to confuse you, there are two places in Word where you can set tab stops. The first is the Ruler, shown in Figure 13-1. The second is in the Tabs dialog box. Most folks use the Ruler, but for some Tab options you must go to the Tabs dialog box.

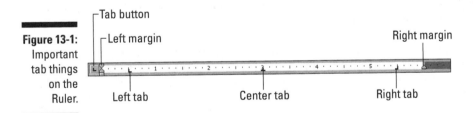

Figure 13-1: Important tab things on the Ruler.

The Ruler is the first choice for setting tabs because of the Tab button on the left side (refer to Figure 13-1). The Tab button sports one of Word's five different types of tab stops. Here's the brief rundown (which you don't have to memorize):

The most common tab is the left tab, the plump L. This tab works like the Tab key on a typewriter: Press the Tab key and the new text appears at the next tab stop. No mental hang-ups here.

The center tab stop centers text on the tab stop. This is strange, which is why it's covered later in this chapter in glorious detail. See the section, "Center Me, Tab."

The right tab causes text to line up right-justified at that tab stop. This tab gives you leeway to do some fancy paragraph justification on a single line, some of which is demonstrated in the section, "Right On, Tab," later in this chapter.

The decimal tab aligns numbers by their decimals. This proves to be a great boon to anyone printing up a list of prices. See the section, "The Amazing Decimal Tab," later in this chapter.

The ugly stepsister of the Tab family is the Bar tab. I'm sure there were a few hoots in the Word programming lab the day they named this one. See the section "Paying the Bar Tab," somewhere a few pages to the right of here.

Clicking the Tab button displays one of the above tab stops. Click the button a few times to watch it change from one type of tab stop to the other.

Also included in the Tab button, though they're not really tab stops, are the Left Indent and Hanging Indent items. Why they put them there, I'll never know. Chapter 12 shows you better ways to indent a paragraph, anyway.

The following sections describe the various tab stops and how they can be used in your documents.

How to Set a Tab Stop

To set a tab stop, you generally follow these steps:

1. Click the Tab button until you find the type of tab you want.

For example, click the Tab button until the standard Left tab — Big "L" — appears (see the margin).

2. Click in the Ruler were you want the tab stop placed.

This is the tricky part. You must click right in the middle of the Ruler. For example, to put a tab stop at 1¼-inches you position the mouse pointer as shown in Figure 13-2.

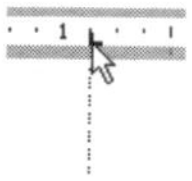

Figure 13-2:
Setting a
left tab.

You can drag the tab stop left or right. As you drag, notice a line that extends down into your document's text (refer to Figure 13-2). That line tells you *exactly* where text lines up for that tab stop.

Release the mouse button to set the tab.

3. **To set another tab stop, repeat Step 2.**

   You set a new tab stop every time you click in the Ruler. The type of tab displayed on the Tab button determines what kind of tab you set.

4. **When you're done, just click in your document to set the toothpick cursor and type away.**

Pressing the Tab key zooms the toothpick cursor over to the tab stop — at 1.125 inches as shown in Figure 13-1. (That's 1⅛-inches for those of you who don't follow the stock market.)

✔ The best thing about setting tabs and using the Tab key is that they line up text *exactly* with the tab stop. Pressing the spacebar doesn't do that.

✔ Setting the tab affects only the paragraph the toothpick cursor is in. If you want to set the tabs for multiple paragraphs or an entire document, you must select a block and then set the tabs.

✔ Removing a tab stop is as easy as dragging the tab (the Fat "L" or other tab character) from the Ruler. That's right, you can drag a tab stop down from the Ruler into your text to remove it.

✔ The "phantom" tab stop you may see when you select a block appears when there is a tab set in one of the paragraphs but not all of them. You can remove the phantom tab stop by dragging it off the ruler, or click the tab stop with the mouse to set it for all the selected paragraphs.

Setting Your Standard Left Tabs

Left tabs are the standard, typical, boring types of tabs most everyone uses. But why are they left? Left over? Left out? Leftist?

Left tabs are called such because text typed after you press the tab aligns its left side to the tab stop. Figure 13-3 illustrates this concept. See how each bit of text lines up its left edge with the tab stop in the figure?

Figure 13-3:
Lining up
text on a
left tab.

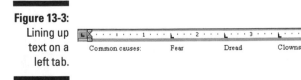

To make a new left tab stop for your current paragraph, follow these steps:

1. **Type the paragraph you want to stick the tabs into.**

   I'm a fan of typing the text *first*. That's because one tab stop does the trick. Just type your text, pressing the tab key once — no matter how far you eventually want the text to go over. Too many people press the Tab key three or four times. That's okay, but it's inefficient. Word is smarter than that. Use the Tab key only once, then use the Ruler to set the tab stop. Trust me, this is the best way to work things. (See the sidebar, "One tab will do.")

2. **Make sure that the toothpick cursor is in the paragraph you want to change.**

3. **Choose the left tab stop from the Tab button.**

   Keep clicking the Tab button until the Left tab appears, as shown in the margin.

4. **Click the mouse in the Ruler where you want a new tab stop.**

   For example, in Figure 13-3, the first tab stop is set at 1.5 inches, the second at 2.5 inches, and the third at 3.5 inches.

One tab will do

If you plan on setting tab stops, then you'll do yourself a favor by pressing the Tab key *only once* between each item you want to tab out. This is something you must learn, but the benefits are that your document is cleaner and editing is less frustrating.

As an example, the figure below shows how text lines up before I set the tab stops. I just pressed the Tab key once after each word — and I clenched my teeth knowing that things weren't lined up as I want them:

> Vitamins: A   B   Chocolate

Note that Word used ½-inch tab stops naturally, but that's not what I want. Instead, I set the tab stops as shown below *after* writing the text:

> Vitamins: A   B   Chocolate

Note how the text now lines up as I want. I used only one tab between each item and no spaces.

You may not see the advantage to doing it this way right now. However, if you ever have to go back and edit the document or rearrange the tab stops, you'll appreciate that there is only one tab between them. Trust me.

Center Me, Tab

The center tab is a unique character. It's normally used with only a single word or just a few words. What it does is allow you to center that word (or those words) on a line of text without centering the entire paragraph. Here's a demo:

1. **Start a new paragraph, one containing text you want to center.**

   Okay, you probably won't type a whole paragraph for a center tab. In fact, that would be very unusual. Instead, the best example for this is typing a header or footer — a single line of text. (See Chapter 15, "Formatting Documents" for more information on headers and footers.)

2. **Press the Tab key.**

   See the sidebar "One tab will do" for information on why I insist on using only one tab key to get to a tab stop.

3. **Type the text to center.**

   A chapter title, your name, or whatever text you type will be centered on that line when you set a center tab stop.

4. **Press Enter.**

   This ends the line. Now you're ready to set the center tab.

5. **Click the mouse to put the toothpick cursor in the line you just typed.**

6. **Click the Tab button until the center tab appears.**

   The center tab is shown in the margin. It looks like an upside-down "T."

7. **Click the mouse in the middle of the Ruler to set the center tab.**

   Your text should line up as shown in Figure 13-4. See how the text, "My Great American Novel" appears centered on the center tab? The paragraph is still aligned to the left, but that tiny bit of text is centered.

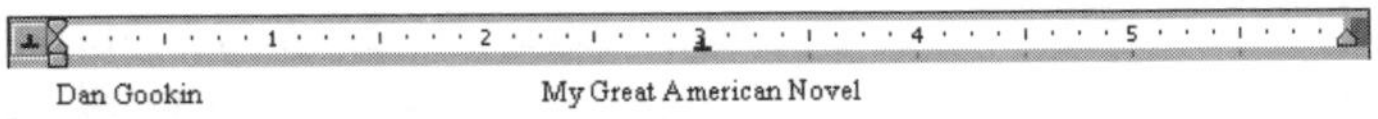

Figure 13-4:
A bit of text
is centered
with the
center tab.

Dan Gookin   My Great American Novel

✔ Center tabs are best used on a single line of text, usually by themselves. There's no restriction on this; you can use as many center tabs in a line as you like. I just haven't seen it done that way.

 ✔ Most often you'll use center tabs in headers and footers. See Chapter 15, "Formatting Documents."

 ✔ Obviously, centering a paragraph beats the pants off of using a center tab stop in most cases. In fact, the only time I find center tab stops useful is when I create headers or footers.

Right On, Tab

The right tab is a creature that aligns text to the right of the tab stop, not the left. Figure 13-5 shows how a right tab stop lines up text using an example from the previous section.

Figure 13-5:
A right tab
stop.

Dan Gookin   My Great American Novel   April 9, 1999

 ✔ To set a right tab stop, choose the Right tab from the Tab button on the Ruler. Then click in the Ruler where you want the right tab to be.

 ✔ Figure 13-5 shows the right tab on the right side of a heading. After setting the right tab, I pressed the Tab key and then typed the date.

 ✔ Typing text at a right tab stop pushes the text to the left (opposite of normal), which keeps the text aligned to the right stop.

 ✔ As with a center tab stop, the right tab stop is best used on a line by itself, usually in a header, footer or some type of document title as shown in Figure 13-5.

The Amazing Decimal Tab

I love decimal tabs. Without them, columns of numbers would never match up. This is a serious boon to anyone who writes a financial summary report, as shown in Figure 13-6.

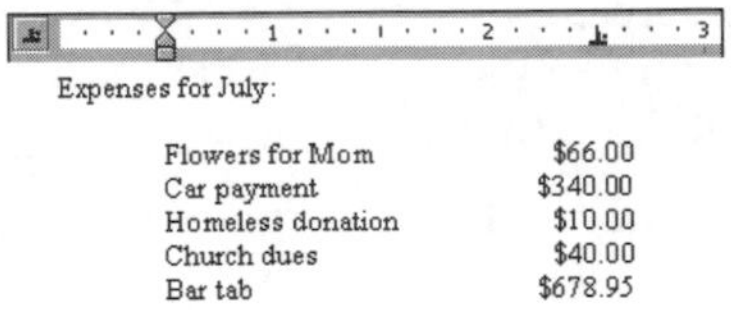

Figure 13-6.
Lining up
numbers
with the
decimal
tab.

Expenses for July:

Flowers for Mom	$66.00
Car payment	$340.00
Homeless donation	$10.00
Church dues	$40.00
Bar tab	$678.95

The best way to set a decimal tab is to format the first paragraph before you type. Click the Tab button until the decimal tab appears. Then click the Ruler to set the tab, as shown in Figure 13-6.

 Typing with a decimal tab works like this: Type whatever text you type before the tab (if any), then press the Tab key. The toothpick cursor lines up with the decimal tab stop. Type the first part of the number and the text moves to the left. Press the period (decimal) and the second part of the number — the cents part — moves to the right. Everything lines up.

 If you need to rearrange things (perhaps the columns are too close together), select all the lines with numbers as a block. Use your mouse to slide the decimal tab left or right on the Ruler. You can then re-align the numbers in the selected block all at once.

Paying the Bar Tab

After nine versions of Word (which is really only five versions, but ask me later), the word-processing gurus at Microsoft finally decide to add a bar tab. What gives? Aren't there enough puns in this program?

Setting a bar tab puts a vertical line in your document at that tab stop, as shown in Figure 13-7.

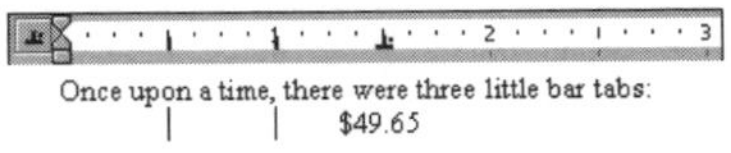

Figure 13-7:
Mystic bar
tabs.

Once upon a time, there were three little bar tabs:

		$49.65

The bar tab doesn't actually set a tab stop. If you press the Tab key the toothpick cursor doesn't hop over to the bar. For example, in Figure 13-7, when I pressed the Tab key at the start of the second line, the toothpick cursor went to where the Decimal tab stop was set. So this leaves me kind of numb and cold on the concept of a bar tab, though it does have a pretty effect. Pretty useless.

Using the Tabs Dialog Box

Setting tabs in the Ruler is fine for most folks. I like it because you can actually see the effect the tab has on your text and can drag the tab stop to make adjustments. For purists, however, there is the Tabs dialog box.

Call forth the Tabs dialog box by choosing Format⇨Tabs from the menu. The Tabs dialog box appears in all its glory, as shown in Figure 13-8.

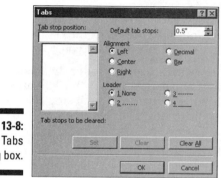

Figure 13-8:
The Tabs
dialog box.

Working with this dialog box is an awkward thing, most likely because the Ruler just makes so much more sense for setting tabs. But suppose you have some really uptight editor who wants you to set your tab stops at 1.1875 and 3.49 inches. If so, the Tabs dialog box is the only place to do it.

Setting a tab in the Tabs dialog box

To set a tab in the Tabs dialog box, follow these steps:

1. **Summon the Tabs dialog box.**

   Choose Format⇨Tabs from the menu.

2. **Enter the exact tab stop position in the Tab Stop Position box.**

   For example, type **1.1875** to set a tab at exactly that spot.

3. **Choose the type of tab stop from the Alignment area.**

   The standard tab stop is Left. Other tab stops are covered elsewhere in this chapter.

4. **Click the Set button.**

The Set button is what creates the tab stop — not the OK button. After clicking Set, your tab stop is placed in the list below the Tab Stop Position dialog box.

5. **Continue setting tabs.**

   Repeat Steps 1 through 3 for as many tabs as you need to set.

6. **Click OK.**

   You're returned to your document with the new tab stops visible on the Ruler.

✔ If you need to set a row of tabs, say, each three-quarters of an inch apart, type **0.75"** into the Default Tab Stops box, then click the OK button. Word automatically figures the tab stops and sets them for you.

✔ For setting precise tab stops, type measurements for each tab stop into the Tab Stop Position box. For example, type **1**, click the Set button; type **1.67**, click Set; type **2.25**, click Set, and so on. Each tab stop is added to the list of tab stops in the Tabs dialog box. Click OK to set the tab stops for your paragraph.

✔ If you make a mistake, click the tab stop you want to remove and then the Clear button.

✔ You must click the Set button to set a tab. I don't know how many times I click OK thinking the tab stop is set and it's not.

Killing off a tab stop in the Tabs dialog box

To remove a tab stop using the Tabs dialog box, click the tab in the list below the Tab Stop Position box. Then click the Clear button.

Clicking the Clear All button in the Tabs dialog box removes all tabs from the Ruler.

You can also zap all your tab stops at once by summoning the Tabs dialog box (Format⇨Tabs) and clicking the Clear All button; then click OK.

Setting Fearless Leader Tabs

One thing you can do in the Tabs dialog box that you cannot do with the Ruler is set a leader tab.

A *leader tab* produces a row of dots when you press Tab. You see these tabs all the time in indexes and tables of contents. Word gives you the choice of three different leaders:

Fearless dot leader tabs 147

Zipper line leader tabs - - - - - - - - - - - - 147

U-boat underline leader tabs _____147

To set up a fearless leader tab, follow these steps:

1. **Position the toothpick cursor on the line where you want your leader tabs.**

   For example, say you're asked by your city's government to index the phone book. You're starting the index in a new document in Word.

2. **Set a Left tab stop on the Ruler.**

   Choose the Left tab stop from the Tab button, then click the mouse on the number 3 on the Ruler. This sets a tab stop 3 inches in from the page's left margin. A plump L appears on the Ruler.

3. **Choose the Format⇨Tabs command.**

   The Tabs dialog box appears, as shown in Figure 12-3.

4. **Select the tab stop you want to leader-ize from the Tab Stop Position list.**

   In this case it would be the tab stop set at 3 inches.

5. **Choose the style of fearless leader tab you want.**

   Click the appropriate style — dotted, dashed or underline as presented at the beginning of this section. My personal favorite is the dotted underline, which you can select by pressing the Alt+2 key combination.

6. **Click Set.**

   You'll forget this step the first time you try this on your own. And you'll wonder why it didn't work. That's when you'll return here to re-read this sentence.

7. **Click OK.**

8. **Type the text to appear before the tab stop:**

   `Last names beginning with the letter A`

9. **Press the Tab key.**

   Zwoop! The toothpick cursor jumps to your tab stop and leaves a trail of, well, "stuff" in its wake. That's your dot leader (or dash leader or underline leader).

10. **Type the reference, page number, or whatever:**

Letter A

11. **Press Enter to end that line.**

You can adjust the tab stops after setting them if some of the text doesn't line up. Remember, to adjust the tab stops for more than one paragraph at a time, you need to select everything as a block. See Chapter 6.

The word "tab" appears in one form or another 286 times in this chapter.

Chapter 14

Formatting Pages

• •

In This Chapter

▶ Setting the page/paper size

▶ Choosing Landscape or Portrait layout

▶ Setting margins for your document

▶ Automatically numbering your pages

▶ Changing page numbers

▶ Using a hard page break

• •

*L*arger than a word! More cumbersome than a paragraph! Look, up on the screen! It's a sheet of paper! No! It's a window! No! It's a *page*.

In keeping the trend of going from small to big, the next step in the formatting circus is to format a page of information. Pages have a certain size, orientation, and margins plus page numbers. All of that is covered here in a neat and tidy manner that entertains while it informs.

How Big Is My Page?

How many angels can dance on a sheet of paper? Well, it depends on the size of the paper, of course — not to mention the type of dance.

Most printing takes place on a standard, 8½-x-11-inch sheet of paper. That's what Word defines as a "page" on which you can format margins and other page-formatting whatnot. But Word isn't burned to the frying pan on using only that size paper. No, Word lets you change the paper size to anything you want — from a teensy envelope to a sheet of paper big enough to make the bed with.

The paper-size setting stuff is done in the Page Setup dialog box. The following instructions tell you how to change the size of the paper you're printing on.

1. **Position the toothpick cursor at the top of your document.**

   It doesn't have to be the top of your document. You can change the page size in the middle of your document if you like. Most of the time, however, you'll probably want the new page size for your entire document.

2. **Choose the File⇨Page Setup command.**

   The Page Setup dialog box appears.

3. **Make sure that the Paper Size tab is in front.**

   See Figure 14-1 to ensure that what you see on the screen is right. If not, click the Paper Size tab.

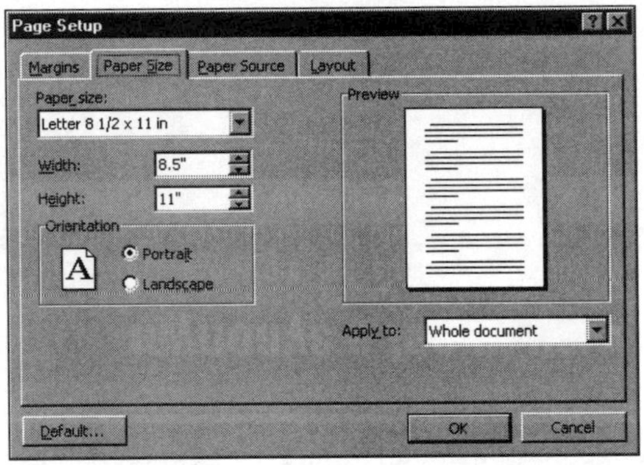

Figure 14-1:
The Page Setup dialog box, Paper Size part.

4. **Click the Paper Size drop-down list.**

   The list drops down to reveal a host of paper sizes.

5. **Select a new paper size from the list.**

   For example, `Legal 8 1/2 × 11` is for legal-sized paper. Other standard sizes are listed there as well.

   Most PC printers are capable of printing on several different sizes of paper. Weird sizes, though available in the list, may not be compatible with your printer — not to mention that you need that specific paper size to print on; Word can't make an 8 ½-x-11-inch sheet of paper another 3 inches longer.

   Select this new paper size by clicking it with your mouse.

6. **Select Whole Document or This Point Forward from the Apply To drop-down list.**

   Select Whole Document to have the new paper size apply to your entire document. Choosing This Point Forward applies the new paper size to the current page (where the toothpick cursor is) onward.

If you're using document sections, select the This Section option to have the new paper size apply to the current section. Sections are covered in Chapter 15.

7. Click OK.

Okay. Type away on the new size of paper.

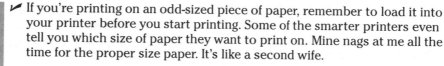

✔ If you're printing on an odd-sized piece of paper, remember to load it into your printer before you start printing. Some of the smarter printers even tell you which size of paper they want to print on. Mine nags at me all the time for the proper size paper. It's like a second wife.

✔ If the paper you're printing on isn't shown in the drop-down list, you can enter the measurements yourself. First select Custom Size from the Paper Size drop-down list. Then type the paper's width into the Width box and the height into the Height box.

✔ Keep an eye on the Preview window in the Page Setup dialog box. It changes to reflect the new paper size.

✔ Refer to Chapter 30, "Your Basic Letter and Envelope," for information on printing envelopes. (There's a special command for doing that; no sense in finagling a new paper size here.)

The Wide and Narrow Choice

Word usually prints up and down on a piece of paper — which is how everyone is used to reading a page. However, Word can print sideways (or long-ways) on a page as well. In this case, the page's orientation is changed; rather than up-down, the paper is printed sideways.

The technical, I'm-an-important-word-processing-expert terms for the two paper orientations are Portrait mode for the up-down paper and Landscape mode for sideways. A portrait picture is usually taller than it is long to accommodate our faces — unless someone has large ears on a jug-like head. Landscape is for those lovely oil paintings of seascapes or lakes and trees that are wider than they are tall — the kind Bob Ross used to paint (may he rest in peace — sniff, sniff).

To make Word print the long way on a sheet of paper — the Landscape mode — do the following:

1. Choose File⇨Page Setup.

The Page Setup dialog box appears. Make sure that the Paper Size panel is forward if it's not already (press Alt+S to summon it). Refer to Figure 14-1.

2. **Choose Portrait or Landscape from the Orientation area.**

   The sample document and the tiny icon change to reflect the document's perspective.

3. **Click OK.**

Avoid printing standard documents in Landscape mode. Scientists and other people in white lab coats who study such things have determined that human reading speed slows drastically when people must scan a long line of text. Reserve Landscape mode for printing lists, tables, and items for which normal paper is too narrow.

As with changing the paper size, you can have Landscape or Portrait mode apply to an entire document, from a certain point forward, or to a selected section within your document. See the previous section for more information.

Marginal Information

Every page has margins. They provide the air around your document — that inch of breathing space that sets off the text from the rest of the page. Word automatically sets your margins at 1 inch from the right, left, top, and bottom of the page. Most English teachers and book editors want margins this size because they love to scribble in margins (they even write that way on blank paper). In Word, you can adjust the margins to suit any fussy professional.

To change the margins, follow these steps:

1. **Position the cursor where you want the new margins to start.**

   If you're changing margins for part of your document, it's best to set the new margins at the top of the document, top of a page, or beginning of a paragraph (or the beginning of a new formatting section). If, on the other hand, you want to change the whole document, where you place the cursor doesn't matter.

2. **Choose the File⇨Page Setup command.**

   The Page Setup dialog box appears, as shown in Figure 14-2. Click the Margins tab if it's not up front (as shown in the figure).

3. **Enter the new measurements for the Top, Bottom, Left, and Right page margins.**

   Type the new values in the appropriate boxes. For example, typing a value of **1"** in all the boxes sets all margins to 1 inch. Entering a value of **2.5"** sets a 2½-inch margin. You don't need to type the inch symbol (").

   The Preview window shows you how your margins affect the page.

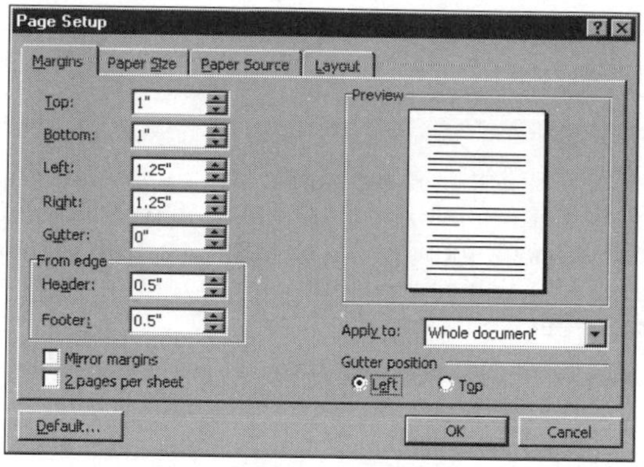

Figure 14-2:
The Page
Setup
dialog box.

4. **Choose Whole Document, This Point Forward, or This Section from the Apply To drop-down list.**

   • *Whole Document* changes the margins for your whole document, boot to bonnet.

   • *This Point Forward* means the new margins take place from the toothpick cursor's position, onward.

   • *This Section* means the margins apply only to the current section. (See Chapter 15 for more information on sections.)

5. **Click OK.**

   Your new margins are enforced.

✔ If you want to print on three-hole paper, set the left margin to 2 or 2.5 inches. This setting allows enough room for the little holes, and it offsets the text nicely when you open up something in a three-ring notebook or binder.

✔ Keep in mind that most laser printers cannot print on the outside half-inch of a piece of paper — top, bottom, left, and right. This space is an absolute margin; although you can tell Word to set a margin of 0 inches right and 0 inches left, text still does not print there. Instead, choose .5 inches minimum for the left and right margins.

✔ The Gutter box inside the Page Setup dialog box applies more to documents printed on two pages and intended to be bound in a book-like format. The Gutter box is a bonus margin that appears on the left side of right-facing pages and vice versa. No need to put your mind in the gutter.

✔ The Mirror Margins item is used for printing pages to be bound together. That way the margins on the left-facing page will match (or, more accurately, be a mirror-image of) the margins on the right-facing page.

✔ The 2 Pages Per Sheet item is nifty: Choose Landscape from the Paper Size panel, then click 2 Pages Per Sheet. You'll notice in the Preview window how Word splits a sheet of paper down the middle with pages on either "side." This is a nifty trick for creating a brochure or greeting card.

✔ If your homework comes out to three pages and the teacher wants four, bring in the margins. Set the left and right margins to 1.5 inches each. Then change the line spacing to 1.5. Refer to the section "Changing line spacing" in Chapter 11. (You can also choose a larger font; check out the section on text size effects in Chapter 10.)

Page Numbering

Time to repeat the word-processing mantra:

Your word processor will number your pages for you.

Your word processor will number your pages for you.

Your word processor will number your pages for you.

Honest. Word does it all. It sticks the page number on the page and keeps the number there no matter how many pages you have or how much you add to or delete your text. There's nothing for you to do, other than tell Word where on the page to stick the page number. Please, oh please, don't manually number anything in a word processor!

Where to stick the page number?

The question is not *can* Word put a number on your page, but *where* should the number go? If you follow these steps, you can direct Word to put the page number just about anywhere on the page. (Well, anywhere *logical*.)

1. **Choose the Insert⇨Page Numbers command.**

   The Page Numbers dialog box, shown in Figure 14-3, appears.

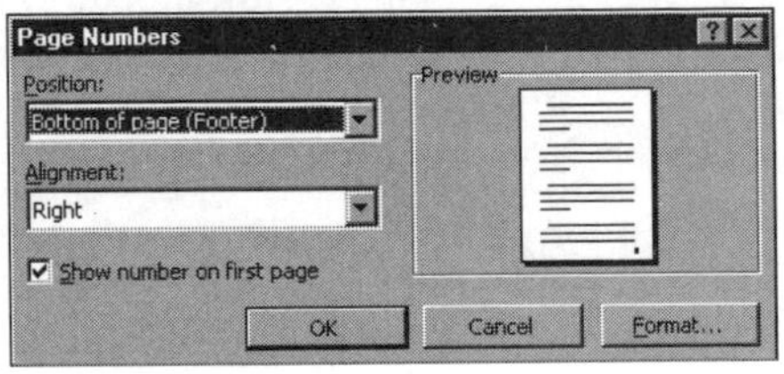

Figure 14-3: The Page Numbers dialog box.

2. **Pick a position for the page number.**

   Word can stick the page number at the top or bottom of the page. Choose that from the Position drop-down list.

   The page number can appear to the right, left, center or inside or outside of your text. Choose the position from the Alignment drop-down list.

   Ponder this situation carefully and keep an eye on the Preview box.

   If you want to get fancier page numbers, click the Format button in the Page Numbers dialog box. Doing so opens the Page Number Format dialog box (see Figure 14-4). From there, you can select various ways to display the page numbers from the Number format drop-down list — even those cute little iis and xxs.

   If you don't want a page number on your first page (say, the title page), deselect the Show Number on First Page check box by clicking in it (in the Page Numbers dialog box, Figure 14-3). That tells Word not to stick an ugly "1" on the bottom of your pristine title page.

3. **Choose OK.**

   The page numbers are inserted.

You can also create page numbering by sticking the page number command in a header or footer. See Chapter 15 for more information. (If you do end up putting the page number in a header or footer, you don't have to use the Page Numbers command.)

Starting off with a different page number

To start numbering your pages with a new page number, heed the instructions in the previous section to conjure up the Page Numbers dialog box. That must be done first since, obviously, there's no need to change page numbers when your document doesn't have them in the first place. Like, duh.

Follow these steps:

1. **Click the Format button in the Page Numbers dialog box.**

   Clicking this button opens the Page Number Format dialog box, shown in Figure 14-4. (Refer to the preceding section for the commands to summon the Page Number dialog box.)

2. **Select the Start At radio button.**

   Type the page number you want to begin with into the box. You can also press the arrows to wheel up and down. Whee!

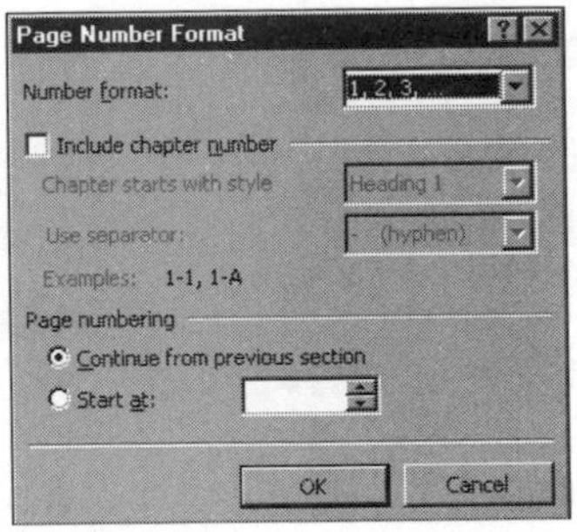

Page Number Format

Number format: [1, 2, 3, ...]

☐ Include chapter number

Chapter starts with style [Heading 1]

Use separator: [- (hyphen)]

Examples: 1-1, 1-A

Page numbering

◉ Continue from previous section

○ Start at: [   ]

[OK] [Cancel]

Figure 14-4:
The Page
Number
Format
dialog box.

3. **Click OK to close the Page Number Format dialog box.**

4. **Click OK to close the Page Numbers dialog box.**

You see the new page numbers reflected on the status bar's little nonsense line. Time to fool everyone into thinking page one is really page 20!

This procedure is something that you may want to do for the second, third, or later chapters in a book. By setting a new page number, the page numbers in all chapters are continuous.

It's Been a Hard Page Break

You can choose two ways to start a new page in Word, the horribly-wrong-yet-obvious way and the impressively neat way:

- ✔ **Horribly wrong:** Keep pressing the Enter key until you see the row o' dots that denotes the start of a new page. Yes, this works. But it's horribly wrong.

- ✔ **Impressively neat:** Press Ctrl+Enter. Voilà! New page.

Pressing Ctrl+Enter inserts a *hard page break* into your document, demanding that Word begin a new page On That Very Spot. This is the preferred way to start a new page.

This line shows a Word hard page break (in Normal view):

--Page Break--

In Print Layout view, the hard page break looks like a new sheet of paper:

Keep these things in mind when you're dealing with hard page breaks:

✔ You can also insert a hard page break by choosing Insert⇨Break from the menu. Choose Page break from the list and click OK. That's a lot of steps, however, and Ctrl+Enter is what most people use all the time.

✔ The hard page break works just like a regular page break does, although you control where it lives in your document: Move the toothpick cursor to where you want the hard page break and press Ctrl+Enter.

✔ Pressing Ctrl+Enter inserts a hard page-break *character* in your document. That character stays there, always creating a hard page break no matter how much you edit the text on previous pages.

✔ You can delete a hard page break by pressing the Backspace or Delete keys. If you do this accidentally, just press Ctrl+Enter again, or you can press Ctrl+Z to undelete.

✔ If you set hard page breaks, remember to use Print Preview to look at your document before you print it. Sometimes the process of editing moves text around, making the hard page breaks unnecessary and awkward. See Chapter 9 for more information on the Print Preview command.

✔ Don't fall into the trap of using hard page breaks to adjust your page numbering. You can use the power of the computer to alter your page numbers without having to mess with page formatting. See "Where to stick the page number?" earlier in this chapter.

Chapter 15

Formatting Documents

• •

• •

*D*ocument is an important word. It carries weight. Funny, you wouldn't think of a silly letter to your niece as something heavy, important, or legal-sounding. But in Word, the big picture is the document. My wife keeps my Honey-Do list as a document on her computer. I suppose that means it must somehow be important.

As far as formatting is concerned, a document is not the same thing as page. No, formatting a document is a *big picture* thing. In fact, a lot of the information in this chapter isn't necessary for most of the documents you create (the silly ones). But when you go nuts some day, or say the urge hits you to *really* flaunt your knowledge of Word, this chapter will be your boon companion.

Breaking Up Your Document into Sections

Many of Word's formatting commands affect an entire document. For example, most of the page formatting commands covered in Chapter 14 are typical document-wide commands: margins, paper size, orientation, and other what-not. And the header and footers you can add to a document (covered in this chapter), also apply to a whole document.

If there ever comes a time when you need to change a document-wide format, such as paper orientation or centering a page, then you need to break your document up into sections.

The sections I'm talking about here are not the various parts of your research paper, or anything like that: These sections are formatting things. In fact, people reading your final printed document won't be aware that you broke up your document into formatting sections at all. They'll just see a fancy document.

A *section* is basically an area in your document whose formatting is independent of the rest of your document, so that the page formatting in one section is independent of the page formatting in another area. For example, to create a unique title page, put that page in its own section. A sideways table would also be its own section.

Finally, the subject of sections is generally considered an advanced Word topic. Most people never use them. Only on rare occasions have I had the need to break up a document into sections. So if you want, you can freely skip this information.

> ✔ Sections are used to create many of the interesting and fun types of documents covered in Part IV of this book.

> ✔ See Chapter 20, "Building Tables," for information on putting a sideways table into a document.

Give me a break

Breaking up your document isn't hard to do. Word has carefully placed all its breaking commands into a handy Break dialog box. To summon the dialog box, choose Insert⇨Break from the menu.

Figure 15-1 shows the Break dialog box. The top group of breaks are text breaks, the bottom group are section breaks.

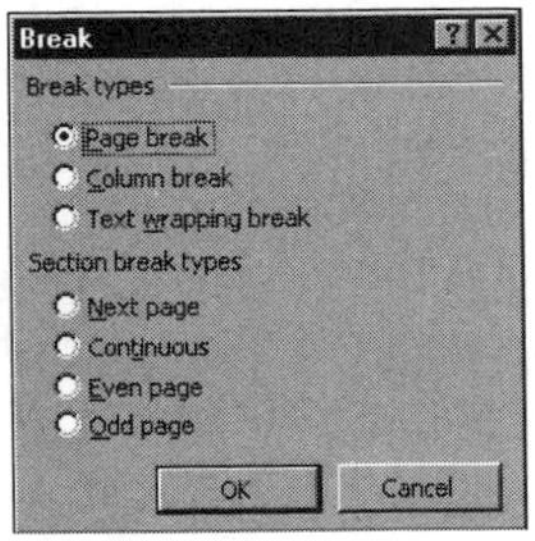

Figure 15-1:
The Break
dialog box.

Break

Break types
- ● Page break
- ○ Column break
- ○ Text wrapping break

Section break types
- ○ Next page
- ○ Continuous
- ○ Even page
- ○ Odd page

[OK]   [Cancel]

To insert a new break, choose that break type from the list and click OK. For example, you insert a hard page break into a document by choosing Page Break and clicking OK — even though the Ctrl+Enter key combination works just as well.

- ✔ See Chapter 14 for more information on starting a new page with a page break.
- ✔ See Chapter 21, "Marching Columns of Text," for information on a column break.
- ✔ I have no idea what a text wrapping break is.
- ✔ The various section breaks are covered in the next section.

Taking a section break

Section breaks are inserted in your document where the page formatting changes. For example, after a title page.

The best way to use the section breaks is to insert them first and then do your page-level formatting (or even typing). Creating a section break is like telling Word to treat one (or more) pages in your document separately.

As an example, suppose you're creating a title page on a new document. Before doing any typing, create the title page as follows:

1. **Choose the Insert⇨Break command.**

   The Break dialog box opens, as shown in Figure 15-1.

2. **Select the Next Page option from the Section Breaks panel.**

   The Next Page option works like a hard page break; it inserts a page break *and* a section break into your document. This is the most common form of section break, since most of the formatting items you're working with are at the page level.

3. **Click OK.**

   In Print Layout view, the new section looks like a hard page break. In Normal view, the section break looks like this:

   ===========================Section Break (Next Page)===========================

The next step in the process is to move the toothpick cursor up to the first page (the title page in the previous section), and format that page according to your needs.

✔ You can use the Continuous Section break to mix formatting styles within a page. For example, if you have columns of text sharing a page with regular text, the Continuous Section break is the ideal way to separate the individual formats. See Chapter 21 for more information.

✔ You can use the Even Page and Odd Page options to start the next section on the next even or odd page. For example, if the document you're writing will be bound, you may want certain sections to start on the right or left side of the bound hardcopy. (I don't know anyone who uses these options.)

✔ Section breaks also provide a great way to divide a multipart document. For example, the title page can be a section; the introduction, Chapter 1, and Appendix A all can be made into separate sections. You can then use Word's Go To command to zoom to each section. Refer to Chapter 3 for more information on the Go To command.

Deleting a section break

You can delete a section break with the Backspace or Delete keys. If you do this accidentally, you lose any special formatting you applied to the section. In this case, press the Undo shortcut, Ctrl+Z, before you do anything else.

Beware of creeping format! If you formatted a special page and then delete the section break, that special page formatting may "fall through" to the rest of your document. Always use Print Preview before you print to ensure everything looks good. See Chapter 9.

The Joys of Headers and Footers

In construction, a header is a buncha wood over a doorway or window. In baseball, a double-header is two games in a row (and a boon for seat cushion sales). In a document, a header is the text you see at the top of every page. The header's little brother is the footer, which is text that appears on the bottom of every page in a document. Word does 'em both.

✔ Headers usually contain things such as your name, document name, the date, page number, title, and phone numbers. ("Hurry! Buy now! Operators are standing by!")

✔ Headers can also be called "eyebrows." Weird, huh?

✔ Footers can include page numbers, a chapter or document title, and odor-eaters.

✔ Footers are not the same thing as footnotes. See Chapter 23 for the low-down on footnotes.

Adding a header or footer

Headers and footers can make any document shine. You don't need to use them both; you can use just one or the other. Either way, the same command is used to add or play with them.

To add a header or footer, follow these steps:

1. Choose <u>V</u>iew⇨<u>H</u>eader and Footer.

Word tosses you into a special version of the Print Layout view that shows the Header and Footer areas of your document roped off. Also visible is the floating Header and Footer toolbar. Witness Figure 15-2 for an example.

Figure 15-2:
A sample
header
with the
Header and
Footer
floating
toolbar
thing.

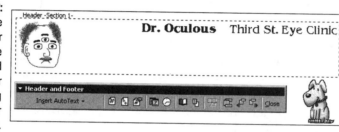

Header -Section 1-

Dr. Oculous Third St. Eye Clinic

▼ Header and Footer
Insert AutoText ▾

2. Click the Switch Between Header/Footer icon to choose either the Header or Footer for editing.

Clicking the button switches you back and forth between the header and footer.

3. Enter your header or footer text.

Any text you type can be formatted using any of Word's text and paragraph formatting commands, including tabs. (See Chapters 11, 12, and 13.)

Word preformats the headers and footers in any document with Center and Right tabs at the center and far right of the Ruler. This allows you to press the Tab key, type some text, and have the text automatically centered at the bottom (or top) of each page. This tab stop isn't required, but it's mighty thoughtful of Microsoft to set it up that way.

4. Use the buttons in the Header and Footer toolbar for special items.

Hover the mouse pointer over each button to see a brief explanation of its function (just like on the big toolbars!). These buttons are described in detail in the sidebar "The Header and Footer toolbar unbuttoned."

For example, you can press the Tab key and then click the Insert Page Number button to put a page number in the center of a footer.

You can use the Insert AutoText drop-down list to put AutoText items into the header or footer. One of the entries is - PAGE - which inserts one of 12 types of page numbers into your header or footer.

5. Click the Close button after you're done.

You're back in your document.

In Print Layout view, you can see the header or footer displayed in "ghostly gray" text. In Normal view, you cannot see any header or footer, even though it's still there. (You can also use the Print Preview command, as covered in Chapter 9, to see the header or footer.)

You can put anything in a header or footer that you can put in a document, including graphics (see Figure 13-6). This capability is especially useful if you want a logo to appear on each page. See Chapter 22, "All about Figures," for information on Word and graphics.

✔ You don't have to go to page 1 to insert a page number in the header. Word is smart enough to put the proper number on the proper page no matter where you're editing the header in your document.

✔ In Print Layout view you can quickly edit any header or footer by double-clicking its ghostly gray image.

✔ You probably want to put some text in front of the page number because a number sitting all by itself tends to get lonely. You can get real creative and type the word **Page** and a space before you click the # button, or you can come up with some interesting text on your own.

✔ To insert the current date or time into the header or footer, click the Date or Time buttons on the Header and Footer toolbar.

✔ Don't forget to use the Switch Between Header and Footer button to alternatively edit headers and footers.

Odd headers for odd pages, even headers for even pages

Word lets you put two sets of headers and footers in your document, if you like: one set for odd pages and another for even pages. For example, this book is formatted that way. The header on even pages contains the page number and the part title. The header on odd pages contains the chapter number and title, then the page number. You can do that too! (And then you can apply for a high-paying job in the Production Department of IDG Books Worldwide!)

To force Word to accept two sets of headers and footers, obey these steps:

1. Choose View➪Header and Footer.

This displays any headers or footers in your document and also the Header and Footer floating toolbar thing (refer to Figure 15-2).

2. Click the Page Setup button on the Header and Footer toolbar.

The Page Setup dialog box opens, Layout area forward as shown in Figure 15-3.

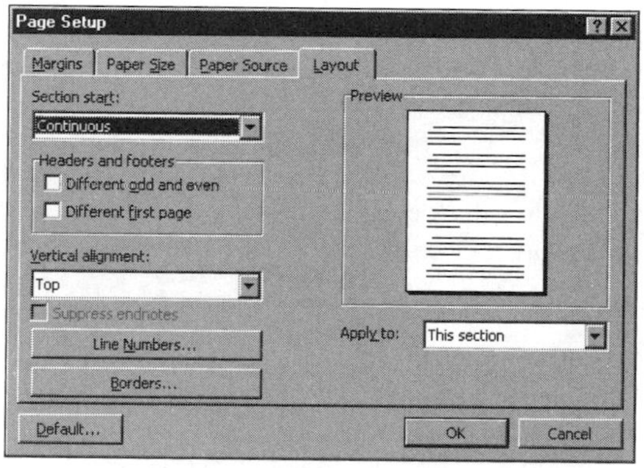

Figure 15-3:
The Page
Setup dialog
box, Layout
area.

3. Select the Different Odd and Even check box in the Headers and Footers panel.

This tells Word that you want two sets of headers and footers, one for odd pages and one for even pages.

4. Click OK.

You're returned to the header/footer editing mode, but notice how the header or footer now says `Odd Page` or `Even Page` before it?

5. Create the odd (or even) header or footer.

Refer to the previous section for notes on making a header or footer.

6. Create the even (or odd) header or footer.

Click the Show Next button to see the next footer in your document, or you can click the Show Previous button. These two buttons cycle you through the various odd or even headers or footers in your document.

7. Click the Close button when you're done editing the headers and footers.

This odd-even stuff has nothing to do with the last number in your car's license plate or the last number in your address.

But I don't want a header on my first page!

To prevent the header or footer from appearing on the first page of text, which usually is the title page, you need to use the Page Setup dialog box as described in the previous section.

In the Page Setup dialog box, select the Different First Page check box; then click OK.

 When you return to edit the headers and footers in your document, click the Show Previous button until you find the first header, titled `First Page Header`. Leave that header (or footer) blank.

This procedure places an empty header on the first page; the header appears on all the other pages as ordered. You can also use this option to place a different header on the first page — a graphic, for example.

Multiple header and footer madness — beyond odd and even pages!

A header is a section-long thing. For most documents, which are one section, that's fine. But suppose for some reason you need multiple headers in your document. Or maybe you just need to turn the headers "off" for a section of text — say some graphic images appear in the middle of your document and you don't want your header interfering. If so, then you need multiple headers (starting headers, no headers, then the starting headers again). To do that, you need to split your document into sections.

By using sections, you can have several different types of headers and footers floating throughout your document, one set for each section. The new section's headers and footers are completely different from the previous (or next) section's. And changing a header in one section doesn't affect any other section in the document.

Refer to the section "Breaking Up Your Document into Sections," earlier in this chapter, for more information on sections.

TECHNICAL STUFF

The Header and Footer toolbar unbuttoned

There are a baker's dozen of buttons on the Header and Footer floating palette of button joy. This table shows the official picture, title, and function for each of them:

Button	Official Button Name	Purpose in Life
Insert AutoText ▾	Insert Auto Text	Allows you to choose an AutoText entry to insert into the document (see Chapter 7)
	Page Number	Inserts page number into the header or footer
	Insert Number of Pages	Inserts the length of your document in pages (use with the page number to make a "page ⅓" type of footer)
	Format Page Number	Opens the Page Number Format dialog box (see Figure 14-4)
	Date	Inserts current date into header or footer
	Time	Inserts current time into header or footer
	Page Setup	Grants you access to Word's Page Layout dialog box
	Show/Hide Document	Allows you to view the main document's text along with the header or footer
	Same as Previous	Copies previous header or footer to this header or footer
	Switch Between Header/Footer	Like the name says
	Show Previous	Views previous header or footer
	Show Next	Views next header or footer
Close	Close	Returns you to your document and closes the Header and Footer screen

Chapter 16

Working with Styles

. . . .

In This Chapter

▶ Finding your styles

▶ Creating a style

▶ Assigning a style to a shortcut key

▶ Changing a style

▶ Using a style

▶ Using the Heading styles

▶ Managing styles

. . . .

*L*ike trying to do Walt Disney World in a day, Word's formatting commands can be overwhelming. Sure, if you're just doing one type of document — like trying to visit only the Disney/MGM Studios in a day — it's not a problem. But if your document contains lots of different things, you'll probably spend more time formatting than writing. That's as bad as spending more time riding the bus at WDW instead of riding the rides (which can be fun if you're under 5).

To ease the formatting chore, Word uses *styles*. A style is nothing more than a collection of formatting information. So if your paragraph is in Times New Roman at 12 points, left-justified with tabs at .5 and 2.0, you can apply those settings to any paragraph by using a style. That's what this chapter tells you how to do.

Where Your Styles Lurk

In Word, styles can be found in one of two places: On the formatting toolbar and in the Style dialog box, obtained by choosing the Format⇨Style command.

You'll probably end up choosing styles from the toolbar. The Style dialog box is where you'll create and edit styles for your documents.

Styles on the toolbar

The easiest way to see and use the styles available in a document is to use the drop-down list on the Formatting toolbar — the one that says Normal — as shown in Figure 16-1.

You may need to arrange your toolbars to see the Styles drop-down list. See Chapter 29, "Modifying Word's Appearance," for help.

The styles you see in the list are the ones you can use in your document. In Figure 16-1 you see the standard styles Word applies to every new document. There are five of them: Default Paragraph Font, three Heading fonts, and Normal. Someone else added any additional styles you see in your Style box.

The way the styles appear in the list gives you a hint as to their format. For example, the Heading fonts are bold and of a specific size and weight, but the Normal font appears in 10-point Times New Roman.

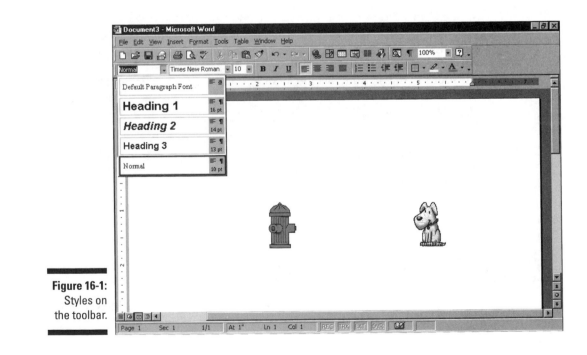

Figure 16-1:
Styles on
the toolbar.

The point size of the text used in the style appears in the gray box to the right of the style name. The four lines tell you how the paragraph is aligned: Left, Center, Right, or Justified. And the a indicates a text style whereas the ¶ indicates a paragraph style.

To choose a style, just select it from the list. All text in the current paragraph and new text you type takes on the attributes of that style. The new style also affects any selected blocks of text in your document.

- ✔ The standard styles are kept in a document template Word uses for all new documents. The name of the template is NORMAL (or NORMAL.DOT), and it's discussed in the next chapter.

- ✔ Hey! Those lines next to the style name (in the gray box) look an awful lot like the alignment buttons on the toolbar. Weird.

- ✔ The Heading styles are not the same thing as headers and footers, covered in Chapter 15. Headers appear on the top of a page. Heading styles are used for chapter and section titles.

Using the style command

For more control over your styles there's the Style dialog box. Summon it by choosing Format⇨Style. Figure 16-2 shows you what's up.

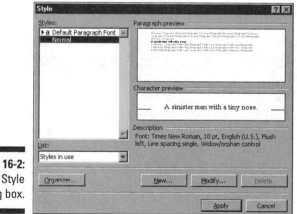

Figure 16-2:
The Style
dialog box.

The Styles list displays available styles in your document (minus the Heading styles for some reason I can't figure out). When you choose a style in the list, that style is previewed in the Paragraph and Character preview windows. A description of the style appears in the Description area.

The Description area tells you how the style is defined — which paragraph and text formatting commands are contained inside the style. One simple style can contain a wealth of formatting information. Applying that style can save you gallons of time.

- ✔ The Style dialog box is best used to create or edit styles. The New button is used to create a new style; the Modify button edits an existing style.

- ✔ The Normal style is the style Word uses for any new document you create.

- ✔ Styles can be deleted from the list by clicking them once with the mouse, then clicking the Delete button. Deleting unwanted styles keeps the style drop-down list brief and makes it easier to find a particular style.

- ✔ You cannot delete the Normal, Default Paragraph Font or any other standard Word fonts. Also beware: You cannot undelete styles!

Creating a New Style

I hate the Normal style. I suppose they could have called it the "Vanilla" style, but I'm one of the 40 percent of the population that likes vanilla ice cream. And calling it the "Boring" style would show too much humor for a Microsoft product. No, Normal is it. And Normal stinks.

The following sections show you how to create some new styles for your document, something better than Normal.

Creating a style based on a paragraph you already formatted

When I write a letter, I use my own style. I call it Body. The Body style. I use the Body style for most everything I write because I think it's pretty: 12-point Souvenir (a font I bought).

Make sure the Style drop-down list is visible on the toolbar (refer to Figure 16-1). If it's not, rearrange the toolbars so you can see the drop-down list.

To create your own style, experiment by creating a sample formatted paragraph first:

1. **Type a paragraph of text.**

   Or you can simply work with any paragraph of text already in your document. Basically you just need something on the screen to see how your formatting works.

2. Mark your paragraph as a block.

See Chapter 6 to find out how to mark a block of text.

3. Format the block.

Select your character formatting. Select a font and select a point size to make the text big or little. See Chapter 11 for more information on character formatting.

Stick to fonts and sizes for your character formatting; avoid bold, italics, or underline unless you want them applied to *all* of the text in the paragraph.

Select the paragraph formatting. Choose Left, Right, Center, or Justified alignment, pick indents and so on. See Chapter 12 for the full list of what you can do.

4. Press Ctrl+Shift+S.

This key combination activates the Style drop-down list on the Formatting toolbar. The current style displayed (most likely "Normal") is highlighted.

5. Type a new name for your style.

A brief, descriptive, one-word name does nicely.

For example, if you create an indented paragraph that you want to use to list things, name the style List. Or if you create a special musical style, name it Liszt. Or you can create a Body style, as I have.

6. Press Enter.

The style is added to Word's repertoire of styles for your document.

The style you created now applies to the paragraph you typed (on which the style is based); any additional paragraphs you type also take on that style. And you can apply the style to other paragraphs.

✔ Give your style a name that describes the style's function. Names like Indented List or Table Body Text are great because they make it easy to remember what they do. Names like Ira or Gopple-bop are somewhat less desirable.

✔ The styles you create are available only to the document in which they're created.

✔ If you create scads of styles you love and want to use them for several documents, you need to create what's called a template. Chapter 17 covers this procedure in "Creating a Document Template to Store Your Styles."

✔ You may have to tweak some things in your style. If so, you'll need to use the Style dialog box. See the section "Changing a style" later in this chapter.

Creating a style in the Style dialog box

Using the Style dialog box to create a style is handy — providing you're well-versed with all of Word's style commands, including some I introduce in the next part of this book. In any event, the following steps glide you through the trips and traps of using the Style dialog box to make up a style.

1. **Choose Format➪Style.**

   The Style dialog box appears (refer to Figure 16-2).

   Notice that you don't have to create a new paragraph or anything to format for this step. Basically you just boldly march forth and build the style from scratch.

2. **Click the New button.**

   The New Style dialog box opens, as shown in Figure 16-3.

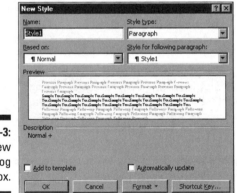

Figure 16-3:
The New
Style dialog
box.

You can save time by basing your new style on an existing style. For example, if you have a heading style that's nearly the same as your text style, though with a larger, bold font, you can choose the original style from the Based On drop-down list. Then you need only make modifications to that style rather than create the whole thing from scratch.

3. **Choose formatting options from the Format button's menu.**

   Clicking the Format button pops up a menu. From that menu you can select any of Word's formatting commands, most of which are covered in this part of the book and a few of which are in the next part.

   As an example, choose Font from the Format button's menu. The Font dialog box appears, allowing you to make character formatting selections for your style.

Choose the Paragraph item from the Format menu to make paragraph formatting selections.

Continue selecting formatting options from the Format button's menu as necessary.

Remember, the steps here assume you *know* which formats you're putting into the style. If you don't know, then you're better off using the techniques described in the previous "Creating a style based on a paragraph you already formatted" section.

4. **Click OK after setting the Font, Paragraph, and other formatting options from the Format button's menu.**

5. **Enter a name for your style into the Name box.**

   The Name box is in the upper-left corner of the New Style dialog box.

   Make the name memorable — something other than "Style1" or whatever lame choice Word makes. For example, type "Title A" for an A-level title in your document.

   Word warns you if you use a name already given to a style. Use another name.

6. **Click OK to create the style.**

   The New Style dialog box goes away. The style you created appears in the Styles list in the Style dialog box.

7. **Click the Close button to return to your document.**

   Or, if you want to apply the new style to the current paragraph (or a selected block of paragraphs) in your document, click the Apply button.

Creating a character-only style

Most of the styles you'll create in Word format at the paragraph level. To create a style that contains a lot of complex character formatting, you should create a Character style. This type of style is flagged by an underlined *A* (**a**) in the Style list.

For example, if you have a centered block of text and only want to change the font to big, ugly text, you can do so by selecting the Big Ugly character-only style, which leaves the paragraph formatting alone.

To create a character-only style, follow the steps outlined in the previous section. However, after Step 2, in the New Style dialog box, choose Character from the Style Type drop-down list. This gears everything in the New Style dialog box to accept only character and font-related formatting stuff. Then, continue working the New Style dialog box as described in the previous section.

✔ When you create a character-only style, the Format button's menu has only three options available: Font, Border, and Language.

✔ The special character styles don't affect any paragraph formatting. Selecting a character style only changes the font, style, size, underlining, bold, and so on.

✔ A section in Chapter 19 is titled "Creating That Shocking White-on-Black Text." Refer to it for information on creating a white-on-black character style.

✔ Also refer to "Stealing Character Formatting," in Chapter 18, for a quick method of applying font formats.

Giving your style a shortcut key

Styles allow you the advantage of quickly formatting a paragraph of text. Style shortcut keys make formatting even better because pressing Alt+Shift+B to get at the Body style is often faster than messing with the Style drop-down list or dialog box — especially when you have a gob of styles you're messing with.

To give your style a shortcut key, follow these steps:

1. **Choose Format⊅Style.**

2. **Select the style for which you want a shortcut key.**

   Highlight that style in the list by clicking it once with the mouse.

3. **Click the Modify button.**

   The Modify Style dialog box appears (and it looks just like the New Style dialog box, shown in Figure 16-3).

4. **Click the Shortcut Key button.**

   A cryptic Customize Keyboard dialog box appears. Don't waste any time trying to explore here. Just move on to Step 5.

5. **Press your Shortcut key combination.**

   Using Ctrl+Shift+*letter* or Alt+Shift+*letter* or Ctrl+Alt+*letter* key combinations is best, where "letter" is a letter key on the keyboard. For example, press Ctrl+Alt+B for your Body style shortcut key.

   You'll notice that the key combination you press appears in the Press New Shortcut Key box (see the middle left side of the dialog box). If you make a mistake, press the Backspace key to erase it.

6. **Check to see that the combination isn't already in use.**

   For example, Word uses Ctrl+B as the Bold character formatting shortcut key. This key combination appears under the heading `Currently Assigned To`, which shows up under the Press New Shortcut Key box. Keep an eye on that box! If something else uses the shortcut key, press the Backspace key and go back to Step 5.

   As an interesting aside, the key combination Ctrl+Shift+B also applies Bold text format. My opinion: Feel free to use that combination for one of your styles since Ctrl+B is easier to type for Bold anyway.

   If the key combination isn't used by anything, you see `[unassigned]` displayed under the `Currently Assigned To` heading.

7. **Click the Assign button.**

8. **Click the Close button.**

   The Customize dialog box sulks away.

9. **Click the OK button.**

   The Modify Style dialog box huffs off.

10. **Click the Close button in the Style dialog box.**

    Congratulations; you now have a usable shortcut key for your style.

    I use the Ctrl+Alt key combinations along with a letter key for my style shortcuts. When I write a magazine article, Ctrl+Alt+B is the Body style; I use Ctrl+Alt+T for my "type this stuff in" style and Ctrl+Alt+C for my Caption style. The notion here is to make the shortcut keys kinda match the style name.

Changing a style

Styles change. Bell bottoms may come back. Again. And though my wife thinks I'm nuts, I believe my Chuck Taylors will very soon be a popular accessory for the upwardly savvy. Oh, but let me not get sidetracked.

Times New Roman — the bane of the Normal style — is a wonderful font . . . if you still wear an undershirt or bow ties and think that Meringue is an ex-Nazi who lived in Brazil. Still, Times New Roman is a workhorse used by everyone for almost everything. Maybe you want to put this font out to pasture and use a different font in your Normal style. If so, you can change it.

Here are the instructions for changing a style — any style, not just the Normal style.

1. **Choose the Format⇨Style command.**

   Well, Howdy Mr. Style dialog box, how are the wife and kids?

2. **Select a style to change from the Styles list.**

   Click that style once with your mouse.

3. **Click the Modify button.**

   The Modify Style box erupts on the screen. It looks just like the New Style dialog box (refer to Figure 16-3), but it says "Modify Style" instead.

4. **Change the style.**

   Use the Format button to access the Font, Paragraph, Tabs, Border, Physique, R_x . . . whatever dialog boxes to give the style a new appearance.

5. **Click OK in the Modify Style box after you're done.**

6. **Oh, and click Close in the Style dialog box to get back at your document.**

✔ Changing a style affects every dang doodle paragraph in your document that uses that style.

✔ In a way, changing a style is cool; if you need to indent the first line in every paragraph, just modify the style. When you leave the Styles dialog box, all the paragraphs magically change. Neat-o.

✔ If you do change the Normal style for good, you need to edit the NORMAL.DOT template. This is covered in Chapter 17.

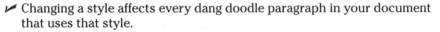

The Follow Me style

In the New Style (or Modify Style) dialog box you find a drop-down list called Style for the Following Paragraph. You can use that list to have Word automatically change styles for you.

For example, when I write a new chapter in a book, I start off with the Chapter Title style. The very next style I use is Chapter Number, always followed by the Intro Paragraph style. In the Modify Style dialog box, I changed the Chapter Title style so that the Chapter Number style

appears in the Style for following paragraph list. That way, after I press the Enter key to end my Chapter Title, the very next style automatically changes to Chapter Number.

Normally Word tries to use the same style, paragraph after paragraph. That's okay. In the body of my text, I choose the Body style to follow all Body styles. If I need to change it, I can do so manually from the Style drop-down list on the toolbar.

Proper Style Application

You don't use a style as much as you apply it. The character and paragraph formatting carefully stored inside the style is applied to text on-screen, injected into that text or block like a stern shot of pickle juice. (Doesn't that make you want to squirm?)

Step-by-step, applying a style is easy:

1. **Decide what text you're applying the style to.**

   If it's a paragraph already on-screen, just stick the toothpick cursor somewhere in that paragraph. Or you can select a block. Otherwise, the style is applied to any new text you type.

2. **Select a style from the Formatting toolbar.**

   Click the down-arrow button beside the first drop-down list — the "Normal" list. Select your style from that list.

   From the keyboard, press Ctrl+Shift+S and then the down-arrow key to see the styles. You see a gaggle of styles displayed, some displayed as they will appear in your document. (See Figure 16-1.)

"Uh, what does the Modify Style dialog box mean?"

As you're goofing with styles, you may stumble upon the Modify Style dialog box shown here:

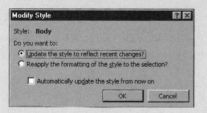

What this dialog box tries to say is, "Excuse me, but you selected some text and a style, but they don't match. Should I pretend that the style should match the text from here on, or should I reformat the text to match the style?" An interesting question.

Choosing Update the style to reflect recent changes? means that you want to change the style to match the selected text in your document. You probably don't want to do this.

The other option is Reapply the formatting of the style to the selection. Equally confusing, this option means that Word formats your highlighted text to match the style you selected. You probably want to choose this option; it keeps your style intact.

As a final word, be thankful for Word's Undo command. No matter what you select in the Modify Style dialog box, the Undo command returns your text to normal (or the way it was before).

✔ Remember the differences between paragraph and character styles. You cannot apply a paragraph style to just a single word in a paragraph; the style takes over the whole paragraph instead.

✔ You can also apply a style by using a shortcut key. Refer to the properly numbered instructions in the preceding section for the details.

✔ To apply a style to your entire document, choose Edit➪Select All. Then select the style you want for everything.

Using the Built-in Heading Styles

There are three (or more) built-in Heading styles available in Word. You can, and should, use these styles if you plan on breaking up your text with different headings.

For example, this chapter has main headings, such as "Proper Style Application," and then subheadings, like "Giving your style a shortcut key." The main headings are formatted with the built-in Heading 1 style. The subheadings are formatted with the Heading 2 style.

Granted, the Heading styles are boring as they come out of the box. But you can change them to suit your document's needs. Refer to the section, "Modifying a style," for information on changing a style's look and smell.

There are a few advantages to using the Heading styles. The first is that you see the headings when you drag the elevator button in the scroll bar. Also, you can use the browsing buttons (below the vertical scroll bar) to hop through your document, stopping at various Heading styles. All this is covered back in Chapter 3, if you're interested.

Honestly, though, you don't really have to use the Heading styles. There are those advantages mentioned above. But if you really want to create your own, fun styles, don't let the Heading styles get in your way.

✔ Heading styles, like the Normal and Default Paragraph Font styles, cannot be deleted from your document.

✔ There are actually many Heading styles Word can use, from Heading 1 on down through Heading 9. These mostly come into play when you use Word's outlining feature. See Chapter 25, "Working with an Outline."

Managing All Your Various Styles

Styles can be like trading cards. And they should be! If you create a great style, it's nice to use it in several documents. This can be done without re-creating the style (and even without using a document template, which is covered in the next chapter).

| Organizer... |

To trade or manage all the styles you have in Word, you need to use the Style Organizer. Choose Format⇨Style from the menu. In the Style dialog box (refer to Figure 16-2), click the Organizer button. The Organizer dialog box appears, as shown in Figure 16-4.

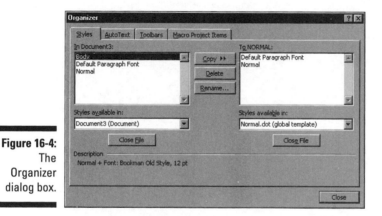

Figure 16-4:
The
Organizer
dialog box.

The purpose of the Organizer is to manage styles (and other things, but this chapter is on styles). You can do that by moving styles between various documents and document templates in Word.

For example, in Figure 16-4 you see the styles available in your document on the left. On the right are the styles that appear in the NORMAL.DOT document template. (NORMAL.DOT is a file that contains all Word's standard settings.)

| Copy ▶▶ |

To copy styles between two documents, use the Copy button. Choose a style from either side of the dialog box and click the Copy button to copy it to the other side.

To choose another document or template, click the Close File button. That button changes to the Open File button, which you can then use to open any Word document on disk. Once open, a list of styles in that document is displayed in the window.

Click the Close button when you're done managing the styles.

✔ As you can see, the Organizer dialog box is also used to organize your AutoText entries, toolbars, and macros (which are an advanced topic not covered in this book). Just as with styles, you can copy AutoText entries or special toolbars from one document to another, or between document templates in the Organizer dialog box.

✔ Also see Chapter 17 on just exactly what a document template is.

Chapter 17

Working with Templates

A template is a pattern you follow to create something. For example, the Department of Transportation uses these huge STOP templates that they lay down at intersections. The workers just spray paint over the template and a huge STOP appears on the roadway. I remember being 11 and playing with my friend's dad's architecture template. There were patterns for couches and TVs and pianos. And toilets. I designed a house with 85 toilets 'cause you never know. . . .

A Word template works like any other type of template. It's basically a skeleton of a document to which you can add text. The template contains styles primarily, though it can also contain text, and graphics, and even its own toolbar. This chapter covers all that (save for the toolbar part, which is covered in Chapter 29).

Ode to the Document Template

Document templates are handy things to have. I use one for sending faxes, writing letters, and so on. This book has its own "Dummies Style" template that contains all the text styles used in this book. Whenever I need to start a new chapter, I use the File⇨New command and choose "Dummies Style" from the list. It's handy, and it keeps my annoying editor off my back.

It's worth your time to create a template for every type of document you use regularly. The following sections tell you how.

> ✔ Unless you choose otherwise, Word uses the Normal document template, also known as NORMAL.DOT.

> ✔ My advice is to create your document first, and then build the template based on the created document. Only if you're really well-versed with Word's formatting and style commands should you attempt to create a template from scratch.

Creating a document template

You create a document template like you do any new document. Start by creating a new document in Word:

1. Choose the File⇨New command.

You must choose the New command from the File menu; clicking the New button on the Standard toolbar doesn't do the job.

The New dialog box opens, numbing your brain because it's just way too complex (see Figure 17-1).

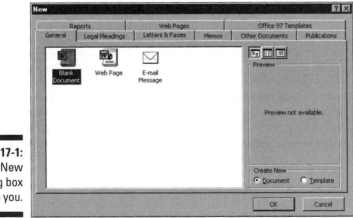

Figure 17-1:
The New dialog box stuns you.

2. Select a template to base your new template on.

Locate the Blank Document template in the General tab. (It should be the first template listed in the New dialog box, as shown in Figure 17-1.) This is the base upon which you're creating your new template — a blank slate, in this case.

If you select a template other than Blank Document, the new template you create will be based on that existing template. For example, if you have a Letterhead template, you can select it to create another letterhead-type of template, or a template for a specific letter you write.

No matter what, you must select a template to base your new template on before you can continue with Step 3.

3. **Click the Template button.**

   In the Create New area (lower-right corner of the dialog box), there are two radio buttons: Document and Template. Clicking the mouse on the Template button puts a little dot there.

4. **Click OK.**

   You see what looks like a new document on-screen. Don't be fooled! It's really a document template thing. (The title bar of the new document indicates that you are working on a template; it lists the template's name until you save your document.)

5. **Create the styles for your new document template.**

   Following the instructions for creating styles in Chapter 16, create the styles you want to use for documents in this particular template.

   For example, when I'm writing a play I have one style for the lines the actors say and another for stage directions. Add a title or two, and those are all the styles I need for my script template.

6. **Save the document template to disk; choose File⇨Save As.**

   The Save As dialog box appears. Note that you're saving the template in a special folder on disk. Don't change this unless you really, *really* know what you're doing.

7. **Type a name for your template.**

   Keep in mind that you should be descriptive with the name. Oh, and you don't need to use the word "template" in the name because Word keeps track of that for you.

   Be clever with your template names. I send out all my letters by using the LETTER template; faxes start with the FAX template. These filenames are accurate, brief, tasteful, and they describe the types of templates that they represent. Do the same, and your Word guru will smile in a delightful manner.

8. **Click OK.**

   The template file is saved to disk.

9. **Close the template document.**

Now you can use the template when you create a new document, which is covered later in this chapter.

- Remember the purpose of a template: To store styles and often-used information in a single place.
- You can find more information on saving stuff to disk, including all-important filename info in Chapter 8.
- Word keeps all its templates in the following folder:

```
C:\WINDOWS\Application Data\Microsoft\Templates
```

Creating a template complete with text

There's no rule that says your document templates must contain only styles. Word's templates can also store text, especially text you may use over and over again in certain types of documents. For example, a common type of Word template may contain letterhead, which allows you to use that template for your correspondence.

For example, your Letter template may contain your letterhead information.

To create a template complete with text, follow these steps:

1. **Do everything outlined in the preceding section, Steps 1 through 5.**

   Gee, a direction like that saves the author a lot of typing energy molecules.

2. **Before saving your document template to disk, type some text that you want to be part of the template.**

   Anything you type will be saved to disk along with the template's styles.

   For example, if you're creating a letter template, why not put in some of the items you use every time you compose a letter? (For my office letterhead, I adjust the page margins and paragraph indent so that the text doesn't overwrite the beautiful illustrations on the paper.)

   Figure 17-2 shows a sample company letterhead type of template that not only contains text but also exciting graphics.

3. **Save the template to disk, as outlined in the preceding section.**

   Give it a clever name, something like LETTER or LETTERHEAD or even NEWSLETTER.

- You can store lots of text in a document template if you like — anything you normally type into a Word document. However, the idea here is to be brief. A specific template isn't as useful as a general one.

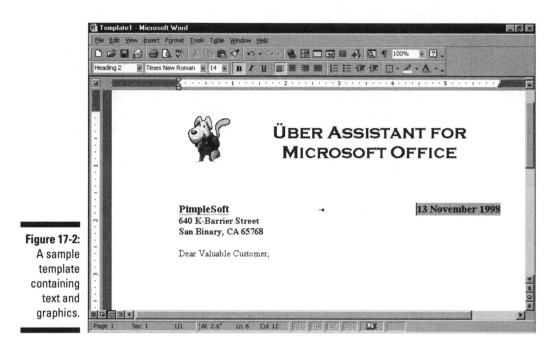

✔ Great template idea: A fax letter cover page. Choose one of the existing templates in the Letters & Faxes panel, click Template in the Create New area of the dialog box, and then modify the existing template, customizing it for your own use.

✔ Refer to Chapter 22 for information on stuffing graphics into a document (which of course means you can also stuff graphics into a template).

✔ Please refer to Chapter 26 for information on Mail Merge — a distinct concept from document templates, although the two can be easily confused.

Using a Document Template

Oh, this is really dumb. To use a document template, follow these steps:

1. **Choose File⇨New.**

    The New dialog box opens.

    You must use the File⇨New command to see the New dialog box; pressing Ctrl+N or clicking the New button on the toolbar just doesn't do the trick.

2. **Select the template you want from the assortment presented.**

First look for the tab that describes the kind of document you want to create. If you're using your own templates, however, they should all live in the General panel. Pluck out the proper template for whatever job you're trying to do.

Word may ask for the Office 2000 (or Word 2000) CD when you choose a new template. If so, insert the CD into your CD-ROM or DVD drive and follow whatever instructions are on the screen. (This is part of Word's new "update as you go" technology. There are vague allusions to that on the software box.)

(You may notice allusions to Word's new "update as you go" philosophy on your software box.)

The Blank Document template is Word's own boring normal template (which should be renamed Yawn).

3. **Click OK.**

Word starts up a document, complete with that template's information, fonts, styles, and whatnot, all ready for use. You can take advantage of any styles stuffed into the template and view, use, or edit any text saved in the template.

✔ Opening a document with a template does not change the template; your new document is merely using the template's styles and any text it already has. To change a template, refer to the next section.

✔ Golly, don't templates make Word kind of easy? Only, of course, if the entire document template and style fiasco hasn't already sent you on the road to the Betty Ford clinic.

Changing a Document Template

Changing or editing a document template is identical to changing or editing a normal document. The difference is that you open a template instead of a document. It's a minor difference, but a big deal since templates, after all, are not really documents.

1. **Open the template by choosing File➪Open.**

Yes, this is the normal Open command and it displays Word's famous Open dialog box. Nothing new here. Yet.

2. **In the Open dialog box, choose Document Templates from the Files of Type drop-down list.**

You can find the Files of Type drop-down box in the bottom center of the Open dialog box.

This option directs Word to list only document templates in the Open dialog box file window.

3. **Find your template folder.**

Here is the path you need to take to find your templates folder:

- Look in drive C. Use the Look In list to pluck out your (C:) hard drive.

- Open (double-click) the WINDOWS folder.

- Open the Application Data folder.

- Open the Microsoft folder.

- Open the Templates folder.

- Open a beer.

The Templates folder should store any templates you created in the General tab. If not, you can open additional folders, such as the Letters & Faxes or Other Documents folders, to look in there.

4. **Open the template that you want to edit.**

Double-click its filename.

Sticking the current date into a template

Any text that you type into a template becomes a permanent part of that template. This situation isn't good news when you want to add the date to a template, as today's date may differ from the date you actually use on the template. Fortunately, there is a solution. Though the procedure is a bit cumbersome, the following steps enable you to set an updating date *field* into your template:

1. **Position the toothpick cursor where you want the date.**

2. **Choose Insert⇨Date and Time. The Date and Time dialog box appears.**

3. **Select the way you want your date to look from the Available Formats list. Me? I like the format "25 December 1999" myself.**

4. **Click the Update automatically button.**

5. **Click the OK button.**

Your template now has a date field in it, as shown in Figure 17-2. The date looks like regular text — except when the toothpick cursor is on it, in which case the text grows gray shading, telling you it's a *date field.*

See Chapter 13 for information on setting a Right tab stop (refer to Figure 17-2), which allows your date to appear aligned on the right margin of the page.

When you open the template, it appears in Word just like any other document — though it's really a template. (Sneaky.)

5. **Make your changes.**

   You edit the template just as you would any other document. Bear in mind that it is a template you're editing and not a real document. Any style changes or text editing affect the template and are saved to disk as a template again.

6. **Save the modified template by choosing File⇨Save.**

   Or choose File⇨Save As to assign the modified template a new name and maintain the original template.

7. **Close the template document by choosing File⇨Close.**

Any changes that you make to a document template do not affect any documents already created with that template. The changes do, however, affect any new documents you create.

Editing the NORMAL.DOT Template

The Normal template is a special beast. Referred to as NORMAL.DOT (its old MS-DOS filename), the Normal template is where Word contains all the settings made for any New document you create with the Ctrl+N shortcut or by clicking the New button on the toolbar.

NORMAL.DOT appears in the New dialog box (refer to Figure 17-1) as the Blank Document template.

So why is this important? Because you can change the Normal template if you want to change the standard font and size (and whatever other formatting) Word uses when it opens a new document. I've gotten many letters from readers asking how to do this.

For example, if you want all your documents to start with the Souvenir font at 12 points, edit NORMAL.DOT:

1. **Choose File⇨Open.**

2. **Browse to the C:\WINDOWS\Application Data\Microsoft\Templates folder.**

   That's where Word keeps its template files.

3. **Choose NORMAL.DOT and click OK.**

   The file will be named NORMAL or NORMAL.DOT, depending on how you have Windows set to show filenames.

4. **Edit the Normal style to whatever font, size or paragraph formatting you want.**

   Choose Format⇨Style. Select the Normal style. Click the Modify button. Use the menus on the Format button to edit the style to whatever you wish. (Follow the instructions found in Chapter 16 for more information on editing a Style in Word.)

5. **Close the NORMAL.DOT file when you're done.**

   This saves the NORMAL.DOT file back to disk, making your changes permanent.

You're set for life.

Chapter 18

Formatting and Spiffing-Up Tricks

· ·

In This Chapter

▶ Reviewing your document's formats

▶ Playing with page number fields

▶ Using color text

▶ Centering a page on the up and down

▶ Having fun with click-and-type

▶ Borrowing character formatting

▶ Using the various AutoFormat commands and tricks

▶ Using Word's wizards

· ·

*N*othing perks up a yawning document like some highly caffeinated formatting. This whole part of the book is dedicated to the formatting task, including the benefit of creating styles and using templates to make the job easier. Now it's time for some fun.

This chapter contains tips and tricks designed to make your formatting chores easier. The sections in this chapter are a grab-bag of useful tidbits I've collected in my many years as a Word user. Some of these techniques may not appear useful to you right now, so flag this chapter for later consumption, when you're ready to absorb the knowledge nuggets that follow.

What's Going on with This Formatting!?

Ah, the mystery format! You're scanning through your latest masterpiece when you notice — right there, mocking you — a paragraph that doesn't seem to fit. Something's amiss with the formatting, but what? To see what's going on with a chunk of text, you could try to lodge the toothpick cursor in that paragraph and then select various formatting commands until you discover which way is up. Needless to say, this is an awkward way to discover your document's formatting.

A nifty trick to pull on any mystery part of your document is to press the Shift+F1 key combination. The mouse pointer changes to look like an arrow-question mark (see the margin).

Now click any character in any word in any paragraph. Word displays a pop-up cartoon bubble (see Figure 18-1) that describes exactly what the heck is going on with the formatting.

You can continue to click text to check its formatting as long as you like. Press the Esc key to cancel the mouse-pointer-as-a-question-mark mode.

✔ You can use the formatting summary displayed in the cartoon bubble to see what needs fixing or just to see how the formatting was done.

✔ The Shift+F1 key activates Word's point-and-shoot help. Click anything in Word's window to see help on that item.

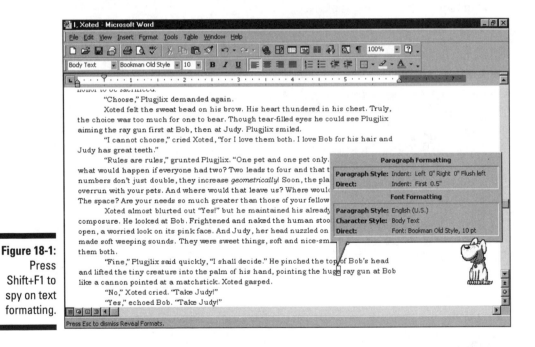

Figure 18-1:
Press
Shift+F1 to
spy on text
formatting.

Let Word Do the Work for You

Once again, Word can do many things for you, things that some users may do in other, less efficient ways. To help you with formatting chores, I've gathered tips on stuff that Word can make short work of. These are things many Word users may toil with in awkward ways. Why bother? Word can do it for you!

Love them automatic page numbers!

Sticking a page number in a document a page at a time is silly. Word can put the page number in for you, and then you don't have to worry about whether the page numbers are correct after you move stuff around. And I'm not talking about only putting page numbers in the header or footer, as I describe in Chapter 14. You can put a page number anywhere in your document that your heart desires.

For example, you could type something like "This is page . . ." and insert a code that tells Word to insert the current page number. In the case of this book, the current page number is 215. So in your document, you'd see `This is page...215`. If, in the process of editing, however, the sentence moved to the next page, Word would automatically change the number to reflect this; you'd then see `This is page...216`.

To insert a page number that Word automatically updates, move the tooth-pick cursor to where you want the page number placed. Choose Insert➪Field. (You may have to click the down-arrow to see the Field command in the menu.) This displays the Field dialog box, as shown in Figure 18-2.

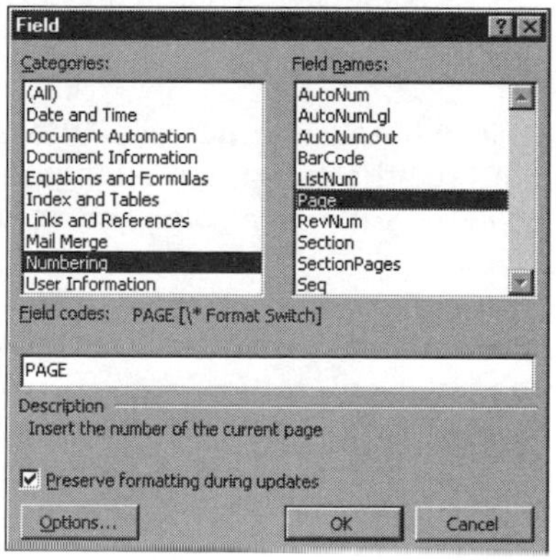

Figure 18-2:
The Field
dialog box.

In the Field dialog box, select Numbering from the Categories list and Page from the Field Names list. Click OK to insert the current page field into your text.

If you want to insert the total number of pages in your document, such as "This is page 5 of 18," select Document Information from the Categories list and NumPages from the Field Names list. Click OK.

The field you insert into your document looks like normal text, but it's not! The information in the field is updated as you update your document. That way, the page number you insert is always accurate.

- ✔ See Chapter 14 for information on sticking the page number in a more traditional spot in your document.
- ✔ Chapter 15 covers putting page numbers in a header or footer.
- ✔ You cannot edit the page number field. You can only delete it: Do so by selecting the entire field as a block, and then pressing the Delete key.

Color your text to make it easy to find

In Word, you can change the color of your text because fonts have a color setting. Normally, Word selects the cryptic "Automatic" color, which means that the text is colored black-on-white (or whatever color your printer naturally prints things in). Text color can be changed, however.

Unless you have a color printer, don't expect your text to print in color. That's one thing. Another thing is that colored text is a lot easier to find on the screen. For example, when I write, I color text purple if I plan on returning later to update it or if I need to check it again later. That makes the text easier to find when I'm reading or reviewing the document.

To change text color, select the text as a block and then click the down arrow by the Font Color tool on the toolbar (see the margin). Clicking the down-arrow displays a drop-down color palette. Choose a color and your text takes on that color.

If the Font Color tool already shows the color you want to paint your text, then just click the tool to change the text's color.

To remove colored text, select it as a block and choose Automatic from the Font Color tool's palette.

Don't forget these tricks!

Here are a few of the formatting tricks I mention in other parts of the book — this is the stuff I want to really drive home:

✔ Always use Ctrl+Enter to start a new page.

✔ Use tabs to line up your text. Never use spaces.

✔ Always use one tab between columns to line them up. That makes editing the information easier should you have to do it.

✔ You can quickly undo any character formatting with the Ctrl+spacebar key combination.

Centering a Page, Top to Bottom

Nothing makes a document title nice and crisp like having it sit squat in the middle of a page. I mean here the middle between the top and bottom of the page as opposed to the middle between the left and right of the page. To achieve this feat, follow these steps:

1. **Move the toothpick cursor to the start of your document.**

   The Ctrl+Home key combination moves you there instantly.

2. **Type your document's title.**

   It can be on a single line or on several lines.

3. **After the last line, choose Insert⇨Break.**

   The Break dialog box appears.

4. **Select the Next Page option from the Section Breaks panel.**

5. **Click OK.**

   This inserts a next-page section break, ensuring that your title page is separate from the rest of your document, both literally and in the formatting sense as well.

   If you're in Normal view, a double-dashed line indicates the section break. In Print Layout view, the new page appears graphically on the screen. (In any event, you can use Print Preview to confirm that you have a new page.)

6. **Format the title.**

   Select the title line(s) and apply proper text and paragraph formatting; you'll probably want the text bold and the paragraphs centered, but don't let me unduly influence you.

Avoid the temptation to use the Enter key to add space above or below your title. Right now, the title sits by itself at the top of the page. That will be fixed in a jiffy.

7. Choose the File⇨Page Setup command.

The Page Setup dialog box appears.

8. Click the Layout tab.

The Layout part of the Page Setup dialog box appears, as shown in Figure 18-3.

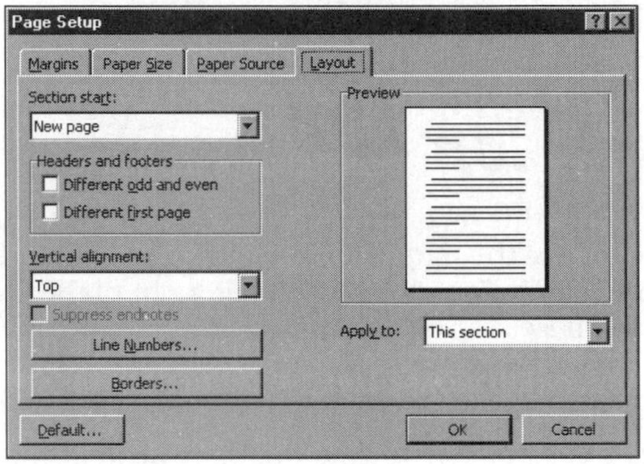

Figure 18-3: The Layout part of the Page Setup dialog box.

9. Choose Center from the Vertical Alignment drop-down list.

10. Click OK.

You may or may not see visual evidence on-screen that you centered a page. To be sure, click the Print Preview tool on the toolbar and, yes, you're a confirmed page-centerer.

Click the Close button to return to your document from the Preview window.

Splash Around with Click-and-Type

The stereotype of the mad modern artist is of a person wearing a beret standing before a huge, blank canvas with a bucket of paint. "Toss a little here," they say, throwing paint up in the corner. Then they get another bucket, "Toss it here," they say as they toss more paint in the middle. And so on. You get the idea.

You get a chance to be your own mad artist with Word's amusing and some-times useful click-and-type feature. Like throwing paint on a canvas, click-and-type lets you splash text around your document wherever you want it — almost. Formatting rules be damned!

To use click-and-type, show your document in Print Layout view by choosing View⇨Print Layout from the menu. Also, click-and-type works best on a new document (so press Ctrl+N to summon a new window if you just want to play around).

As you move the mouse pointer around the blank page, you'll see it change. This tells you how text "splashed" on that part of the page will be formatted.

As you move the mouse pointer around the blank page, the cursor changes. The different cursor types tell you how text "splashed" on that part of the page will be formatted.

Double-click with this type of pointer and you get an indented paragraph, left-aligned on the page.

Double-click with this type of pointer to set a left-aligned paragraph. The paragraph is set on the page wherever you double-click.

Double-clicking in your document with this pointer creates a center-aligned paragraph at that very spot.

Double-clicking with this pointer (can you guess) sets Word up to do a right-aligned paragraph. Wow.

There are many other click-and-type tricks as well, and double-clicking with a click-and-type mouse pointer changes your document's formatting in interest-ing ways. The best way to discover this is just to mess with click-and-type. It really is amazing.

✔ I prefer *not* to use click-and-type, primarily because I know all the other formatting commands. If you grow to understand and use click-and-type, more power to you. But for true control, the other formatting commands mentioned in this part of the book beat click-and-type hands down.

✔ If you really are splashing-and-dashing with click-and-type, consider changing the zoom for your document, zooming out to make the whole thing easier to see. See Chapter 29.

Stealing Character Formatting

Speaking of mad painters, the paintbrush tool on the Standard toolbar can be used to *paint* character styles, copying them from one bit of text to another in your document. Here's how:

1. **Jab the toothpick cursor in the middle of the text that has the character (font) formatting that you want to copy.**

   The toothpick cursor must be in the midst of the word, not to the left or right (but it doesn't have to be in the exact middle, just "in the word"). If it's not, this trick won't work.

2. **Click the Format Painter button on the Standard toolbar.**

   You may need to rearrange the toolbars to see the Format Painter. See Chapter 29.

   The cursor changes to a paintbrush/I-beam pointer, depicted in the margin. This special cursor is used to highlight and then re-format text in your document.

3. **Hunt for the text that you want to change.**

4. **Highlight the text.**

   Drag the mouse over the text you want to change — paint it. (You must use the mouse here.)

   Voilà! The text is changed.

Mad, modern artists can also make use of the following tips and tidbits:

- ✔ The Format Painter works only with character formatting, not paragraph or page formatting.

- ✔ To change the formatting of multiple bits of text, double-click the Format Painter. That way, the format painter cursor stays active, ready to paint lots of text. Press the Esc key to cancel your Dutch Boy frenzy.

- ✔ If you tire of the mouse, you can use the Ctrl+Shift+C key command to copy the character format from a highlighted block to another location in your document. Use the Ctrl+Shift+V key combination to paste the character format elsewhere. Just highlight the text in your document and press Ctrl+Shift+V to paste in the font formatting.

- ✔ You can sorta kinda remember Ctrl+Shift+C to copy character formatting and Ctrl+Shift+V to paste because Ctrl+C and Ctrl+V are the copy and paste shortcut keys. Sorta kinda.

- ✔ Don't confuse the Format Painter with the highlighting tool, which is described in Chapter 30.

Using AutoFormat

Word's AutoFormat command has absolutely nothing to do with formatting in the sense of font or paragraph formatting. No, what AutoFormat really does is clean up your document, remove excess spaces, add spaces where needed, apply Heading formats to what it thinks are your document's headings, and other minor housekeeping chores. Yes, it removes the slop most of us add to our documents without thinking about it.

Before AutoFormat can do its job, you need to create the document's text. Write! Write! Write! Write your letter, memo, chapter, poem, whatever. Then follow these steps:

1. **Save your document to disk.**

   This step is most important, and saving your document is something you should be doing all the time anyway. So, save your file one more time before you use AutoFormat. Refer to Chapter 8 for details on saving documents.

2. **Choose Format⇨AutoFormat.**

   You may have to click the down-arrows at the bottom of the menu to find the AutoFormat command. The AutoFormat dialog box appears, as shown in Figure 18-4.

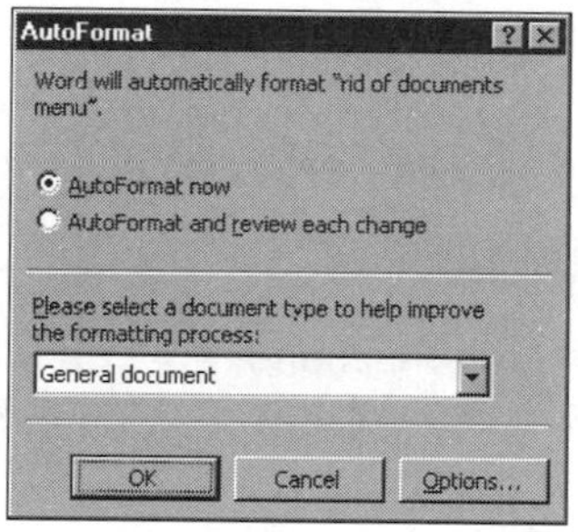

Figure 18-4:
The
AutoFormat
dialog box.

3. **Click OK.**

   Ook! Eep! Ack!

4. **Formatting completed.**

   Word has carefully massaged and adjusted your document. You may find new headings, bulleted lists, and other amazing, whiz-bang things automatically done to your text.

Hey! AutoFormat created a list of helpful bullets right here in the text:

✔ If you like, you can click AutoFormat and review each change button in the AutoFormat dialog box to see exactly what needs to be done before AutoFormat does its job.

✔ If your text is kinda boring, it won't appear as though AutoFormat did anything. Don't despair. AutoFormat is good at creating headings and bulleted lists, but it can't read your mind.

✔ You can always use the Undo command if you detest what AutoFormat did to your document. (Alas, there is no Detest command.)

✔ The AutoFormat tool has nothing to do with formatting your document, as in character or paragraph formatting.

✔ If you're interested in formatting your document automatically, refer to the section on wizards later in this chapter.

Automatic Formatting as It Happens

Sometimes Word can be so smart it's scary. A long time ago, just having a program remind you to save before you quit was thought to be miraculous. But now . . . why just the other day Word reminded me that I forgot to floss the night before and, boy, though that blackberry cobbler looked tempting, I am several stones over my ideal weight. Scary stuff.

Making the automatic formatting thing happen as you work

You must direct Word to be smart. The program cannot do it on its own. To take advantage of the many automagical things Word can do, follow these steps:

1. **Choose Format⇨AutoFormat.**

   The AutoFormat dialog box exposes itself on the screen.

2. **Click the Options button lurking in the bottom-right corner.**

   The AutoCorrect dialog box appears. (Microsoft had to stick the AutoFormat stuff somewhere. They both start with Auto. And they both have a capital letter in the middle.)

3. **Click the AutoFormat As You Type tab.**

   What you see looks something like Figure 18-5.

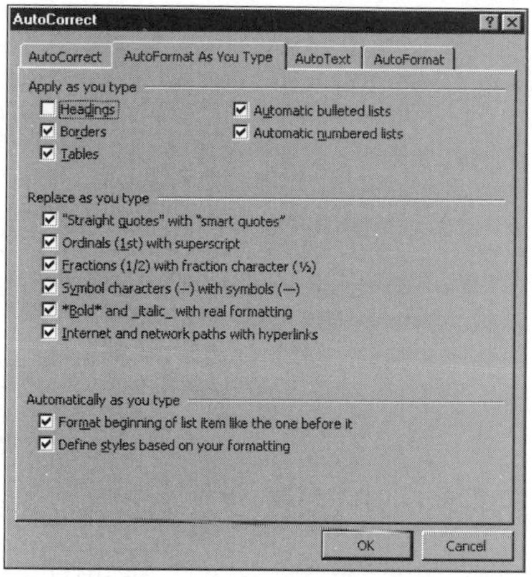

AutoCorrect

AutoCorrect | AutoFormat As You Type | AutoText | AutoFormat

Apply as you type
- ☐ Headings
- ☑ Borders
- ☑ Tables
- ☑ Automatic bulleted lists
- ☑ Automatic numbered lists

Replace as you type
- ☑ "Straight quotes" with "smart quotes"
- ☑ Ordinals (1st) with superscript
- ☑ Fractions (1/2) with fraction character (½)
- ☑ Symbol characters (--) with symbols (—)
- ☑ *Bold* and _italic_ with real formatting
- ☑ Internet and network paths with hyperlinks

Automatically as you type
- ☑ Format beginning of list item like the one before it
- ☑ Define styles based on your formatting

[OK] [Cancel]

Figure 18-5:
The
AutoCorrect
dialog box;
AutoFormat
front and
center.

4. Because you don't know what the options do, check them all on.

Hey! They *are* already all checked! Word comes out of the box with the AutoFormat options checked. If they're not checked, most likely someone configured Word to work differently. Whatever. Make sure all the options are selected, and click to check any that aren't checked.

5. Click OK and then click OK again.

Close both the dialog boxes you left hanging open. Now you're ready to start playing, beginning in the next section.

And now a word from your Word bullet-point tips:

✔ Make sure that you switch on the Headings, Borders, Tables, Automatic Bulleted Lists, and Automatic Numbered Lists items before you work through the remaining sections in this chapter.

✔ The AutoFormat as You Type and AutoFormat panels contain similar items. The AutoFormat as You Type panel is for on-the-fly corrections. The AutoFormat panel, however, is for the AutoFormat command's settings.

✔ The "Straight Quotes" with "Smart Quotes" Replace option tells Word to change the boring straight quote marks into the more stylish "double" and 'single' style quote marks. Face it: The " and ' smell of Smith Corona.

✔ The Ordinals (1st) with Superscript option tells Word to change your text so that when you type **2nd**, the program immediately formats it as 2nd. No pencil could ever be that smart.

✔ The Fractions option replaces the number-slash-number combination with a fraction character — like 1/2 with ½. Again, you lose a degree of dorkiness in your text.

✔ The Symbol Characters (—) with Symbols (—) option is a little less obvious. What it does basically is turn specific letter or key combinations into symbols. For example, with this option on, when you type **TM**, Word automatically changes those letters into a trademark symbol, like so: ™. There must be a list of symbols and key combinations somewhere, but I've yet to find it.

✔ Okay, they're found in the Tools⇨AutoCorrect dialog box.

✔ The *Bold* and Underline option comes in handy when you use Word to compose e-mail messages (though I've yet to figure this one out fully).

✔ Internet and Network Paths with Hyperlinks and everything after it: Don't bother. Check it later on. Maybe someday it will help.

Automatic numbered lists

The best way to understand the AutoFormat-as-you-type adventure is to *live* it. Heed the following steps:

1. **Start a new document in Word.**

   The simplest way to do that is to press the Ctrl+N key combination. No messing around here.

2. **Type the following:**

   ```
   Things to do today:
   ```

   Press the Enter key to start a new line. Then type:

   ```
   1. Sell kidneys.
   ```

   Now — prepare yourself — press the Enter key to end that line. You see the following:

   ```
   1. Sell kidneys.
   2.
   ```

   Not only does Word automatically give you a 2, but it reformats the previous line as indented text. Amazing. Stupendous. Definitely worth $25 of the purchase price.

3. **Deal with your annoying Assistant.**

   Because starting a numbered list may or may not be what you want to do, your annoying Assistant appears to ask a question of you (see Figure 18-6). Keep typing your document if you want to keep numbering your list or choose No, change it back to how it was if you don't want a numbered list.

Figure 18-6:
Your
annoying
Assistant
asks what's
next.

4. **Keep typing your list.**

   Word adds a new number every time you press the Enter key to start a new paragraph.

5. **Press Enter and then Backspace when you're done.**

   When you finish, press the Backspace key after you press Enter the last time. Word instantly forgets that it was helping you out and returns to its original, rude mode.

This trick also works for letters (and Roman numerals, too). Just start something with a letter and a period and Word picks up at the next line with the next letter in the alphabet and another period.

Automatic headings

This is simple. To stick an automatic heading into your document, type the heading and then press the Enter key twice. No need to apply any formatting; your Assistant asks if you want to convert the paragraph to a heading. Choose that option from the Office Assistant's cartoon bubble and you're on your way.

- ✔ See Chapter 15 for more information on the Heading 1 style. You can change this style to be more suitable to your document if you like.

- ✔ Personally, I think this is a silly option. For me, it's easier to format my own headings, primarily because I use A, B, and C level headings, and this trick doesn't apply to those lesser headings.

Automatic borders

In the old Smith Corona days of yore, we would fancy up our documents by woodpeckering a line of hyphens, underlines, or equal signs. It brings back kind of a sentimental tear to the eye, especially for me, because I pressed the keys so hard that ripping the paper out of the typewriter often ripped the paper in two. Not with a word processor, though.

If you want a single-line border, right margin to left across your page, type three hyphens and press the Enter key:

- - -

Then press the Enter key. Word instantly transmutes the three little hyphens into a solid line. (Office Assistant may pop up and ask if you need help; choose a help option or just keep typing.)

Want a double line? Then use three equal signs:

===

Press the Enter key and Word draws a double line from one edge of the screen to the next.

Chickening Out and Using a Wizard

You're off to see the Wizard, the wonderful Wizard of Word. . . .

A wizard enables you to create a near-perfect document automatically. All you need to do is select various options and make adjustments from a handy and informative dialog box. Word does the rest of the work. This is so easy it should be a sin.

To use a Word wizard, follow these steps:

1. **Choose File⇨New.**

    This command opens the New dialog box (refer to Figure 17-1).

2. **Select a wizard.**

    A number of wizards come prepackaged with Word. Of course, none of them hides in the General panel. To find a wizard, click another panel in the New dialog box, for example, the Letters & Faxes panel.

    Wizards live along with templates, though the wizards have the word "wizard" in their name and they're identified by a unique icon (see the margin). You can find the Fax Wizard, Letter Wizard, Memo Wizard, Lizard wizard, gizzard blizzard, and so on.

    Whatever wizard you select, highlight it in the template list, then click the wizard's icon once with your mouse. For example, the Letter Wizard in the Letters & Faxes panel helps you create one of many different types of letters.

3. **Click OK.**

   Word hums and churns for a few minutes. It's thinking — no doubt a painful process. Give it time.

4. **Optionally, be enlightened by the Wizard dialog box.**

   The more advanced wizards will quiz you. You'll see a dialog box displayed and be asked a bunch of questions to assist the wizard in creating your document.

   The more advanced wizards quiz you, giving you a dialog box with a bunch of questions for you to answer. The wizard uses your answers to help create your document.

   Some wizards merely create a blank document for you to complete. Just fill in the sections that say something like [type the recipient's name here] with the proper information and you're on your way.

- Wizard. Wizard. Wizard. It's one of those words that gets weirder and weirder the more you say it.

- Even though a wizard created your document, you still must save it to disk after you're done. In fact, most wizards may just start you on your way. After that point, you work with the document just like any other in Word. Don't forget to save!

- The Tools menu offers a Letter Wizard item. If you choose this command, follow your Office Assistant's advice and answer the various questions in the dialog box.

- Some wizards even fill in text for you. These are super-cheating wizards. The Stephen King wizard, for example, writes his books for him in under a day.

Part III
Sprucing Up Your Document

In this part . . .

Word is more than a mere word processor. (If it weren't, this book would be over now.) Compared to a car, a word processor is like a Chevy. Word, on the other hand, is all forms of transportation. There are just so many interesting and outrageous things Word can do I had to create this entire part of the book in which to put them. It's a bunch of random, occasionally-useful-but-often-useless tricks and whatnot. Fit them all under the category of sprucing up your document.

Chapter 19

Borders, Boxes, and Shading

· ·

· ·

*T*here is a warm, fuzzy border between word processing and desktop publishing. Traditionally, word processors dealt with words and added some formatting to make things less ugly. Desktop publishing brought in graphics and design elements beyond the power of most word processors. Today the distinction between the two isn't so clearly drawn.

As an example, ten years ago being able to draw a box around your text was considered too advanced for a mere word processor. Ah, but Word is no mere word processor. This chapter covers the box-drawing topic, along with shading your text and adding pretty borders to everything.

Boxing Your Text

Remember that controversial movie a while back, *Boxing Helena*? That movie wouldn't have been such an issue, and it certainly would have been less creepy, had Dr. Cavanaugh done the following:

> Helena

There. Nothing to it. The following sections tell you how to box anything in your document, from mere words to paragraphs to full pages o' text.

Boxing in small bits of text or paragraphs

Word allows you to stick a box around any bit of text or paragraph in your document. For example, you can box in a title, or draw a box around an "aside" paragraph or sidebar, or put a box around a single word. No matter, whatever you're boxing up, follow these steps:

1. **Choose the text you want to box.**

   It's best to select the text you want to put into a box: either a word, a few words, several paragraphs, or an entire page.

   If nothing is selected as a block, Word boxes in the paragraph the tooth-pick cursor is blinking in.

2. **Choose the Format➪Borders and Shading command.**

   The Borders and Shading dialog box opens. Make sure the Borders tab is chosen, as shown in Figure 19-1. (If not, click that tab with the mouse.)

3. **Select the type of border you want from the Setting column.**

   Four preset, easy-to-use, pop-n-fresh border styles are available; don't bother with the Custom style until you fully figure this out. Just click the style of paragraph border you want. My favorite is Shadow.

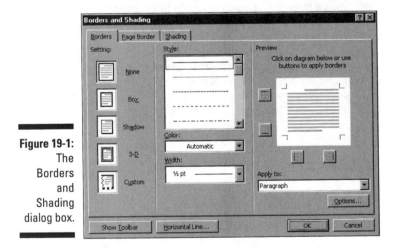

Figure 19-1:
The
Borders
and
Shading
dialog box.

Optionally you can choose a line style from the Style list.

The Color drop-down list sets the border color. (The "Automatic" color is black.)

The Width drop-down list sets the line width.

Observe the Preview window to see how the border affects your text.

4. **Choose Text or Paragraph from the Apply To list.**

   Word is usually smart with this. If you select only one word or any bit of text less than a paragraph, Word assumes you want to box in only that text. Even so, you can choose Paragraph or Text from the list.

5. **Click OK.**

   Your text now has a box around it.

Putting a border around pages of text

Not only can you rope titles and paragraphs, but you can put a border around each page in your document. Now that may sound hokey, but if you're making a newsletter or award or something cheesy like that, the border can come in handy.

To stick a border around your document, choose Format⇨Borders and Shading and then click the Page Border tab to view that panel. I'm not including a figure here because this panel looks and operates just like the Borders panel; see the previous section for more information.

The only difference you find in the Page Border panel is the Apply To drop-down list in the lower-right corner. Before you click OK, you need to tell Word which parts of your document need a page border. Then click OK.

   ✔ Select Whole Document from the Apply To list to have a border on every page.

   ✔ Other options in the Apply To list deal with sections in your document. For example, if you want to border only one page out of many, you need to make that page its own section. Refer to Chapter 15 for more information on creating a section break in your document.

Making partial boxes

In Figure 19-2, the newsletter's title is boxed in with using the Borders and Shading dialog box, but notice that it has lines only on the top and bottom. To make that happen with your title or any other text, follow Steps 1 and 2 as outlined in the section, "Boxing in small bits of text or paragraphs." With the Borders and Shading dialog box on the screen, do the following:

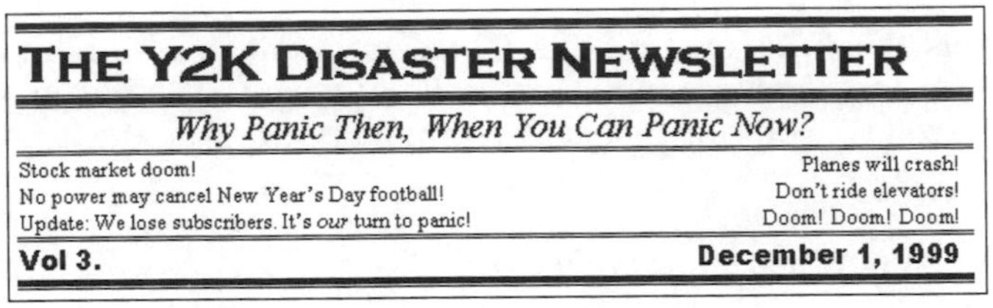

Figure 19-2:
A docu-
ment title
with bor-
ders at the
top and
bottom.

THE Y2K DISASTER NEWSLETTER

Why Panic Then, When You Can Panic Now?

Stock market doom!   Planes will crash!
No power may cancel New Year's Day football!   Don't ride elevators!
Update: We lose subscribers. It's *our* turn to panic!   Doom! Doom! Doom!

Vol 3.   **December 1, 1999**

1. **Click the Box icon to put a box around your text.**

   Yeah, this isn't how you want to end up, but it's how you must start. (Just click once — don't double-click here.)

2. **Select a line style from the Style panel in the Paragraph Borders and Shading dialog box.**

   You can choose from several thicknesses and double- or single-line patterns, as shown in Figure 19-2. In fact, notice how paragraphs in that figure have different line styles for the top and bottom lines.

   Use the Preview box to ensure your changes match the line style you select.

   You can also mess with the Color and Width doohickeys if you feel like it. Oh, play, play, play. What's the point in doing any work?

3. **Now focus on the Preview box.**

   The box tells Word where to put lines around your text — top, bottom, left, right, middle, and so on.

4. **Click the mouse on the left and right sides of the border in the Border preview box.**

   Or you can click the left and right border buttons. Either way it eliminates the lines on the outside of your text.

5. **Click OK after you finish making your box.**

   The box is now missing two sides, so it's really not much of a box at all and will probably spill all of its contents if you tip the page the wrong way, so be careful.

Using the Border Button on the Toolbar

If you ever need to slap down a quickie border on your paragraph (or in a table), you can take advantage of the Border button on the toolbar and its handy palette o' options.

Just click the down-arrow by the button, and you see a selection of line types — top, bottom, outside, and so on (see Figure 19-3). Pick one from the list and whichever paragraph the toothpick cursor is on, or whatever text is selected, grows that line.

Figure 19-3:
Your paragraph border selection, courtesy of the toolbar's Border button.

- ✔ The line style that's currently selected in the Borders and Shading dialog box is applied when you click the Border button on the toolbar.
- ✔ So, if you don't like the line style, choose Format⇨Borders and Shading from the menu to change it.
- ✔ To remove all borders from a paragraph, click the Border button on the toolbar and click the No Border button.
- ✔ The Border button on the toolbar only affects text, not the entire page. For that, see "Putting a border around pages of text" elsewhere in this chapter.

Giving Your Text Some Shade

The neatest Border dialog box effect of them all is shading. You can shade text, and parts of your document, like a title, as Figure 19-4 shows. You can shade text or a title with or without a border around it. Use these steps:

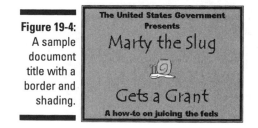

Figure 19-4:
A sample document title with a border and shading.

1. **Mark your text or title as a block.**

   Refer to Chapter 6 for efficient block-marking instructions. If you want the shaded area to cover more than the title line, highlight the lines before and after the title.

2. **Choose Format⇨Borders and Shading.**

   The Paragraph Borders and Shading dialog box appears, but . . . .

3. **Make sure that the Shading panel is up front.**

   Click the Shading tab with your mouse if it's not. The Shading panel jumps to the front, as shown in Figure 19-5.

Figure 19-5:
The Shading panel in the Borders and Shading dialog box.

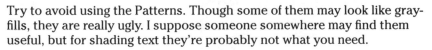

4. **Select a shading value from the Fill palette.**

   The first three rows of the palette (below the "No Fill" choice) give you shading options for your text in percentages of black, from white to all black in various increments. (The other options are for colors, which your printer may or may not be capable of producing.)

   The best values to select for shading your text are 10 percent, 20 percent, or 30 percent. I prefer 20 percent because it prints well on my laser printer.

    Try to avoid using the Patterns. Though some of them may look like gray-fills, they are really ugly. I suppose someone somewhere may find them useful, but for shading text they're probably not what you need.

5. **Click OK.**

   Your text appears shaded on-screen. Everyone will wonder how you did it.

✔ Nope, just because you visited the Border dialog box doesn't mean that you have to put a border around your text.

✔ If the shading stinks (and we're all allowed a little latitude for screwing up here), you can remove it. Just follow the steps outlined previously, but select None in the Shading panel in Step 5. Oh, and you can always use Ctrl+Z, the Undo command, to chicken out of anything.

✔ At the bottom of the drop-down list of styles, you can find some shading patterns as well. Ooh! And look at the colors! Choose something to match the drapes.

TIP

✔ Shaded titles look best when they're at the top of your first page — not on a page by themselves.

Creating That Shocking White-on-Black Text

After shading, the next most fun thing to do is print white text on a black background. This is a very bold move and stands out prominently in your text — like being hit in the face with a cinder block. So don't use this technique casually.

> Gentlemen, please refrain from firing your guns during the performance.

To produce white-on-black text, you must do two things. First, you must create a black background; and second, you must create white-colored text. Here is how you create a black background:

1. **Mark your text as a block.**

   It's best to start with text you've already written. At some point here, you will have black text on a black background, which you cannot see. If you already have the text written, it is easier to see after you're done. (See Chapter 6 for block-marking instructions.)

2. **Choose Format⇨Borders and Shading.**

   The Paragraph Borders and Shading dialog box appears.

3. **Making sure that the <u>S</u>hading panel is forward.**

   Click the Shading tab if it's not. The Shading dialog card reshuffles itself to the top of the pile (see Figure 19-5).

4. **Click the black square in the Fill area.**

   That's the first square in the fourth column; you can see the word Black in the box to the right of the color grid.

5. **Click OK to exit the Borders and Shading dialog box.**

Now you don't see anything on-screen because you have black text on a black background. (Actually, with the block highlighted, you see what looks like a large white block floating over a black block. Don't freak!)

With the block of text still highlighted, you need to change the text color to white. This step is done by using the Text color tool on the formatting toolbar.

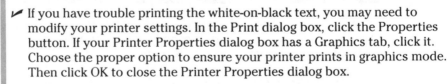

1. **Click the Font Color tool on the toolbar.**

   A drop-down palette appears.

2. **Choose White.**

   It's the last square in the palette, bottom right. (If you point the mouse at the square long enough, a bubble with the word "White" appears.) Click that square to color your text white.

   You can now unhighlight your block. The text appears on-screen and printed in white letters on a black background.

   ✔ Word 2000 is (actually) smart about displaying white-on-black text, especially when that text is selected. You'll never "lose" the text on the screen.

   ✔ I don't recommend reversing vast stretches of text. White text on a black background prints poorly on most computer printers. This stuff is best used for titles or to highlight smaller blocks of text.

   ✔ If you have trouble printing the white-on-black text, you may need to modify your printer settings. In the Print dialog box, click the Properties button. If your Printer Properties dialog box has a Graphics tab, click it. Choose the proper option to ensure your printer prints in graphics mode. Then click OK to close the Printer Properties dialog box.

   ✔ You can use the white-on-black text sample you created to make a white-on-black character style in Word: Put the toothpick cursor in the white-on-black text. Choose Format⇨Style from the menu. Click the New button. (You'll see the white-on-black style described in the Description area.) Type a name for the style in the Name box. Choose Character from the Style type drop-down list. Click OK to close the New style dialog box, then the Close button to close the Style dialog box. See Chapter 16 for more information on styles.

Chapter 20

Building Tables

A table is a piece of furniture with four legs on which you set things — but not your elbows when Grandma is watching. In Word, a table is a collection of items all lined up in neat little columns and rows. In the primitive days, you made tables happen by using the Tab key and your handy frustration tool. Face it: Making things align can be maddening — even in a word processor and even if you think that you know what you're doing.

Coming to your rescue, of course, is Word. "It's Table Man, Ma, and he's here to rescue us!" Word has an able Table command. (Well, honestly, it has two or three of them.) Using primitive skills you learned while watching art programs on PBS, you too can create elegant and interesting tables anywhere in your document. This chapter gives you all the details.

Why Use Tables?

And so the debate rages: Should you stick information into a table or just use a bunch of tabs to line things up?

Okay, it's not a debate. It's probably nothing you've ever thought about before, but it's ponderable.

If you have short bits of text you need to align in columns, use tabs:

Child	*Gift*	*Thank-You Sent*
Susan	Jawbreaker	Yes
Will	Shrunken head	Yes
Al	Rubber snake	No

This type of "table" works great for small words. But when you have larger bits of text, you need to create an official table in Word. This chapter tells you how to go about that.

- ✔ Use a table whenever you have information that can be organized into rows and columns.

- ✔ Each cubbyhole in a table is called a *cell*. Into the cell, Word lets you put text (any amount) or graphics.

- ✔ Unlike working with tabs, Word's tables can be resized and rearranged to fit your data. In other words, if you plan on modifying the information later, it's best to use a table as opposed to a brief list formatted with tabs.

- ✔ Alas, Word does not have a handy Chair command. (Although rumor has it that Microsoft is working on barstools.)

Splash Me Down a Table

Tables are "drawn" into your document using the handy Table and Borders button. Basically you draw the table first, then fill in the rows and columns later. And it doesn't matter if there's already text in your document; drawing the table moves any existing text out of the way to make room for the table.

To splash down a table in the middle of your document, follow these steps:

1. Click the Tables and Borders button.

After you click the button (shown in the margin), the Tables and Borders tool palette appears, floating over your text. See Figure 20-1. This palette contains buttons for building tables as well as options from the Borders and Shading dialog box (see Chapter 19).

Figure 20-1:
The Tables
and
Borders
palette.

If you weren't previously in Print Layout view, Word switches you there automatically. (You cannot splash down tables in Normal view.)

2. **Ensure that the Draw Table button is "on" in the Tables and Borders palette.**

The Draw Table button should be active (looking like it's pressed down), unless you've done something else between this step and the previous step (which would have been naughty of you). If the Draw Table button isn't on, click it.

The mouse pointer changes to a pencil, which I call the *pencil pointer*.

3. **Drag the mouse to "draw" the table's outline in your document.**

Start at the upper-left corner of where you envision your table and drag to the lower-right corner, which tells Word where to put your table. You'll see an outline of the table as you drag down and to the right (see Figure 20-2).

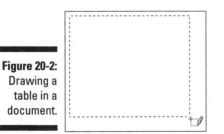

Figure 20-2:
Drawing a
table in a
document.

Don't worry about making the table the right size; you can resize it later.

Notice that any text you already have in your document moves aside to make room for the new table.

4. **Use the pencil pointer to draw rows and columns.**

As long as the mouse pointer looks like a pencil, you can use to it draw the rows and columns in your table.

To draw a row, drag the pencil pointer from the left side to the right side of the table.

To draw a column, drag the pencil pointer from the top side to the bottom side of the table, as shown in Figure 20-3.

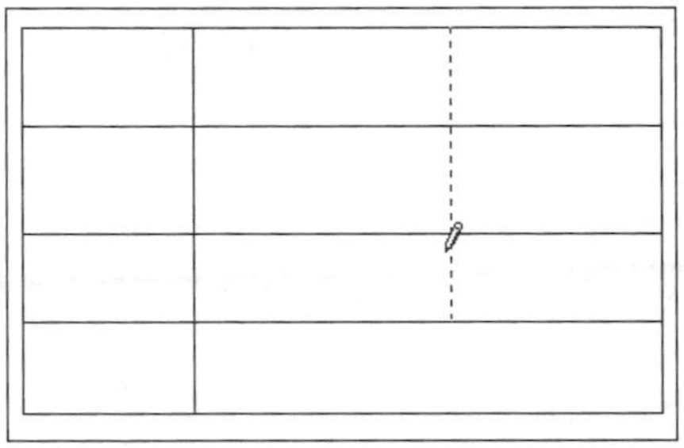

Figure 20-3:
Drawing a
column.

As you drag the pencil pointer, a dashed line appears showing you where the new row or column will be split. Figure 20-3 shows how your table is shaping up. Also notice that you can split columns or rows into more cells simply by dragging the pencil pointer inside a cell and not across the entire table.

Again, don't worry if you have too many or too few rows or columns. You can add or delete them later, as you see fit. And don't worry about things being uneven; you can rearrange your rows and columns later.

5. **Click the Draw Table button when you're done creating the table's rows and columns.**

   This turns off table-creating mode and switches you back to normal editing mode. Now you can fill the text into your table or modify the table or whatever.

The Tables and Borders dialog box is nifty to have hanging around while you're working in a table. To get rid of it when you're done, click its X button (upper-right part of the window) to make it go thither.

Adding text to the table

Enter text into the table as you would enter text anywhere in Word. Here are some pointers:

- ✔ Cells grow longer (taller) to accommodate extra text you type into them.

- ✔ You can press the Enter key to start a new paragraph in a cell, or use Shift+Enter to start a new line of text.

✔ Use the Tab key to move from cell to cell in your document.

✔ If you press the Tab key in the last cell in the table, you create a new row of cells.

✔ The Shift+Tab combination moves you backward between the cells. (This is easier than using the arrows keys, which dawdle in any text a cell may contain.)

✔ Text in a cell is formatted using the font dialog box, just as normal text is formatted in your document.

✔ Each cell is its own unit as far as paragraph formatting goes. To align or indent an entire row or column of cells, choose Table⇨Select and then choose Column or Row for the sub-menu to select a column or row, respectively.

✔ You can also select columns by holding the mouse cursor above the column until the cursor changes shape to a down-pointing arrow. Point the arrow at the row and click the left mouse button. You can select multiple columns by dragging the mouse across them.

✔ Clicking the mouse thrice in a cell selects all text in that cell.

✔ Graphic images can also be pasted into cells.

Messing with the table

After the table is splashed down into your document, you can mess with it in uncountable ways. The following pointers suggest merely a few of them:

✔ On the upper-left corner of the table is the Move Thing. It allows you to move the table elsewhere in your document. Just drag the Move Thing with the mouse. However:

✔ As with dragging anything with the mouse, you're probably better off cutting and pasting the table if you plan on moving it more than a few lines up or down (or left or right). Put the toothpick cursor in the table and choose Table⇨Select⇨Table from the menu to select the table for cutting and pasting.

✔ Point the mouse between a row or column to re-size that row or column. When you find the "sweet spot," the mouse pointer changes to look like the Redimensioning Doohickeys, shown in the margin. Then just drag the mouse left or right or up or down to change the table.

The following tips assume you have the Tables and Borders palette floating in Word's window. If not, choose View⇨Toolbars⇨Tables and Borders from the menu.

- ✔ To erase a line between two cells in a table, choose the Erase tool and click the line you want to remove. If the two cells both contain text, then Word simply tacks the contents of one cell onto another.

- ✔ Use the Line Style and Line Weight drop-down lists to set the style and thickness of the lines in the table. After choosing a style and thickness, use the Draw Table (pencil) tool to click a line in the table, which changes it to the new style.

- ✔ You can further modify your table with the Insert Table button. Clicking the down-arrow by the icon displays a menu of various table-related commands for inserting columns or rows or for automatically adjusting the table's dimensions.

- ✔ To utterly remove the table from your document, click the mouse inside the table and then choose Table⇨Delete⇨Table. The table is blown to smithereens.

Making a Table Out of Text Already in Your Document

After you realize the glory of tables, you may desire to convert some of the tab-formatted text in your document into a table. Or, actually, you may just want to put any text into a table because you become obsessed with tables and not seeing any text in a table makes you frustrated and angry and the little people are screaming and the sky is yellow and . . .

[*The author has been asked to calm down. The remaining sections in this chapter are being written by the author's assistant, Trixie. Ed.*]

To convert text already in your document into a table, first select the text (which Dan wrote about in Chapter 6). Next, choose Table⇨Convert⇨Text to Table. The Convert Text to Table dialog box appears, as shown in Figure 20-4.

Figure 20-4:
The Convert
Text to Table
dialog box.

> **Convert Text to Table**
>
> Table size
> Number of columns: 1
> Number of rows: 4
>
> AutoFit behavior
> ○ Fixed column width: Auto
> ○ AutoFit to contents
> ○ AutoFit to window
>
> Table format (none)   AutoFormat...
>
> Separate text at
> ○ Paragraphs   ○ Commas
> ○ Tabs   ○ Other: -
>
> OK   Cancel

If your text is already in a table-like format using tabs, then choose the Tabs item from the bottom of the dialog box. Click OK to perfectly create the new table.

If your text isn't formatted with tabs, choose the number of rows you want from the top of the dialog box. Click OK and Word creates the table with the number of columns you want. Your text appears in the first column of each row.

Oh, and you can use this command's twin, T_able➪Con_vert➪Ta_ble to Text to convert a table into plain text back in your document. [*But I don't want to go into any details about that just now, seeing how upset it would make this book's true author. Trixie.*]

A Quick Way to Cobble a Table Together

 To quickly create an empty table in your document you can use the Insert Table button on the toolbar (see the margin). This button appears when the toothpick cursor is in a blank part of the document; otherwise the button is used to insert rows into a table.

Clicking the Insert Table button displays a drop-down list thing. Drag the mouse through the thing to tell Word how big a table you want to create, such as the 2-row by 3-column table shown in Figure 20-5.

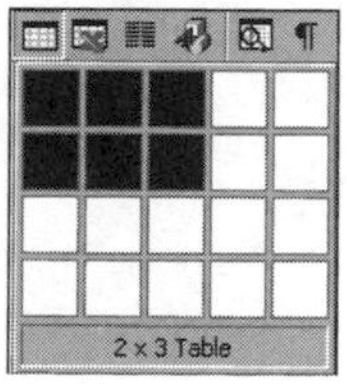

Figure 20-5:
The Insert
Table drop
down thing.

2 x 3 Table

Automatically Spiffing-Out Your Table

 Word contains a deep well of formatting tricks, some of which you can use on any old table you create to make it look really, really spiffy. [*Ed: "Spiffy" sounds like a word Dan would use. Trix.*] This trick, the AutoFormatting trick, lets you create a table then use a special Word command to customize your table.

Stick the toothpick cursor in any table, preferably one you've already filled in. Then choose Table➪Table AutoFormat from the menu. The Table AutoFormat dialog box appears, as shown in Figure 20-6.

Just keep your eyeballs focused on the sample table shown in the Preview window. Then click your mouse on each consecutive item in the Formats scrolling list. Each one of those items automatically spiffs up your table to look like the sample shown in the Preview window.

After you find a table format you like, click the OK button.

You can goof around with other options in this dialog box in your own spare time.

[*Ed. Again "goof" sounds like Dan. Trix.*]

[*T: Yes, it does. K.*]

Chapter 21

Marching Columns of Text

Columns — especially those you can see right on your screen — are one of those features all the magazines, gurus, and other pseudo-pundits demanded for their word processors. Do we need them? No. Can Word do them? Yes. Do you want to mess with them? Sure, why not? If columns can make the Greeks and Romans famous, why not you?

This chapter covers the methods in word for mustering your text into columns.

Why Do Columns?

Columns are interesting, yes. But necessary? Probably not. While they may spice up a dull document, the only time I've ever really used columns was when I plagiarized Shakespeare and created my own script for *A Midsummer Night's Dream*.

Okay, so Shakespeare is dead and I put his name on it so it wasn't plagiarizing, but you get the idea: The script just fit better running down two columns on a page. Other than that, I've never used columns.

Before I divulge my Word column secrets, here's a healthy bit of advice: The best way to make columns happen is by using a desktop publishing package, such as PageMaker or QuarkXPress. Those programs are designed for playing with text and they make columns much easier to use than Word does.

Splitting Your Text into Columns

To start columns in your document, follow these steps:

1. **Move the toothpick cursor to where you want the columns to start.**

   If your document already has text in it, put the toothpick cursor at the start of the first paragraph you want to appear in columns.

   If you haven't yet written the text to put into columns, that's okay. Just follow along with Step 2.

2. **Choose the Format⇨Columns command.**

   If the Columns command isn't visible, click the down-arrow at the foot of the menu to see it.

   The Columns dialog box opens, as shown in Figure 21-1.

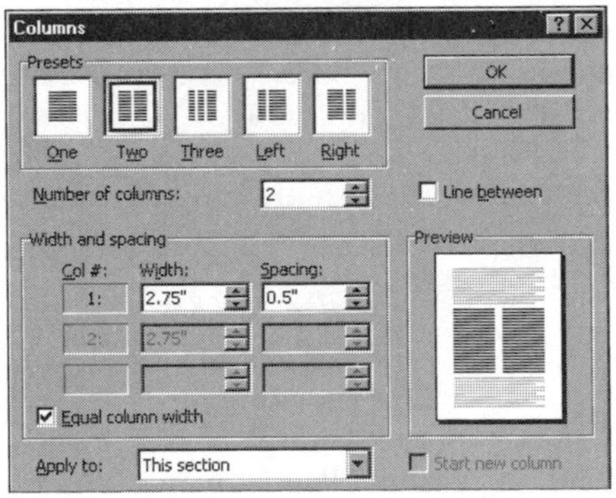

Figure 21-1:
The
Columns
dialog box.

3. **Choose a column style from the Presets area.**

   Two columns are sufficient enough to impress anyone. More columns make your text skinnier and harder to read.

   Note the Preview area, which shows how your document is (or will be) affected by your column choices.

   If you want more than three columns, you need to specify them in the Number of Columns list.

Specific column adjustments can be made in the Width and spacing area of the dialog box.

If you want a pretty line between the columns of text, check the Line between box. (The dialog box says Line Between, not Pretty Line Between.)

4. **Choose where you want to apply the columns from the Apply To drop-down list.**

   You can choose to apply the columns to the Whole document, from the toothpick cursor's position forward (This point forward) or to the current section (This section).

   The Apply To drop down list only displays two options at a time; use the up or down buttons to see the other options (though the This Section option may not be available if your document doesn't use sections).

5. **Click the OK button.**

   Okay!

What you see on the screen depends on how Word displays your document. If you switch from Normal to Print Layout view, then you see the columns right there on the screen.

If you're using Normal view, you'll see a Section Break (Continuous) type of page break in your text, and then one skinny column. That's simply how Word displays columns in the Normal view. Choose View➪Print Layout to see the columns in real life.

- Instead of using the cursor movement keys to move the toothpick cursor between columns, use the mouse instead. It's much easier to point and click in a column than watch the toothpick cursor fly all over the page.

- The space between columns is called the gutter. Word sets the width of the gutter at .5" — half an inch. This amount of white space is pleasing to the eye without being too much of a good thing.

- The three-column text format works nicely on Landscape paper. This method is how most brochures are created. Refer to Chapter 31, "Brochures and Greeting Cards" for more information.

- Word's text and paragraph formatting also applies to text and paragraphs in columns. The difference is that your column margins — not the page margins — now mark the left and right sides of your text for paragraph formatting.

- See Chapter 15 for more information on breaking your document up into sections.

- Even though you can apply columns to specific sections in a document, Word does let you turn the column mode on and off throughout a document without having to use sections. See "Undoing columns" which is, oh — it's right here!

Undoing columns

According to Word, there is no such thing as not having columns in your document. No, when you have "normal text," Word just thinks you have only one column on a page. Funny, huh?

To remove columns from your document, move the toothpick cursor to where the columns start. (Choose View➪Print Layout from the menu to help you find the exact spot.) Then follow the steps in the previous section, but choose only one (1) column for the page in Step 3. Then choose Whole Document in step 4. Click OK.

If you have a document that has columns in it, but you want to return to normal text, move the toothpick cursor to where you want the columns to stop. Then repeat the steps in the previous section: choose one column in Step 3. And choose the This Point Forward menu option in Step 4. Click OK.

Using the Columns button on the toolbar

In a hurry? You can use the Columns tool. Click the tool, and a baby box of columns appears. Click and drag the mouse to indicate how many text columns you want. When you release the mouse button, the columns appear.

Inserting a Column Break

Word's columns run continuously, down one side of the page, then to the top of the next column. To split things up, you can use a column break.

For example, to stop one column in the middle of the page and have the next column start at the top of the page, put the toothpick cursor in the column you want to break, usually at the end of a paragraph. Then choose Insert➪Break. Choose Column Break from the list; then click OK. The column the toothpick cursor is in stops at that point, and the next column continues at the top of the page (or top of the next page).

See Chapter 14 for more information on inserting breaks into a document.

Chapter 22

All about Figures

*T*hey say a picture is worth a thousand words. So I suggested to my editor that I could convert this chapter into one giant image and be done with writing for the rest of the week. Unfortunately, he's being difficult, so I'm forced — against my will — to write about graphics using awkward text. Oh the pain. . . .

Most of the time, your documents will be text. Occasionally, you may want to spice things up with an image. Word is more than willing to help you. Images fit in nicely with your text, and Word lets you move them and reshape them and manipulate them in a variety of interesting and obscure ways, several of which this chapter touches upon. No degree in art or drawing skills is necessary!

"Where Can I Find Pictures?"

You can add a graphic to any Word document in several ways:

- ✔ Copy the image from a graphics program (or a Web page) and then paste it into your document wherever the toothpick cursor happens to be
- ✔ Insert a clip art image
- ✔ Insert any image file from your hard drive
- ✔ Insert the image from a scanner or video camera attached to your PC
- ✔ Create the image using one of Word's mini-programs
- ✔ Tape a picture to your monitor

I've used just about all these methods for putting pictures into my documents. Even so, I can't vouch for the last method. Sure, it works just fine as long as you never scroll your screen and your printer has ESP. But there are better ways.

- ✔ To capture an image from the Web, right-click on the image and choose Save Picture As (or Save Image As) from the pop-up menu. After you save the picture on your hard drive, you can insert it into any Word document.
- ✔ Windows comes with a simple painting program called MS Paint. You can use MS Paint to create interesting, albeit primitive, images for use in Word.
- ✔ Putting an image into Word really slows things down. My best advice: Add the graphics last.
- ✔ Word (or Microsoft Office) comes with a batch of clip art pictures you can use. You may have to install the clip art at some point while working in this chapter; keep the Word (or Office) CD handy in case the computer begs for it.

And Here's a Picture!

To stick a graphic image into your document, follow these whimsical steps:

1. **Switch to Print Layout view.**

   If you're not in Print Layout view, switch there now: Choose View⇨Print Layout form the menu. (If you don't do this now, Word will do it when you insert a graphic image.)

2. Position the toothpick cursor in the spot where you want your picture.

If any text is already there, it is shoved aside to make room for the graphic.

Sticking a picture into a Word document is like pasting in one letter of text, though the picture acts like a *very large* letter.

3. Choose Insert⇨Picture.

You may have to click the down-arrows at the foot of the Insert menu to display the Picture command.

Choosing the Picture command displays a submenu full of commands used to insert images into your document, as shown in Figure 22-1.

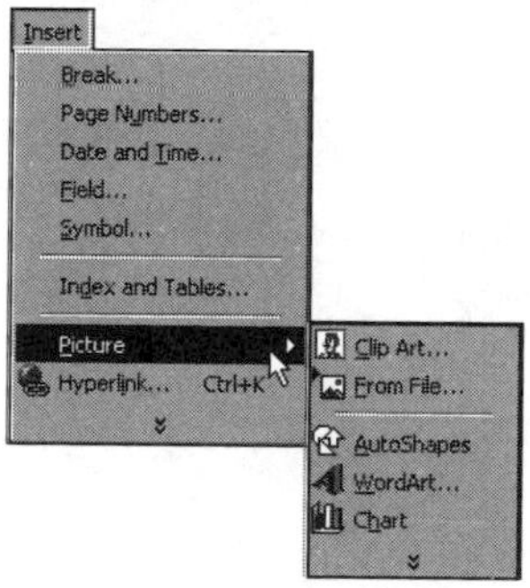

Figure 22-1:
The Insert Picture submenu.

The steps you take next depend on which command you choose from the submenu. The following sections detail the top two options, ClipArt and From File.

✔ Choose ClipArt if you plan on using one of Word's own ClipArt graphics, some of which you may find useful. Continue reading in the section, "Inserting a ClipArt image."

✔ Choose From File if you have a graphics image on disk you want to use, such as something you've saved from the Internet or created in another graphics program. Continue reading in the section "Inserting an image from a file on disk" later in this chapter.

✔ You don't have to use the Insert⇨Picture command if you copy and paste an image. To do that, create the image in another Windows application, select it for copying, and then return to Word and paste it.

Inserting a ClipArt image

Continuing from Steps 1 through 3 in the previous section:

4. **Choose ClipArt from the submenu.**

The Insert ClipArt dialog box appears, as shown in Figure 22-2. Your job is to find some clip art for your document, something suitable.

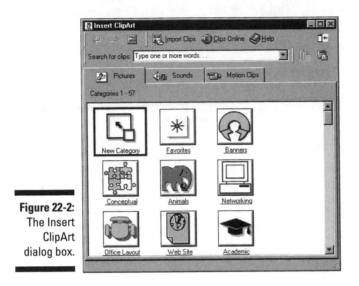

Figure 22-2:
The Insert
ClipArt
dialog box.

5. **Choose a ClipArt category.**

Each "button" in the Insert ClipArt dialog box represents a group of images. Click a button to see thumbnail previews of the images. For example, click the Animals button to see images of various beasts and creatures.

6. **Click the image you want.**

Click once and a pop-up menu appears.

7. **Choose Insert Clip.**

Splat! The image is inserted into your document at the toothpick cursor's location.

8. **Close the ClipArt dialog box.**

Click on its X button in the upper-right corner.

Your next step is probably to adjust the picture, trimming it or moving it about, which is covered in the section "Tweaking the Image," later in this chapter.

✔ Some images are colorful on-screen. Unless you have a color printer, they only print in black, white, and — with a laser printer — shades of gray.

✔ You can't backspace over a graphic. To get rid of it, click it once and press Delete.

Inserting an image from a file on disk

Continuing from the section "And Here's a Picture!" earlier in this chapter (where you'll find Steps 1 through 3):

4. Choose From File from the submenu.

The Insert Picture dialog box appears (see Figure 22-3), which looks like Word's Open dialog box but is geared to hunting down graphic files on your hard drive.

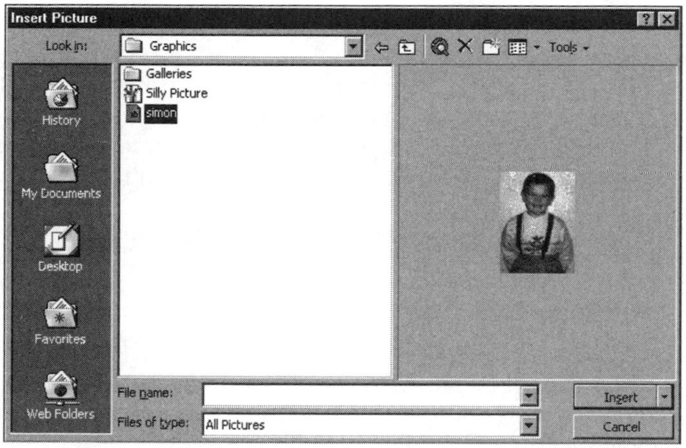

Figure 22-3:
The Insert
Picture
dialog box.

5. Use the dialog box to find the files.

The Insert Picture dialog box starts out looking in the My Pictures folder, which may or may not contain any images. You may have to look elsewhere.

I stick my images in the Graphics folder of the My Documents folder. To get there, I click the My Documents icon on the left side of the Insert Picture dialog box, and open the Graphics folder from there.

6. Choose the graphics file you want to insert.

Click the file once to select it.

To preview an image before you open it, click the down arrow by the Views button in the Insert Picture dialog box; then choose the Preview item. That way you can see a preview of whichever graphics icon you select, as shown in Figure 22-3.

7. Click Insert.

The image is inserted into your document at the toothpick cursor's location.

The picture most likely will need some tuning and tweaking. This is covered in the next section.

> ✔ A cool thing to stick at the end of a letter is your signature. Use a desktop scanner to create your John Hancock. Save it as a file on disk and then follow the previous steps to insert it at the proper place in your document.

> ✔ If you detest the image, you can delete it. Click the image once to select it and then press the Delete key.

Tweaking the Image

Unless you're a graphical pro (in which case you probably bought the wrong book), you need to tweak just about every image you slap into your document. And, ho boy, Word does some frustrating things with images. Fortunately, there's always some hidden way to fix things.

It's always best to work with images in the Print Layout view. Choose View➪Print Layout from the menu.

It also helps to have the Picture toolbar visible when you tweak a graphical image. Choose View➪Toolbars➪Picture from the menu (see Figure 22-4). (The following sections assume this toolbar is visible.)

Figure 22-4:
The Picture
toolbar.

When you click an image to select it, the image grows "handles," one for each side and corner. You use these handles to manipulate the image, as the following sections demonstrate.

After you're done tweaking your graphic, just click the mouse on some text. This deselects the image and returns you to text editing mode. (You may also want to close the Picture toolbar by clicking its X button.)

Moving an image hither and thither

To move an image around on the page, drag it by using your mouse. Drag in the center of the image.

Remember, Word treats graphics like a big letter in a word. The selected graphic fits in anywhere any other character in your document would.

If you'd rather have the image "float" over your text, see the section, "Text wrapping and image floating," later in this chapter.

Changing an image's size

To resize an image, select it and simply grab one of its eight "handles." Drag the handle in or out to resize the image. Figure 22-5 shows an image being stretched to the right.

Figure 22-5:
Grab one of the eight handles to change an image's size.

Grab the top handle to make the image taller or shorter. Grab the side handle to make the image narrower or fatter. The corner handles move in two directions (diagonally) simultaneously.

Cropping an image

In graphics lingo, cropping an image means changing its size without making the image smaller or larger. Grandma does this all the time when she takes pictures of the family; she crops off everyone's head. It's like using a pair of scissors to cut a chunk from a picture.

To crop an image, click it once to select it, then click the Crop tool on the Picture toolbar. You're now in cropping mode, which works a lot like resizing an image: Drag one of the image's handles inward to crop.

I usually use the outside (left, right, top, bottom) handles to crop. The corner handles never quite crop the way I want them to.

After you're done cropping, click the Crop tool again to turn that mode off.

If you don't like the cropping, click the Reset Image button to undo it.

Text wrapping and image floating

The Text Wrapping button on the Picture toolbar controls how your image meshes with the text in your document. You have several choices really, from choosing to stick the picture in your text like a big character to having a ghostly image float behind your text.

To set text wrapping and image floating options, click the image once to select it and then click the Text Wrapping button on the Picture toolbar. A drop-down menu of several text wrapping options appears, as shown in Figure 22-6.

Figure 22-6:
Word's
picture/text
wrapping
options.

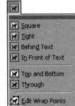

My advice is to *try them all!* Seriously, go through the menu and see how each option affects your image. (You may need to move the image around in your text to see how things change.) One of the options is bound to make your text and graphics appear they way you want them to.

When everything is perfect (or as near as can be expected), click the mouse back in the text to continue editing. (You may need to return to the picture later if you overedit your text, but then again I did recommend at the start of this chapter to add your pictures in last.)

✔ The Edit Wrap Points item works just like the Tight item. However, the image appears in the document with dozens of tiny handles on it. In a dramatic effort to waste serious time, you can drag each handle to adjust how the text wraps around your image. Me? I just select the Tight option and let Word do the work.

✔ Because graphics live on various "layers" in Word you may notice that sometimes your graphics overlap. To move one image in front of or behind another image, right-click that image and choose how you want the images arranged from the Order submenu.

A Caption for Your Figure

Putting a caption on a figure is easy — providing you insert the graphic image into a table.

Start by creating the table. Draw the table in the spot where you want the graphic image and caption. (See Chapter 20 for information on drawing tables.)

Make the table so that it has only two rows, as shown in Figure 22-7. Also, you might want to select "No Border" as the line style — unless you want a border around the figure and caption.

Figure 22-7:
An image
pasted into
a table, cap-
tion in the
second row.

Get a real operating
system.

Insert (or paste) the figure into the top cell. Then type the caption into the bottom cell. Resize the table (or resize or crop the image) so that everything fits nicely.

Select the bottom cell and format it accordingly: Small text, bold, centered (or left-justified), and so on — whatever you feel the caption should look like.

Chapter 23

Creating an Index and Table of Contents

*A*cademic writers sure look smart. Their documents have a table of contents and maybe an index, and any academic worth his salt has tons of footnotes or endnotes or both. Impressive. And you can be smart too, or at least look that way, provided you learn Word's tricks for building a table of contents, index, and footnotes. Some would say that these tricks are pretty advanced stuff. Fie, I say, fie! Keep reading to find out why it just ain't so.

A footnote is not the same thing as a footer. See Chapter 15 for information on footers (and headers).

Creating a Table of Contents

Realizing American's hunger for insider terms, I thought I'd present you with the following: In the book industry, a Table of Contents is known as a TOC, pronounced either *tock* or sometimes *tee-oh-see*. After mastering that term, along with *signature* and *trim size*, you're ready to work for any publishing house in the nation.

More than talking about the TOC, Word lets you actually build a Table of Contents for any document you create — providing, of course, that you format your headings with the proper Heading style. (See Chapter 16 for information on using the various built-in Heading styles.) If you remember to use Word's headings, then building a TOC in Word is cinchy.

Heed these steps to add a TOC to your document — provided you've used the built-in Heading styles:

1. Move the toothpick cursor to where you want the TOC to be.

Me? I put it up front on a page by itself (maybe even a section by itself). See Chapter 15 for information on breaking up your document into sections.

2. Choose Insert⇨Index and Tables.

The Index and Tables dialog box appears.

3. Click the Table of Contents tab.

The Table of Contents part of the dialog box appears, as shown in Figure 23-1.

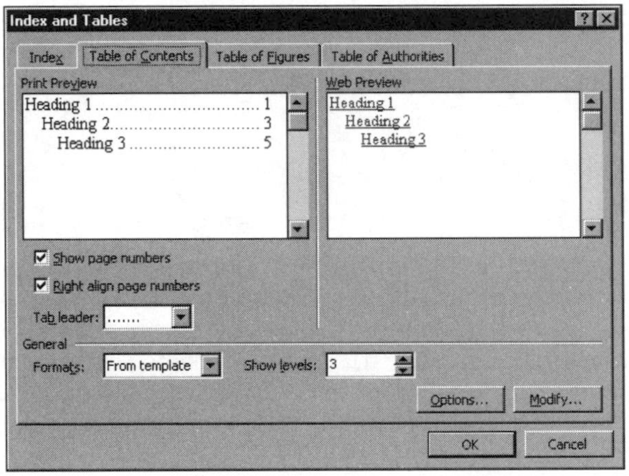

Figure 23-1:
The Index and Tables dialog box, Table of Contents table.

4. Mess around (if it suits you).

Play with the options in the Formats drop-down list and check the various effects in the Print Preview window.

5. Click OK to create the TOC.

Word looks through your entire document and takes everything tagged with a Heading style (whether it's Heading 1, 2, or 3), determines what page it's on, and builds the table of contents for you.

Impressive, huh? The Table of Contents feature saves you a lot of time and effort and works even after you edit things and move stuff around. So, as long as you use those silly Heading styles, creating a TOC is a snap.

Building an Index

At the other end of a document, opposite of the TOC, you typically find an index. There is another clever, publishing industry term for index as well: *index.*

Seriously, an index is more precise than a TOC. It references specific items, tasks, terms, or people throughout a document. Obviously, this is a techie thing; I don't suppose you'll ever index a letter to your mother — and would hope you'd never have a reason to.

Creating an index is a two-part process in Word. The first part is identifying the words or phrases in a document that you want to place in the index. (This implies, obviously, that your document should be written before you index it.) The second part is building the index itself.

To flag a bit of text for inclusion in the index, follow these steps:

1. **Select the text you want to reference in the index.**

   It can be a word, phrase or any old bit of text. Mark that text as a block.

2. **Choose Insert⇨Index and Tables.**

   The Index and Tables dialog box appears.

3. **Click the Index tab.**

4. **Click the Mark Entry button.**

   The Mark Index Entry dialog box appears as shown in Figure 23-2. Notice that the text you selected in your document appears in the Main entry box. (You can edit that text if you wish.)

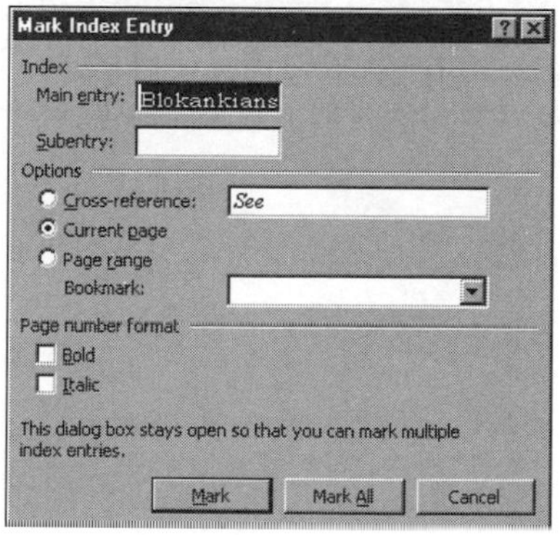

Figure 23-2: The Mark Index Entry dialog box.

5. **Click *either* the Mark button or the Mark All button.**

   The Mark button marks only this particular instance of the word for inclusion in the index. Use this button if you want to mark only instances that you think will benefit the reader the most. The Mark All button directs Word to seek out and flag all instances of the text in your document, creating an index entry for each and every one. Use this option if you'd rather leave it to your reader to decide what's relevant.

   You can mess with other options in the Mark Index Entry dialog box as well.

   When you mark an index entry, Word switches to the "Show Codes" mode, where characters such as spaces, paragraph marks, and tabs appear in your document. Don't let it freak you out. Step 8 tells you how to turn that thing off.

6. **Continue scrolling through your document, looking for stuff to put into the index.**

   The Mark Index Entry dialog box stays open, allowing you to continue to create your index: Just select text in the document, then click the Mark Index Entry dialog box. The selected text appears in the Main entry box. Click the Mark or Mark All button to continue building the index.

7. **Click the Close button when you're done.**

   The Mark Index Entry dialog box goes away.

8. **Press Ctrl+Shift+8 to disable the Show Codes mode.**

   Use the 8 key on the keyboard, not the numeric keypad.

With all the bits and pieces of text flagged for the index, the next step is to create the index:

1. **Position the toothpick cursor where you want the index to appear.**

   Nearly every book has the index at the end, usually on a page by itself. Use the Insert⇨Break command to insert a page or section break for your index. See Chapter 15 for more information.

2. **Choose Insert⇨Index and Tables.**

3. **Click the Index tab.**

   Figure 23-3 shows you what it looks like.

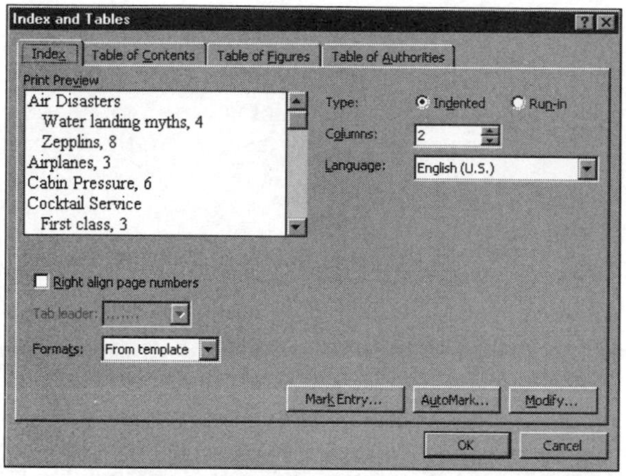

Figure 23-3:
The Index
and Tables
dialog box,
Index thing.

4. Optionally mess with the dialog box.

You can choose an index style from the Formats drop-down list. Use the Print Preview window to see how your choice affects the final product.

The Columns list tells Word how many columns wide to make the Index. Note that 2 columns are standard, though there's no specific reason for that.

5. Click OK.

The index, all nice and neat, is inserted into your document.

Using Footnotes or Endnotes (Or Both)

Do I need to explain what a footnote is and what an endnote is? Probably not. Most folks whose documents require these things know what a footnote is and where and how to put an endnote. So what follows is merely the step-by-steps:

1. Position the toothpick cursor in your document where you want the footnote or endnote to be referenced.

2. Choose the Insert⇨Footnote command.

You may need to click the down-arrows at the bottom of the Insert menu to see the Footnote command.

Choosing the Footnote command displays the Footnote and Endnote dialog box. It's kind of boring, so I'm not putting a figure of it in this book.

3a. Choose Footnote if you're creating a footnote.

3b. Choose Endnote if you're creating an endnote.

You can mess with the Number in the dialog box if you like. Or you can click the Options button to control how and where the footnote or endnote is displayed.

4. Click OK.

If you're using the Normal view, a new "window" magically appears at the bottom of your page.

If you're using the Print Layout view, then the toothpick cursor moves to the bottom of the page, beneath a gray line, ready for you to. . . .

5. Type your footnote or endnote.

You can place in a footnote anything you can place in a document — charts, graphs, pictures, and even text.

6. Continue writing your text.

For the Normal view, click the Close button.

In the Print Layout view you can try using the Shift+F5 command to return to your text, though that may not always work. Instead, use the Go To command to find which footnote (number) you last entered. See Chapter 3.

Here are some non-footnote footnote notes:

✔ To view or edit footnotes in the Normal view, choose View⇨Footnotes. (In Print Layout view, the footnotes appear at the bottom of each "page" on the screen.)

✔ To quick-edit a footnote, double-click the footnote number on the page. The footnote text edit area opens.

✔ To delete a footnote, highlight the footnote's number in your document and press the Delete key. Word magically renumbers any remaining footnotes for you.

✔ You can actually insert graphics into a footnote, just as you can a header or footer. Think how embarrassed those academics will be, seething with jealousy at your wondrously creative, graphical footnotes! Part IV of this book contains information on inserting graphics into your document.

Chapter 24

Inserting Objects

• •

• •

Microsoft has really pushed the boundaries on what a word processor is supposed to do. They pushed into and over desktop publishing, and now they're pushing out into the realm of the obscure. I mean, a word processor that has a drawing mode in it? Much less a drawing mode that is much better than a drawing *program* I used maybe eight years ago. Go figure.

Whatever you think about it, Word does lots and lots of things. They fall under the category of "Inserting objects" since most of the oddball things you can insert into a document (aside from another document) are like graphical images. Also, the commands tend to cling to the Insert menu. Anyhoo. It's all covered here. Or at least the most interesting parts.

Inserting One Document into Another

Sticking one document into the bosom of another document is neither strange, obtuse, nor unnecessary. And it involves no surgery. For example, you may have your biography, résumé, or curriculum vitae in a file on disk, and you want to add that information to the end of a letter begging for a job. If so, or in any other circumstances that I can't think of right now, follow these steps:

1. **Position the toothpick cursor where you want the other document's text to appear.**

   The text will be inserted just as if you typed the whole thing right there with your little, stubby fingers.

2. **Choose Insert⇨File.**

   You may need to click the down-arrows at the foot of the menu to see the File command.

   A dialog box similar to the Open dialog box appears (refer to Chapter 8).

3. **Choose the icon representing the document you want to paste.**

   You can also use the gadgets and gizmos in the dialog box to locate a file in another folder or on another disk drive or even on someone else's computer on the network. Such power!

4. **Click the Insert button.**

   The document is inserted right where the toothpick cursor is.

- ✔ The resulting, combined document still has the same name as the first document.

- ✔ You can retrieve any number of documents on disk into your document, one at a time. There is no limit.

- ✔ These steps allow you to grab a block of text saved into one document and stick the text into another document. This process is often called boiler-plating, where a commonly used piece of text is slapped into several documents. This process is also the way sleazy romance novels are written.

- ✔ Biography. Résumé. Curriculum vitae. The more important you think you are, the more foreign the language used to describe what you've done.

More Fun Things to Insert

Word comes with a host of teensy tiny little programs that let you insert fun and odd objects into your document, spicing up what would otherwise be dull text. The following sections provide merely a whirlwind tour of the most popular teensy tiny little programs. You're encouraged to play with each program on your own to get the proper feel.

Slapping down an AutoShape

AutoShapes are simple images that may come in handy in your document. They're stars, moons, diamonds, green clovers, and other goodies that anyone can "draw" since they're automatically drawn for you! Figure 24-1 shows an example.

Figure 24-1:
An
AutoShape
text box
with the
AutoShapes
toolbar and
a photo of
The Author.

To insert a random or useful shape, choose Insert➪Picture➪AutoShapes. The AutoShapes toolbar appears (shown in Figure 24-1). (Also you're thrown in the Print View mode if you're not there already.)

Each button on the AutoShapes toolbar represents a drop-down menu of shapes. Choose one. The mouse pointer changes to a plus sign. Now "draw" the shape in your document by dragging the mouse. This creates the shape at a certain size and position, though you can resize the shape or move it later if you like.

- ✔ Refer to Chapter 22 for more information on what you can do with a graphic image. (AutoShape images work just like any other graphics in your document.)

- ✔ The text bubbles (shown in Figure 24-1) are produced using the Callouts button on the AutoShapes toolbar. They can contain editable text, which you type into the bubble just as you type text in your document. And, you can format the text in the bubbles, too!

Love That WordArt

WordArt is sadly neglected by most Word users. This is too bad, because WordArt can quickly add a lot of dazzle to your documents. And it's a fun place to waste time.

To put WordArt into your document, choose the Insert➪Picture➪WordArt. The WordArt Gallery dialog box appears, showing you the colors and variety of WordArt you can create and looking a lot like a lipstick display at a cosmetics counter (see Figure 24-2).

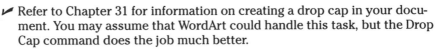

Figure 24-2:
The
WordArt
Gallery lip-
stick case
dialog box.

Choose the style for your WordArt from the gallery; then click OK.

In the Edit WordArt Text dialog box, type the (short and sweet) text you want WordArtified. Choose a font, size, and maybe bold or italics — you know the drill. Click OK when you're done and that bit of text appears as an image in your document.

You can further use the WordArt toolbar to mess with your text. Because this is a "fun" thing, I'll let you explore it on your own.

✔ Like other graphics in your document, WordArt appears wherever the toothpick cursor lurks.

✔ WordArt graphics can be tweaked and twoked. See "Tweaking the Image" in Chapter 22.

✔ You can use the WordArt toolbar to do the following. By clicking the WordArt graphic in your document and then choosing one of the buttons from the WordArt toolbar, you can accomplish feats of derring-do:

• Click the Edit Text button to return to the Edit WordArt Text dialog box to change the WordArt text, font, size, and so on. Click OK after you're done.

• The WordArt Shape button displays a drop-down list of different layouts for your WordArt text — a more detailed version than you can find in the WordArt Gallery. Just select a shape, and your WordArt text is reformatted to fit into that shape.

• If you want to wrap text around your WordArt, click the Text Wrapping button.

✔ Refer to Chapter 31 for information on creating a drop cap in your document. You may assume that WordArt could handle this task, but the Drop Cap command does the job much better.

Drawing pictures in Word (the ultimate word-processing sacrilege)

If you feel the need to break out and draw something in your word processor, you can. Word sports a special Drawing mode that allows you to insert circles, lines, arrows, and other blocky artwork at your whim. Inserting artwork could be the subject of an entire book, so I'm just not going to discuss it here, outside of the minimum information you need to know.

To activate Word's drawing mode, click the mouse on the Drawing button on the Standard toolbar. (You can also choose View⇨Toolbars⇨Drawing from the menu.) This musters the drawing mode toolbar that contains various drawing things, as shown in Figure 24-3.

Figure 24-3:
The
Drawing
toolbar.

The Drawing toolbar is divided into several areas. The middle area contains tools you can use to draw various lines, arrows, squares, and circles. The right area contains controls for colors, line width, and three-dimensional effects.

Oh, go ahead and play. Me? I do graphics in another program entirely. But if you're stuck and have a graphic itch then the Drawing toolbar can help you scratch it.

✔ The Drawing tools are good but best used for simple illustrations. If you need complex or detailed drawings, my advice is to pick up a nice illustration package for your computer. Consult the guy at the software store for more information.

✔ When your drawing is in your document, it behaves like any other graphic. Refer to Chapter 22 for some general graphic-tweaking information.

Inserting Something from Excel

Another something-or-other to insert into your document is a piece of another document created by another program. Right now, Excel is the only other program I can think of. So assume the following:

You're doing a document in Word and you need to paste in a bit of a spreadsheet from something you did in Excel. Let me save you some time: Use the Edit⇨Paste Special command. This displays a host of options for sticking your Excel spreadsheet chunk into Word. Among them:

- ✔ **Microsoft Excel Worksheet Object:** The best option, which provides a link between your Word document and the data in the original Excel document.

- ✔ **Picture:** This option merely puts an image of the spreadsheet into your document, which is good enough for charts or information not expected to change.

- ✔ **HTML Format:** This option is best if your company has decided on HTML format as the standard format for all documents.

Choose whichever option is the most useful to you, then click OK.

You can also just do an Edit⇨Paste to stick the Excel information into your document as if you typed it in yourself. In that case, Word typically builds a table into which the spreadsheet is pasted. See Chapter 20 for more information on tables.

Part IV
Land of the Fun and Strange

In this part . . .

How much would you pay for this word processor? But wait! There's more. . . .

The list of amazing things Word does could never be contained in a single book. I mean outlining? Mail merge? Collaborating with others? Sheesh! This is a word processor?! But I'm getting sidetracked again.

At a loss for a proper place and name under which to store this stuff, I present you with Part IV, Land of the Fun and Strange. In the chapters that follow you'll find an obtuse collection of the weird and bizarre. These are things useful and wondrous, eclectic, and portable. And they've all been mixed in with Word at the subatomic level, so you're stuck with them whether you use 'em or not.

Chapter 25

Working with an Outline

. . . .

In This Chapter

▶ Creating an outline in Word

▶ Adding topics and subtopics

▶ Adding a text topic

▶ Viewing the outline

▶ Rearranging topics in an outline

▶ Printing the outline

. . . .

*T*he daring young man on the flying trapeze better have a net. Without a net, he could have a short career. And audiences forgive a guy when he falls. Really! Enjoy the show, folks! He's got a net!

The daring young man (or woman) on a flying word processor better have an outline. I wouldn't write a book without one. Sure, with short papers and documents you have no need for an outline. (Are you listening, Dr. Tremaine?) But for anything with more than two thoughts, an outline is a blessing. May you read this chapter and be blessed.

Word's Outline Mode

An outline in Word is just like any other document. The only difference is in how Word displays the text on the screen. I'll give you a hint: Outline mode makes solid use of the Heading style — which is terrific since so much of Word assumes you're using the Heading style.

To create a new outline, follow these steps:

1. **Start a new document.**

   Press Ctrl+N or click the New button on the toolbar. (Don't bother with File⇨New because that command adds another, annoying step you don't really need here.)

2. **Switch to the Outline view.**

   Ah. The secret. Choose View⇨Outline or click the Outline View button crowded into the lower-left corner of the window. See Figure 25-1 (though this figure has a lot of text in it that you won't see on your screen right now).

   Two amazing things happen: First, you get to see the Outlining toolbar (it's the third toolbar down in Figure 25-1), which helps you work your outline. Second, a hollow minus sign appears before the toothpick cursor. This minus sign means that you're typing a topic in the outline and the topic has no subtopics.

3. **You're ready to start your outline.**

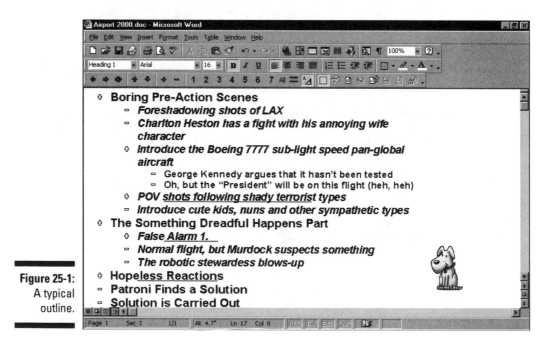

Figure 25-1:
A typical
outline.

All the outlining details are covered in the next few sections. In the meantime, I offer some general facts:

✔ Word's outlining function is merely a different way to look at a document. It's possible to shift back into Normal or Print Layout view, but not really necessary when you're working on an outline.

✔ Don't worry about fonts or formatting while you're creating an outline. Word uses the Heading 1 through Heading 9 styles for your outline. That's okay.

✔ All Word's normal commands work in the outline mode. You can use the cursor keys, delete text, spell check, save, insert oddball characters, print, and so on.

Adding topics to your outline

An outline is composed of topics and subtopics. The main topics are your main ideas, with the subtopics describing the details. You should start your outline by adding the main topics. To do so, just type them out.

In Figure 25-2, you see several topics typed out, each on a line by itself. Pressing Enter after typing a topic produces a new hollow hyphen at which you can type your next topic.

Figure 25-2:
Level one
topics.

- Microsoft Word for Windows 1.0
- Microsoft Word for Windows 2.0
- Microsoft Word for Windows 6.0
- Microsoft Word 95 for Windows
- Microsoft Word 97 for Windows
- Microsoft Word 2000 for Windows
- Microsoft Pencil and Paper

✔ Press Enter at the end of each topic. This tells Word that you're done typing information for that topic and want to move on to the next topic.

✔ Pressing Enter creates another topic at the same "level" as the first topic. To create a subtopic, refer to the next section.

✔ A topic can be a single word, a few words, a complete sentence, or a big paragraph. However, your main topics should be short and descriptive, like in a book's table of contents.

✔ You can split a topic by putting the toothpick cursor somewhere in its middle and pressing the Enter key. That way, *Pins and Needles* can be split into two categories (beneath the *Sharp things* topic, of course).

✔ To join two topics, put the toothpick cursor at the end of the first topic and press the Delete key. (This method works just like joining two paragraphs in a regular document.)

✔ It doesn't matter if you get the order right at first or not. The beauty of creating your outline with a word processor is that you can rearrange your topics as your ideas solidify. My advice is just to start writing things down now and concentrate on organization later.

✔ An outline can be the plot to a novel, a speech you're giving, a recipe, an itinerary, a product development cycle — just about anything that requires more than one thought.

✔ Remember that a topic line should be an individual thought or idea. If your topic is:

```
liver and fava beans
```

you should split it in two:

```
liver
fava beans
```

Use the Enter key to split a topic.

Making a subtopic

Outlines have several levels. Beneath topics are subtopics, and those subtopics may have sub-subtopics. For example, your main topic may be "Things that make me itch," and the subtopics would be what those things actually are.

You don't really *create* subtopics in Word as much as you *demote* main topics.

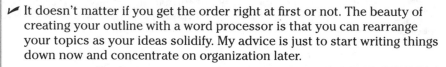

To create a subtopic, simply type your subtopic at the main topic level. Put the toothpick cursor in the topic and click the Demote button on the Outline toolbar.

Instantly, the text in the topic moves over a tab stop, and the style changes to the next Heading style. Both of these visually indicate that you're working on a new topic level.

✔ You can continue creating subtopics by pressing the Enter key at the end of each subtopic — just as you created new main-level topics. Word keeps giving you subtopics, one for each press of the Enter key.

✔ Notice that the main topic (the one the subtopic lives in) grows a + symbol. That's the sign that a topic has subtopics. More on that in the section called "Viewing Your Outline," a bit later.

✔ You can also demote a topic by pressing the Alt+Shift+→ key combination.

✔ Unlike creating main topics, you can get a little wordy with your subtopics. After all, the idea here is to expand upon the main topic. For example, if you're writing a speech, a subtopic would contain a more detailed sketch of your talk. Maybe not the talk itself, just more details.

✔ To make a subtopic back into a topic, you promote it. Put the toothpick cursor in the topic and press Alt+Shift+← or click the Promote button.

✔ See "Viewing Your Outline" for information on looking at different parts of your outline while hiding other parts.

✔ You can create a sub-subtopic simply by repeating the preceding steps for a subtopic. In fact, Word lets you organize on a number of levels. Most outlines, however, typically have maybe 4 or 5 levels max.

Adding a text topic

If you feel the need to break out and actually write a paragraph in your outline, you can do so. Although it's perfectly legit to write the paragraph on the topic level, what you should really do is stick in a text topic using the Demote to Body Text button. Here's how:

1. Press the Enter key to start a new topic.

Do this just as you would create any new topic on a line by itself.

2. Click the Demote to Body Text button.

Or you can press Ctrl+Shift+N. What this step does is change the style to Normal (which is what the keyboard shortcut key does). In your outline, however, that style allows you to write a paragraph of text that isn't a heading. So you can write an actual bit of text for your speech, instructions in a list, or dialog from your novel.

✔ The Body Text style appears with a tiny hollow square by it, unlike topics that have hollow plus or minus signs by them.

✔ If you change your mind, you can promote or demote your Body Text to a topic or subtopic. Refer to the preceding section.

Viewing Your Outline

Unless you tell Word otherwise, it displays all the topics in your outline, top to bottom, everything. But this display really isn't part of the glory of outlining. What makes outlining on a computer special is that if you want to step back and see the Big Picture, you can do so.

 For example, to see all the first-level topics in your outline, click the Show Heading 1 button. All the subtopics and text topics are hidden.

If a topic has subtopics, not only does it have a hollow plus sign by it, but you see a fuzzy line extending out over the last part of the topic name. I haven't met anyone yet who knows exactly what the fuzzy line is supposed to mean.

 If you want to see your outline in more detail, click the Show Heading 2 or Show Heading 3 buttons. Each button displays your outline at a different level.

 The All button is used to expand your outline so that everything can be seen at once.

> ✔ You can open or close individual topics by double-clicking the hollow plus sign with the mouse.

 ✔ Open or expand a topic with the Expand button on the toolbar, or by pressing Alt+Shift+Plus (the Plus key on the numeric keypad).

> ✔ Collapse a topic with the Alt+Shift+Minus key combination. (Use the minus key on your keyboard's numeric keypad.)

> ✔ As your outline nears perfection, you can copy parts of it and paste them into other, new documents. This method is the way some writers create their books and novels; the document is merely a longer, more complete version of what starts as an outline.

Rearranging Topics

Just like shuffling the stack of 3 x 5 cards my high school teachers urged me to use when outlining, reorganizing your topics in a computer outline is a cinch. And it's more fun, too, because you're using a computer and not something that has your mother's recipes on the backside. (And, boy, was she mad!)

To move any topic in your outline, put the toothpick cursor in that topic and then click one of the following buttons:

 ✔ Click the Move Up button (or press Alt+Shift+↑) to move a topic up a line.

✔ Click the Move Down button (or press Alt+Shift+↓) to move a topic down a line.

✔ Click the Promote button (or press Alt+Shift+←) to move a topic left.

✔ Click the Demote button (or press Alt+Shift+→) to move a topic right.

You can also use the mouse to move topics around: Drag the topic by its plus or minus sign and drop it off at the new location. Personally, I don't use this technique because my outlines are rather complex and moving topics in this manner becomes unwieldy.

 It may be a good idea to switch to the All view in your outline before you start rearranging topics. That way you can see where things go and not miss any of the details.

Printing Your Outline

Printing your outline works just like printing any other document in Word. But because it's an outline, there is one difference: Only those topics visible in your outline print.

For example, if you want to print only the first two levels of your outline, click the Show Heading 2 button. This action hides all subtopics and when you print your outline, only the first and second topics print.

 If you want your entire outline to print, click the All button before printing.

The outline shortcut key summary box

When I'm typing, I like my hands to remain on the keyboard. Because of this preference, I discovered the following key combinations that work when playing with an outline. Try them if you dare:

Key Combo	Function
Alt+Shift+→	Demote a topic
Alt+Shift+←	Promote a topic
Alt+Shift+↑	Shift a topic up one line
Alt+Shift+↓	Shift a topic down one line
Ctrl+Shift+N	Insert some body text

Alt+Shift+1	Display only top topics
Alt+Shift+2	Display first- and second-level topics
Alt+Shift+#	Display all topics up to number #
Alt+Shift+A	Display all topics
Alt+Shift+Plus (+)	Display all subtopics in the current topic
Alt+Shift+Minus (–)	Hide all subtopics in the current topic

Chapter 26

You've Got Mail Merge!

*W*elcome to the only chapter in the book the author himself refers to. Now you would suspect that I would *get* this stuff, but I don't! Mail Merge is perhaps the most unnatural thing Word does. It makes you feel like a Neanderthal poking his hand into a fire. *What is that glowing stuff . . . Ouch!*

Fortunately, this chapter explains mail merge and how to do it in a friendly, no-nonsense way. So I'll get to the point as soon as possible.

The Story of Mel Merch (Mail Merge)

Mail merge is the process of taking a single form letter, stirring in a list of names and other information, and combining (merging) everything into a final set of documents, each of which is customized and almost personal.

Wait. I made that sound too easy. Forget what I wrote above. Instead, consider the following terms:

> ✔ **Data Source.** This file contains the names and other information. Word uses the data source to help fill in the blanks in the main document. It's a database of sorts. Say "data source."

✔ **Main Document.** The file that contains the form letter — the fill-in-the-blanks letter — is called the main document. Yeah, I call it the "form letter." Microsoft refers to it as the main document. No, I didn't make this up. Get used to it. Say "main document."

✔ **Fields.** Inside the main document are the fill-in-the-blanks parts, which Microsoft calls fields. These are the places in the main document where information from the data source is stuffed. Information such as the address, "Dear Mr. Snoodle," and anything else that changes from letter to letter goes into a field. Everyone say "fields." Kind of like "Mrs. Fields' Cookies."

✔ **Cookies.** Everyone say "cookies."

✔ **Records.** The fields inside the data source file are grouped into chunks called records. Yes, this is very data-basey. In fact, the data source file is, in a way, a database of sorts. And in a database, fields are grouped into records; a record is composed of the fields containing the name, address, and other information for one person in your data source. Everyone say "records."

Word creates a custom letter by using each of the fields in a record to fill in the blanks in a main document and create a unique document. Everyone say, "Golly, that's awfully complex and pointless for me to memorize. Why don't I just go ahead and work through the remaining sections of this chapter until I get everything right. Then I can forget all this until next time."

✔ Suggested liquor: Bourbon.

Step-by-Step Mail Merging Guide

Start your mail merging mania by choosing Tools➪Mail Merge. This command opens the Mail Merge Helper dialog box, depicted in Figure 26-1. Don't let the dialog box's title fool you.

You mail merge in three steps, as shown in the Mail Merge Helper dialog box. First comes the Main document, and then the Data source, and finally the actual merging.

✔ The Mail Merge Helper dialog box twists and mutates as you step through the mail merging process. Don't be lulled into complacency by its Spartan nature.

✔ Yeah, there are really more than three steps to this whole operation — lots more.

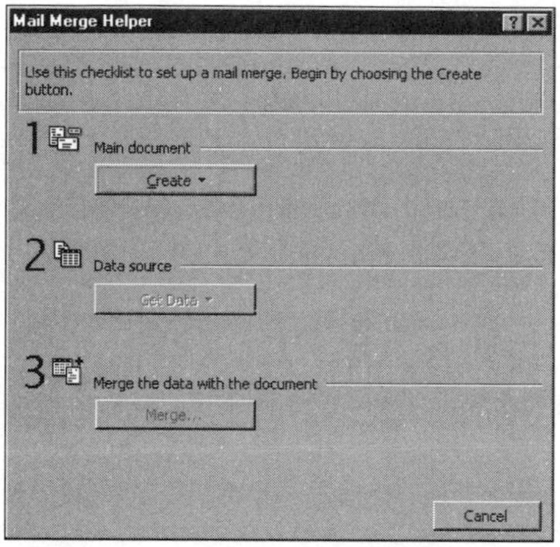

Figure 26-1:
The Mail
Merge
Helper
dialog box.

Preparing the main document

The main document is the fill-in-the-blanks document. Don't freak out if you've already created that document (self-starter, eh?). Just follow along, and I'll show you when to do what:

1. **Click the Create button in the Mail Merge Helper dialog box.**

   It's the only button listed under the big 1 in the dialog box.

2. **Select the Form Letters menu item from the drop-down list.**

3. **Choose how to create your main document.**

   If your main document is all ready to go in Word (meaning that you've written the form letter already and it's right up there on the screen), click the Active Window button.

   If you need to create a new fill-in-the-blanks document, click the New Main Document button.

   An Edit button appears out of thin air, showing up next to the Create button in the Mail Merge Helper dialog box.

4. **Click the Edit button.**

   See? I told you the dialog box gets crowded. It gets worse.

5. **Choose the only item in the new Edit button's menu.**

   The item is Form Letter, followed by Document# item or the name of the document you're already working on in Word.

6. **Edit your document.**

You're now allowed to edit your form letter document. The Mail Merge Help dialog box disappears, and the Mail Merge toolbar shows its ugly face, as shown in Figure 26-2.

✔ The main document contains all the fill-in-the-blanks stuff. Don't bother putting them in just now; you do this task in a later step. However, keep in mind what you want to go where.

✔ In addition to mail merging fields, I inserted an up-to-the-date field in my document shown in Figure 26-2. The date (shown in gray) is created using the Insert⇨Date and Time command. That way the current date always prints.

✔ In my main documents, I usually type in the replaceable, fill-in-the-blanks stuff with ALL CAPS so that I can find the items more easily later (see Figure 26-2).

✔ The new toolbar on your screen (refer to Figure 26-2) is the Mail Merge toolbar. Don't bother messing with it; none of its buttons work at this point. (The attempt is an exercise in frustration, which makes you wonder why the toolbar is there in the first place.)

Mail Merge toolbar

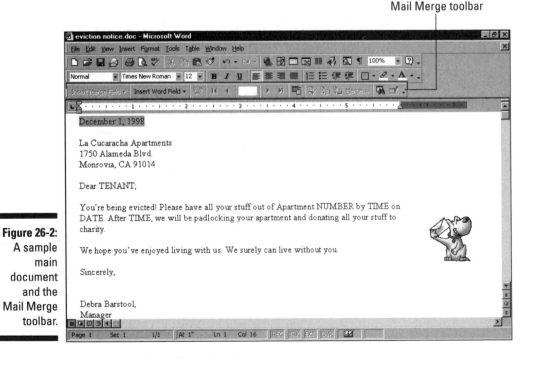

Figure 26-2: A sample main document and the Mail Merge toolbar.

Preparing the data source

A data source is a special file used to store mail merging information, not a "real" Word document. It includes information stored in fields and records. Each field contains a tidbit of text that fills in a blank in the main document. A collection of fields — the tidbits for one form letter — is what makes up a record.

To start a data source, follow these steps:

1. **Click the Mail Merge Helper button on the toolbar.**

   The Mail Merge Help dialog box appears again.

2. **Click the Get Data button.**

3. **Select Create Data Source from the drop-down list.**

   The Create Data Source dialog box appears, full of mirth and merriment (see Figure 26-3). This place is where you create the fields — the fill-in-the-blank items.

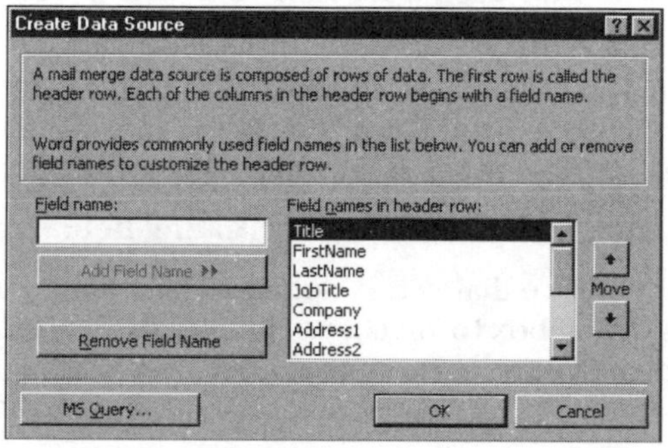

Figure 26-3:
The Create
Data Source
dialog box.

> Create Data Source
>
> A mail merge data source is composed of rows of data. The first row is called the header row. Each of the columns in the header row begins with a field name.
>
> Word provides commonly used field names in the list below. You can add or remove field names to customize the header row.
>
> Field name: [ ]
>
> Add Field Name ▶▶
>
> Remove Field Name
>
> Field names in header row:
> Title
> FirstName
> LastName
> JobTitle
> Company
> Address1
> Address2
>
> Move
>
> MS Query...   OK   Cancel

To be helpful, Word has already dreamt up a whole parade of field names. Your first duty is to erase them all. Unless your fields exactly match Microsoft's samples, these field names do you no good.

4. **Keep clicking the Remove Field Name button until all the names Word concocted in the Field names in header row list are gone, gone, gone.**

   I had to do it 13 times. You may have to click more if you click too fast.

   Don't worry about zapping out Word's preset list of names. There is nothing in there you'll probably need, and if you do need it you'll add it on your own later. In my opinion it was dumb of Microsoft to give you "samples" in this manner. (They reappear each time you mail merge, by the way.)

5. **Type a field name into the Field name box.**

   Here are some suggestions for making this step make sense:

   - Name the field to reflect the kind of information in it. For example, you may want to name the field containing first names something like `firstname`.

   - No two fields can have the same name.

   - A field name must begin with a letter.

   - A field name can contain up to 20 letters, numbers, and under-scored characters.

   - You cannot use spaces or punctuation marks in field names.

   - When entering addresses, always make separate fields for the city, state, and zip code.

6. **Click the Add Field Name button after typing your field name.**

   This inserts the field that you created into the list shown in the Field names in header row box.

7. **Repeat Steps 5 and 6 for each field that you want to include in your data file.**

   In my example in Figure 26-2, I have TENANT, NUMBER, TIME, DATE. I had to go through Steps 5 and 6 four times. For more-detailed form letters, you may be stuck here for an eternity.

8. **Click the OK button when you're done creating field names.**

   The Save As Data Source dialog box appears. This dialog box works just like the Save As dialog box to save a document. In fact, that's what you're doing: saving your data source document to disk. (It can be opened again in Step 3 above, if you ever need to repeat this stuff.)

9. **Give your data source document a name.**

   Be clever. For my eviction notices, I'm calling the file SCUMBAGS. Feel free to use SCUMBAGS for your office Christmas card list.

10. **Click the Save button.**

11. **Am I done yet?**

    No!

12. **Click the Edit Data Source button.**

    The Data Form dialog box appears and . . . you're ready to continue reading the next section.

Adding data to the data source

Because you're obeying step-by-step instructions here, editing the fill-in-the-blanks information — which is technically called "adding data to the data source" — is done via the handy Data Form dialog box, shown in Figure 26-4. The following steps tell you how to fill in the blanks.

Figure 26-4:
The Data
Form
dialog box.

```
┌─────────────────────────────────────────────────────────┐
│ Data Form                                         ? X    │
│ ┌───────────────────────────────────┐  ┌─────────────┐  │
│ tennant:  │Jerry Hewett             │▲ │     OK      │  │
│ number:   │1940                     │  ├─────────────┤  │
│ time:     │noon                     │  │   Add New   │  │
│ date:     │January 2, 2000          │  ├─────────────┤  │
│           │                         │  │   Delete    │  │
│           │                         │  ├─────────────┤  │
│           │                         │  │   Restore   │  │
│           │                         │  ├─────────────┤  │
│           │                         │  │   Find...   │  │
│           │                         │  ├─────────────┤  │
│           └───────────────────────┘▼ │ View Source │  │
│                                        └─────────────┘  │
│ Record: │◄ │ ◄ │1     │ ► │ ►│                          │
└─────────────────────────────────────────────────────────┘
```

1. **Fill in the blanks.**

   Each field in your document needs information. Fill it in.

   For example, in a NAME field, type a name. The same for other fields: type street, zip code, phone number, hat size, and so on. Use the Tab key to move from box to box.

2. **When you've filled in all the blanks, click the Add New button.**

   You don't have to click the Add New button after typing the last record. Instead, go right on to Step 4.

3. **Repeat Steps 1 and 2 for every person to whom you want to mail your form letter.**

4. **After you're done, click the OK button.**

   Clicking OK sends the Data Form dialog box away, saving all the information to disk.

   ✔ Click the Add New button after entering a record; click the OK button only when you're done typing all the records.

   ✔ Data is pronounced DAY-ta.

   ✔ The names for the boxes in the Data Form dialog box are the field names you created in the preceding section.

✔ You can use the Record buttons to scan and modify information that you already entered.

✔ You can use Red Buttons when you wish to be entertained.

✔ If you need to reexamine or edit the data source file, click the Mail Merge Helper button on the Mel Merch toolbar. Click the Edit button under Step 2 (Data Source) and choose the data source item from the list. Click OK to close this dialog box when you're done.

✔ The data source file is secretly attached to your main document. After you go to save your main document, Word asks if you also want to save the data source. Always do so. That way you can reuse the form letter and edit the data source file at any time in the future.

Inserting fields into the main document

The final step before actual merging is to place the fields — the blanks — into your main document:

1. **In the form letter, position the toothpick cursor where you want to place the field.**

   For example, you want a name field after the Dear in your letter's greeting, so position the cursor between the Dear and the colon.

   If you used ALL CAPS words to mark your fill-in-the-blanks stuff (as I did in Figure 26-2), select those placeholders with your mouse; drag the mouse over the ALL CAPS text to highlight it.

   `Insert Merge Field ▾`

2. **Click the huge Insert Merge Field button in the Mail Merge toolbar.**

   A list of your fields drops down.

3. **Select the field you want to place in the document.**

   A special cryptic code is inserted into your document, representing that field. For example, the FIRSTNAME field may look like `<<firstname>>` in the main document. This special code is what Word thinks of as a "blank" for fill-in-the-blanks stuff.

4. **Continue adding fields until the document is complete.**

   Repeat Steps 1, 2, and 3 as necessary to create all the blank spots in your document.

✔ A tad bit of editing may be required after the field. I typically have to add a space, comma, colon, or whatever after fields as Word inserts them.

✔ Don't worry if the formatting looks funny with the `<<Fields>>` in your document. Things get formatted nicely when Word fills in the blanks — after merging.

✔ To delete an unwanted field, select it with the mouse and press the Delete key. You can't use the Delete or Backspace keys by themselves! You must highlight a field and then delete it.

Merge mania!

After creating the main and data files, you're ready to merge away! This is actually the simplest part of all this mail merging nonsense:

1. Save the main document.

Clicking the Save button on the toolbar does this best.

2. Click the Mail Merge Helper button on the Mail Merge toolbar.

Golly, that dialog box has gotten busy. Fortunately, this is the last time it will offend you.

3. Click the Merge button, near the bottom of the dialog box by the third step.

The Merge dialog box appears. *What-ever* . . .

4. Click the Merge button in the Merge dialog box.

As if by magic, Word creates several documents merging your main document with the information that you put into your data source. All the new documents appear, one after the other, on the screen in front of you in Word. Congratulations; you've just merged.

Word merges the names and other information from the data file into the main document and creates lots of little, customized documents in one great big document file. That's what you see on-screen right now. Your options at this point are to review all the documents, save them, or print them. You made it!

The main file appears several times on-screen, with information from the data file plugged into each copy. All files are separated by section breaks or hard page breaks.

✔ The merged documents are tossed into a new file; one that hasn't yet been saved. Save that file now!

✔ If you realize that you missed a few names, you can merge again. To add any extra names you need to re-edit the data source: click the Helper button on the Mel Merch toolbar and click the Edit button under Step 2 for Data Source. Choose the data source item from the list and edit away.

✔ If you missed some fields, you can return to the main document and insert them using the steps described in the section, "Inserting fields into the main document," earlier in this chapter.

✔ You can print right from the screen view of the merged files by selecting File⇨Print.

✔ Now you know how to get those custom, uniquely crafted documents out to the foolhardy who actually think that you took the time to compose a personal letter. Ha! Isn't mail merge great?

✔ Always examine the results of the merge. Some things may not fit properly, and some editing will no doubt be required.

✔ After puzzling through Word's mail-merge feature, tearing through the Heisenberg Uncertainty Principle will be a cinch.

Chapter 27

Collaboration Tricks

● ●

In This Chapter

▶ Slapping down comments in a document

▶ Taking advantage of non-printing text

▶ Highlighting your text

▶ Using revision marks

▶ Comparing two documents

▶ Tracking changes in any document you edit

● ●

*F*or the most part, writing is something you do by yourself. However, there are times when you need (or want) to share your work with others — you want to make sure your proposal is upbeat and nonoffensive, so you run it by someone else. In these instances, you can use some of Word's collaboration tools to help you and your writing partners (or overlords or editors or whomever) communicate.

This chapter covers the Word tricks and techniques that let you happily work with others. This way you and your comrades can cooperatively work on a new antigovernment manifesto, but when the state police come, they'll just arrest one guy.

Adding Sticky Note-Like Comments

Word's comments are like sticky notes for your text. They pop-up on the screen telling those you're working with (or yourself) some useful tidbit or offering advice. And they don't print, which makes them handy to use when working back and forth between two or more people.

To stick a sticky note into your document, follow these steps:

1. **Position the toothpick cursor where you want to make a comment.**

   You can also select a block of text if your comment concerns some specific sentence or phrase.

   Commenting on text is referred to as "making an annotation" or "annotating" the text.

2. **Choose Insert⇨Comment.**

   You may need to click the down-arrows at the bottom of the menu to find the Comment command.

   The screen instantly splits, just as it does when you write a footnote (see Chapter 23). Your initials are inserted into the document, identifying you as the writer of the sticky note, and the text you're commenting on appears in yellow — like it's highlighted.

3. **Type your comment.**

   Enter your comment in the lower portion of the screen, in the comments area. Type away!

4. **Click the Close button after you're done.**

   The annotation area disappears, but the text you commented on remains highlighted. That's your clue that a comment is there.

Repeat these steps to add more annotations to the text.

The beauty of all this is that the annotations remain mute until you want to see them. They don't print, and they show up on the screen as yellow text, which doesn't get in the way (much).

To read a sticky note, just point (don't click) the mouse at it. The mouse cursor changes to the insertion pointer plus a little sort-of sticky note thing (see the margin). Just hold the mouse still and the sticky note pops up on the screen, similar to what you see in Figure 27-1. The name of the person who wrote the note appears, followed by the note's contents.

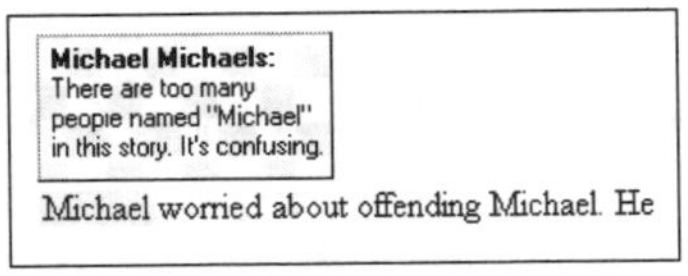

Figure 27-1:
A pop-up note
on the screen.

> **Michael Michaels:**
> There are too many
> people named "Michael"
> in this story. It's confusing.
>
> Michael worried about offending Michael. He

Move the mouse away from the yellow text to make the sticky note disappear.

- ✔ If you want to see all the comments in a document at once, choose View➪Comments from the menu. This action splits the screen (just like it does when you create comments), but shows you every comment. Jump around through your document by clicking the mouse on the initials that start each annotation. For example, click [DG4] to see which part of your text the fourth comment DG made pertains to.

- ✔ Obviously, if the Comments command in the View menu is dimmed, your document contains no comments. Whoopee!

- ✔ To edit a comment, right-click on the mouse on the yellow text. From the shortcut menu that pops up, choose Edit Comment. The screen splits, and the toothpick cursor hops on down to the comment area where you can edit the comment.

- ✔ To delete a comment, right-click on the mouse on the yellow comment text and choose Delete Comment from the shortcut menu.

- ✔ Yes, the comments don't print — and there's no way to get them to print, either. Unless, of course, you select Comments from the Print What part of the Print dialog box. But don't let me ever catch you doing that in real life.

Nonprinting Text

Another way to stuff secret messages into your document is to use Word's hidden text format. As Chapter 11 states, the hidden format makes text invisible in Word. The text doesn't show up on the screen and it doesn't print. But you can still see it! Keep reading. . . .

To hide text — any text — in your document, select the text as a block and hide it: Choose Format➪Font. In the Font dialog box, click the Hidden option in the Effects part of the tab. This hides the text on-screen and when printed, but leaves all the other text (and paragraph) formatting intact. Click OK to apply the hidden text format.

Meanwhile, back in your document, the text you selected is gone! Whew!

To see the hidden text, use the Show command. Click the Show button on the toolbar, or press Ctrl+Shift+8 (the 8 key on the keyboard, not on the numeric keypad). These keystrokes display the hidden text with a dotted underline.

- ✔ To globally unhide text, select your entire document with Ctrl+A, then open the Font dialog box and remove the check mark by the Hidden text attribute. Click OK.

- ✔ Refer to Chapter 6 for more block-marking instructions.

✔ This technique is also good for hiding sensitive parts of a document. For example, you may want to print a report both internally and publicly. Making the internal information hidden ensures that it won't print on the public document.

Whip Out the Yellow Highlighter

Word comes with a text highlighter that lets you mark up and colorize the text in your document without damaging your computer monitor.

 To highlight your text (on-screen, electronically, of course), click the Highlight button on the Formatting toolbar. Click!

 Now you've entered Highlighting mode. The mouse pointer changes to something I can't describe verbally but can picture in the left margin. When you drag the mouse over your text, that text becomes highlighted — just like you can do with a highlighter on regular paper — amazing what those whiz kids at Microsoft come up with. . . .

To stop highlighting text, click the Highlight button again or press the Esc key.

✔ To unhighlight your text, click the down-arrow by the Highlight button and choose None as the highlight color. Then drag over your highlighted text to unhighlight.

✔ To remove highlights from your entire document, press Ctrl+A to select all your text, then choose None from the Highlight button's drop-down list.

✔ You can also highlight a block of text by first marking the block and then clicking the Highlight button. See Chapter 6 for all the proper block-marking instructions.

✔ The highlighted text prints, so be careful with it. If you don't have a color printer, highlighted text prints black on gray on your hard copy.

✔ In addition to the "None" color for erasing highlight marks, you can choose any of the highlight colors available in the Highlight button's drop-down list. And to think that an office supply store would charge you an extra $1.20 for each color.

✔ The yellow highlighter color is almost the same as the yellow used to identify a sticky note. For that reason, if you're using both sticky notes and highlighter, try using a different highlighter color.

Sharing Work with Revision Marks

Every writer jealously guards his text. It's enough that someone must edit, some lowly editor who seethes with jealously over the fact that the noble writer is the one who gets all the fame and glory even though it's the editor who deserves the credit. Oh, editors can be nasty. _[Hey! — Ed.]_ But other writers can be worse.

Revision marks are a way of tracking changes made to your document by evil people. Okay, maybe not evil, but people who change things without first making suggestions. To help protect yourself against such intrusion, you can use one of Word's many revision tracking tools. The following sections outline two ways you can put them to use.

Tracking changes between two versions of the same document

Go ahead and put away the magnifying glass. When someone else returns your Word document to you, it's a cinch to have Word compare the "new" document with your pristine original. Word flags any changes, displaying them for you right on the screen. Here's how:

1. **Make sure that you have the edited (newer) document loaded and on the screen.**

   The original document should be saved to disk. That's okay for now; you don't need to open it. Just open the edited document and have it on the screen in front of you.

2. **Choose Tools⇨Track Changes⇨Compare Documents.**

   You may have to click the down arrows at the menu's foot to see the Track Changes command.

   An Open dialog box appears, though it's named Select File to Compare With Current Document and not Open. Use your finely honed Open dialog box skills to find and select the original document on disk.

3. **Click the Open button.**

   Word thinks long and hard. What it's doing is comparing the document on the screen with the older copy on your hard disk.

4. **Peruse the changes.**

   If you cannot see any changes, choose Tools⇨Track Changes⇨Highlight Changes from the menu. Put a check mark by Highlight Changes on Screen; then click OK.

Ah-ha, the revision-marked-up result! The edited document on your screen is littered with revision marks, showing exactly what changes were made from the original.

Any new text added appears <u>underlined</u>. Text deleted appears ~~crossed-out~~ (the strikethrough-text effect). Unchanged text remains the same. The edited result looks similar to what you see in Figure 27-2.

Yes, it is annoying to read. Oui, oui!

- You can continue to edit the document if you like. After all, it's your document.

- If you want to thumbs-up-or-down each revision, refer to the next section "Reviewing the changes."

- Revision marks can get in the way. To remove them, choose Tools⇨ Track Changes⇨Highlight Changes and remove the check mark by the Highlight Changes on Screen option. Click OK.

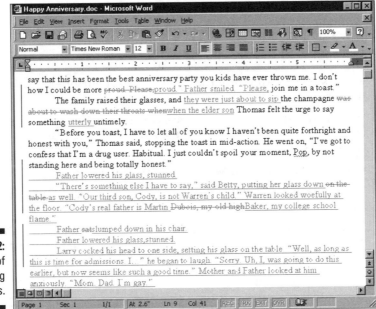

Figure 27-2:
The result of comparing documents.

Reviewing the changes

Don't plow on through a revised document, manually adding and subtracting things. Why not let Word do the work for you? This job is done by the Accept or Reject Changes dialog box, which lets you quickly browse through a document with revision marks to yeah-or-nay each little correction. Here's how:

1. **Move the toothpick cursor to the tippy top of your document. (Press Ctrl+Home.)**

   I'm assuming this is a document that has revision marks, otherwise this operation just won't work. Refer to the previous section for more information.

2. **Choose Tools⇨Track Changes⇨Accept or Reject Changes.**

   The Accept or Reject Changes dialog box appears (see Figure 27-3).

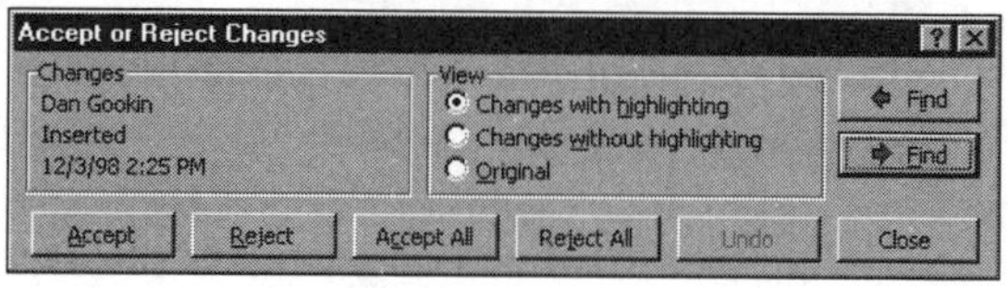

Figure 27-3:
The Accept or Reject Changes dialog box.

3. **Click the Find button.**

   Word ventures out into your document to find the next revision mark, which notes something that has been changed or added to your original document. Word stops at each deletion or addition, highlighting it for you on the screen.

4. **Click the Accept or Reject button.**

   Now pay attention:

   If you click Accept on a ~~strikethrough~~ word or phrase, you're telling Word to remove that phrase, to accept the edit or change from your original document.

   If you click Reject on a ~~strikethrough~~ word or phrase, you're telling Word to _keep_ that phrase in your document.

   If you click Accept on an <u>underlined</u> word or phrase, you're telling Word to _keep_ that addition to your original document.

   If you click Reject on an <u>underlined</u> word or phrase, you're telling Word to remove that addition from your document.

It works if you don't think of strikethrough and underline text together. Just look at each change and think, "Accept or reject?" for each of them.

Naaa! Don't worry about remembering this. Just dog-ear this page.

5. Repeat Step 4 as necessary.

Or you can ignore the change and click the Find button to find the next instance.

6. Click the Close button when you're done.

The Revisions dialog box revises itself outta there.

✔ If you goof, you can click the Undo button in the Accept or Reject Changes dialog box.

✔ You can click the Reject All button to do away with all the revisions or corrections. I mean, to hell with 'em!

✔ Click the Accept All button to keep all the changes at once. I mean, your editor is smarter than you are, and you should just blindly succumb to her superior knowledge.

✔ Going through this process removes all the revision marks from your document. If you want to re-review the revisions, you have to repeat the steps in the previous section for comparing two documents.

✔ Don't forget to save your revised text back to disk.

Tracking changes as you make them

To visually keep track of any modifications you make to a document, even one you created yourself, follow these steps:

1. Open the document you want to edit.

2. Choose Tools➪Track Changes➪Highlight Changes.

The Highlight Changes dialog box appears (see Figure 27-4).

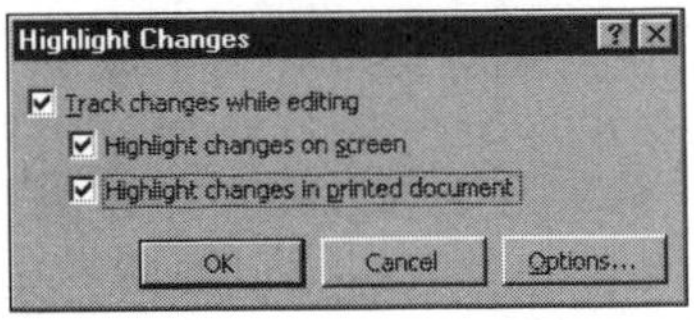

Figure 27-4:
The
Highlight
Changes
dialog box.

Highlight Changes	? X
☑ Track changes while editing	
☑ Highlight changes on screen	
☑ Highlight changes in printed document	
OK	Cancel	Options...

Doing it all at once!

Word sports a great author sharing and review tool, called the Reviewing toolbar. Choose <u>V</u>iew⇨<u>T</u>oolbars⇨Reviewing to display it.

The buttons on that toolbar help you view and find sticky-note comments as well as any revisions made to the document. There's a shortcut button to the highlighter tool, as well as buttons that let you go visit Microsoft Outlook if the edits are so painful it inspires you to write e-mail.

3. Put a check mark in the Track Changes While Editing check box.

You should also make sure that a check mark is in the Highlight Changes on Screen check box.

4. Click OK.

Word is now in change tracking mode.

✔ Different people reviewing your document leave different color revision marks. For example, if you send your document to Kyle and then Kathleen, Kyle's marks may show up in ranting red and Kathleen's in supreme blue.

✔ After you're done editing or reviewing the changes, you can turn off the revision marks. To do this, choose <u>T</u>ools⇨<u>T</u>rack Changes⇨ Highlight Changes and click in the Highlight Changes on Screen check box to deselect it. Click OK to view your document normally.

✔ A quick shortcut for the preceding steps is to double-click the TRK thing on the status bar at the bottom of the screen. When the TRK is bold, revision mark tracking is activated. If you double-click it again, you turn off the revision tracking.

Collaborating on your intranet

One of Word 2000's newest features is Web collaboration. That's where you and several others can actively work on a single HTML (Web page) document at the same time. Nifty, huh? Kind of like gang finger-painting for adults.

Anyway, to get all that to work you need the following: A Web server plus a "discussion server" running the Microsoft Office Extensions. And you need to understand what "intranet" means, and there may be other things required as well.

Obviously Web collaboration is something well beyond the scope of this book. So if anyone reading this does eventually use Word's Web collaboration features, please write in and tell me whether it's fun or not.

Chapter 28

Working with Documents

. . . .

In This Chapter

▶ Making a new folder for your stuff

▶ Changing folders

▶ Using Word's Find command

▶ Opening, saving, or closing groups of files

▶ Deleting or renaming files

▶ Working with non-Word documents and text files

. . . .

*T*he more work you do in Word, the more documents you create — piles of files. And if you don't clean up or organize those piles, then just like manure in a barnyard, you're going to be hip-deep in files in a few weeks. Maybe sooner.

This chapter tackles the subject of files — using and organizing them. It's more of a Windows chapter, so I'll be a little brief on the file management part. Still, you can do a lot of file management right in Word, without ever having to mess with Windows, the Big Momma Operating System.

Also covered: importing and exporting files. No international license is required!

Creating a New Folder

To keep organized, you may need to create new folders for your new projects. For example, suppose that you just started your plan to take over Finland. You're going to need a new folder to put all those memos and letters in.

Here's how you do that:

1. **Summon the Save As dialog box with File⇨Save As.**

   Obviously, having something to save first helps, such as that first letter to the Finnish Parliament.

2. **Click the Create New Folder button.**

   The New Folder dialog box appears.

3. **Type a name for your new folder.**

   Be descriptive. Be creative. Be short and sweet. Be to the point. (Try real hard to achieve this goal if you're a lawyer.)

   Have the folder name reflect its contents.

4. **Click OK.**

   Through the magic of the computer, your new folder is created, sitting right there on the screen for you to marvel at.

5. **Marvel at it.**

6. **Double-click the folder to open it.**

   After all, this is a file-saving exercise here. You open your folder by double-clicking it. The Save As dialog box then displays the contents (nothing).

7. **Continue saving your document.**

   You don't really have to save a document every time you create a folder. You can click the Cancel button in the Save As dialog box to return to your work. The next time you go to save a document (or open one for that matter), you will be using the new folder you just created.

   ✔ You can create new folders in the Save As dialog box but not the Open dialog box. I mean, like duh. If you created a new folder in the Open dialog box, there wouldn't be anything in the folder for you to open. Some people . . .

   ✔ You can get a lot of mileage out of a folder named Junk or Misc.

Using Another Folder

If you go into a folder-creating frenzy, you need to be able to access those folders whenever you want to see the documents they hold, or to save a new document in a specific folder. Here's how you go about it:

1. **Summon the Open command with File⇨Open.**

   Or press Ctrl+O. Soon the Open dialog box swings into full view.

2. **First, see which folder you're currently using.**

   The folder's name appears in the Look In drop-down box at the top of the dialog box. Normally it's the My Documents folder, which is where Word wants to save stuff.

   If you're already in the folder that you want to be in, skip to Step 6 (meaning that you're more-or-less done).

3. **Select the disk drive you want from the Look In drop-down list.**

   If you select a floppy drive, ensure that you have a disk in the drive before you select it.

   If you only have one hard drive, C, select it as well. Looking for your folder from the top down is best.

   Since most folders are kept in the My Documents folder, you can always click the big My Documents button on the left side of the Open dialog box. That zooms you to that folder pronto.

4. **Select your folder from those listed in the dialog box.**

   You may have to scroll through the list to find the folder you want.

5. **Keep repeating Step 4 until you find the folder you're looking for.**

   For example, you may have to open My Documents, then Projects, then Memos to finally see the documents stored in the Memos folder.

6. **Open your document.**

   Click the Open button.

   ✔ Some folders contain other folders. To see their contents, double-click the folder's name in the Open dialog box.

   ✔ Also see Chapter 8 for more information on using the Open dialog box.

   ✔ Each disk in your system has its own set of folders. If you can't find the folder you want on one disk, try another. For example, scope out hard drive D if drive C turns out to be a dud.

Finding Files in Word

Finding files is really a Windows function. Finding files is what Windows does best, but Word can also locate your wayward documents. Too bad finding socks or a clean shirt isn't this easy.

1. **Summon the Open dialog box by choosing File⇨Open.**

   Press Ctrl+O.

2. **Make sure you select Word Documents (*.doc) from the Files of Type drop-down list.**

   If you don't double-check this, Word may find every file on your hard drive (which is dumb) or no files at all (which is sad).

3. **Click the Tools button.**

   Clicking this little guy displays a heretofore hidden menu.

4. **Choose Find.**

   The glorious Find dialog box appears, as shown in Figure 28-1. (If you're an old-time Word user, you'll appreciate seeing this guy again. He was missed in recent versions of Word.)

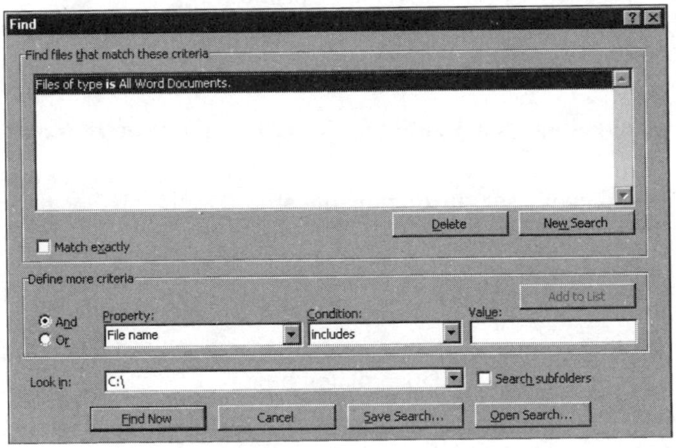

Figure 28-1:
The Find
dialog box.

5. **Choose Text or Property from the Property drop-down list.**

   The most common way to find a file is based on text it may contain, though there are other ways to look for a file in the Find dialog box. The Property drop-down list shows you a bunch of them.

6. **Choose the Includes Words option from the Condition drop-down list.**

7. **Type the text you're looking for in the Value box.**

   For example, I found a nasty letter I wrote to the bank by entering the bank's name in the Value box.

8. **Click Add to List.**

This puts your searching "criterion" up in the top part of the dialog box. At this point you can search, or you can go through Steps 6 through 8 again if you want to be more precise.

9. Choose drive C (shown as `C:\`) from the Look In drop-down list.

Or choose another hard drive to look there.

10. Ensure that Search Subfolders is checked.

If it's not, Word won't find anything. Promise.

11. Click Find Now.

The Office Assistant may ask if you want to install the FindFast program. Click Yes if you like (though you'll need Word's CD). Me? I don't care. . . . (Though Word may *still* demand the CD at this point.)

Word churns and hums.

Eventually, you see a cascading list of folders and documents Word found that match the information you searched for. Everything appears in the Open dialog box.

Or, if nothing was found, no files are displayed.

Deleting a file in Word

Several editions of this book back, there was an index entry for deleting files in Word. Unfortunately, the section telling how to do that was ruthlessly cut! Seeing how I still get mail about it, I thought I'd pass along a few file deleting secrets, just because I'm a nice guy and the editor who cut the deleting files section has since been sacked.

✔ Deleting a file is best done in Windows, by using the Explorer or the My Computer window. Just drag the file's icon to the Recycle Bin, or select the file (or group of files) and press the Delete key. Poof! Easy.

✔ In Word (or in any other Windows program) you can delete files in any Open or Save As dialog box. Those dialog boxes act as mini-Explorer windows. You delete a file by clicking it once with the mouse and pressing the Delete key or the Delete tool in the dialog box.

✔ Since the Open or Save As dialog box acts as a mini-Explorer, you can also rename a file there: Select the file and press the F2 key. Type in the new name, press Enter and you're done. However, Word will not let you rename a file you already have open. Tough luck, eh?

12. **Find your document.**

Use the scroll bar to scan through the list or use some of the hints offered in the following bullets:

- Displaying files after finding them makes the Open dialog box work a bit like Windows Explorer. You can even open and close folders and disk drives by double-clicking them. This capability makes the list a bit more manageable.

- If Word finds no matching files, weep bitterly and curse the computer. Or maybe try again with another word that you're certain is in your file.

Working with Groups of Files

The Open dialog box enables you to work with files individually or in groups. To work with a group of files, you must select them with the mouse, which you do by following the typical Windows procedure for selecting several items in a group:

1. **Press the Ctrl key and click each document you want to select.**

The item becomes highlighted.

2. **Repeat Step 1 for each additional item you want in your group.**

Et cetera.

You can only select a group of files in one folder. However, if you follow the instructions in "Finding Files in Word," earlier in this chapter, you can select files from all over your hard drive.

Opening files

Here's how to open more than one file at a time using the Open dialog box:

1. **Select the file or group of files that you want to open from those shown in the Open dialog box's window.**

2. **Click the Open button.**

The files open, and Word places each into its own document window.

3. **Work away!**

There is a limit on the number of files Word can work with at once. No, I don't know what the maximum number is — but you will! You'll see some odd error message about not enough memory or "heap" space or something bizarre. Don't panic. Close a few windows — maybe even quit Word — and start over.

Saving a gang of documents simultaneously

To save a multitude of documents all at once, you can switch to each window and incant the File⇨Save command. Or you can be sneaky and do the following:

1. **Press and hold the Shift key — either one.**

2. **Choose File⇨Save All.**

   Normally, you choose the Save item. But if you press the Shift key before choosing the File menu, it magically becomes the Save All menu item.

   There is no prompting, and no wait and see. Everything is just saved to disk as fast as your PC can handle it.

   ✔ If a file has not yet been saved, you are prompted to give it a name. Refer to "Saving a Document to Disk (The First Time)" in Chapter 8 for more information.

   ✔ I always use the File⇨Save All command any time I have to get up and leave my computer — even for a short moment, when the phone rings or when aliens land outside and demand Bisquick.

Closing a gang of documents simultaneously

You can conjure up a Close All command just like the Save All command. The difference is that you choose the Close All item from the menu; just press the Shift key (either one) before you click the File menu with your mouse. Then choose the Close All option and — Thwoop! — all your open documents are closed.

Word still asks whether you want to save any unsaved documents before it closes them. See Chapter 8, "Saving a Document to Disk (The First Time)."

Working with Other Document Formats

Word isn't the only word processor in the world (although Microsoft is trying very hard . . .). Other folks use other word processors, and occasionally you may tangle with the files they create. When you do, you need to import their weird word-processing files into Word so that you can do something with them. Likewise, you can export your Word documents into weird word-processing formats.

Another thing worthy of import to or export from Word are ASCII files. These are boring, plain text format files. Because they lack formatting, they come in handy for exchanging files between programs and different computers. Oh, and Windows itself requires plain text files when it's feeling discreet. Droll stuff, but required reading.

Loading a text file

A text file is a special, nondocument file that lacks any formatting or anything creative — kind of like an old Eastern Bloc housing project. You can load this type of document into Word for editing if you like. Follow these steps:

1. **Do the Open command.**

2. **In the Files of Type drop-down box, select Text Files.**

   This tells Word to display only text files in the Open dialog box.

3. **Hunt down the text file you want to load.**

   Use the controls in the dialog box to find the file you want. See the section "Using Another Folder" earlier in this chapter for more information.

4. **Click the text file's icon once with the mouse.**

5. **Click Open.**

   The text file appears on-screen, ready for editing just like any Word document — although the formatting is really cruddy because the file was boring, plain text to begin with.

Word may display a File Conversion dialog box, allowing you to preview how the document appears. Generally speaking, clicking the OK button in this step is your best bet.

✔ Text files are also called ASCII files. ASCII is a technospeak acronym that loosely translates to English as "a text file." You pronounce it *ask-EE*.

✔ Other terms for text files include DOS text file, plain text file, and unformatted file.

✔ You can also use these steps to load information from an alien word processor, such as WordPerfect, or from an older version of Word. Just choose the proper file type from the Files of Type drop-down list. Or choose All Files and just open any old file to see what Word does with it.

✔ Not every text file is a "TXT" file as Word insists. Some have specific names. Generally speaking, when you're told to open such a file, you are given the file's full name, something like CONFIG.INI or something. In those cases, just type the file's name into the File Name text box in the Open dialog box's. Or just find your computer guru and tell her to edit the file for you. Use a can of Surge as a bribe.

Saving a text file

Because some applications need to have files in a text format, you need to train Word in how to save them that way. Otherwise, Word assumes that you're saving a Word document to disk and junks up the text file with lots of curious Word stuff. If you want to save your file as a text file, you've got to be more careful.

First off, any text file you open with Word (see the previous section), is automatically saved back to disk as a text file. Only if you format the file will Word ask if you want to save it as a Word document. Otherwise, just choose File⇨Save and the text document is saved.

If you create a new text document in Word, you must manually direct Word to save it as a text-only document. In the Save dialog box, choose Text Only from the Save as Type drop-down list. Click the Save button and your document is saved.

Word (or the Assistant) may explain that saving the document in Text Only format is, well, bad. Whatever. Click Yes to save the document.

✔ Word really doesn't want you to save documents as text files. It assumes that's not what you want to do, because text files are unformatted and ugly and, honestly, Word is just plain bossy.

✔ Text Only and MS-DOS Text are the same format, mostly likely what you need. The "with line breaks" formats are only needed if you're told to save something to disk in a plain text format "with line breaks."

✔ You can save a document as both a text file and a Word document file. First, save the file to disk as a Word document by selecting Word Document from the Save as Type box. Then save the file to disk as a text file by selecting Text Only from that list. You'll have a text file, which is what you want, and a Word file, which contains secret codes and prints out really purty.

✔ You can use these steps to save a file in any format, not just Text Only. For example, to save a file for Earl, who still uses WordPerfect, choose WordPerfect from the Files of type drop-down list.

✔ Fortunately, the days of having to save things in a text-only format are waning fast.

Chapter 29

Modifying Word's Appearance

• •

In This Chapter

▶ Understanding Word's menus

▶ Working with the toolbars

▶ Displaying toolbars

▶ Rearranging toolbars and floating palettes

▶ Adding a button to a toolbar

▶ Removing a button from a toolbar

▶ Using the Zoom command

▶ Stifling Word

• •

*I*sn't Word a little much? I mean, it's a word processor, right? The main purpose of which is processing words. Yet look at the screen. It's a 747 cockpit of controls, menus, toolbars, and gizmos! Granted, all those buttons and whatnot lie around the big blank part in which you write. But still, there is a lot of *junk* up there on the screen.

With Word 2000, the keen and spiffy boys and girls at Microsoft decided to hand over a bit of interface control to you. You can customize just about everything — from the toolbars to the menus. This chapter shows you what is customizable and how to customize it, plus a few other tidbits about Word's interface.

Jiggling Commands on the Menu

The new "deal" with Word 2000 is that the menu commands you use the most appear toward the top of the menu. So, for example, the more you use the Format⇨Style command, the farther it wiggles its way up to the top of the menu. Interesting.

☒ Beyond the jiggling commands, there are also hidden commands. What Word tries to do is display only the "popular" commands in a menu whenever you click the menu title. The "unpopular" commands (those Microsoft figures you'll rarely use) only appear when you click the down-arrows at the foot of the menu (see margin).

Clicking the down-arrows button displays the entire menu, as shown in Figure 29-1, which also appears if you merely pause to stare at the menu long enough. The normally hidden commands appear to be recessed, like they're tattooed on a second layer of skin.

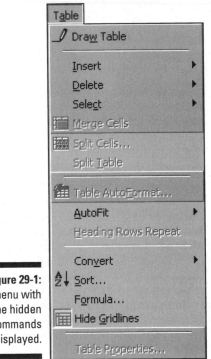

Figure 29-1: A menu with the hidden commands displayed.

Dimmed commands (such as the Merge Cells command in Figure 29-1) are unavailable, not necessarily hidden. Also, the down-arrows and hidden commands may appear on submenus as well.

If you've been reading this book front-to-back, then you should be well acquainted with how the menus work by now. If not, then working the various menus as described throughout this book will familiarize you with them.

Looking for Mr. Toolbar

Word has always had toolbars, but for some reason, now it has Super Toolbars. If you're an old Word hand, then some of these new toolbar concepts may seem strange to you. If you're new to Word, then _everything_ is probably strange to you.

The Standard and Formatting toolbars

The two toolbars Word shows you most of the time are the Standard and Formatting toolbars. The Standard toolbar is shown in Figure 29-2, the Formatting toolbar in Figure 29-3. This is the way they look as Word comes out of the box, although you can always change things.

Figure 29-2:
The
Standard
toolbar.

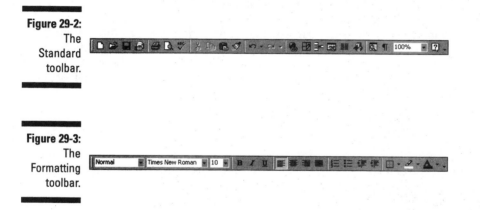

Figure 29-3:
The
Formatting
toolbar.

Two important things to note on these toolbars are the grabber and the toolbar menu.

⌇ The grabber appears on the far left of the toolbar. It looks like a vertical bump. You use the grabber to move or rearrange the toolbar.

▪ The toolbar menu is on the toolbar's far right. It looks like a down-pointing triangle. Clicking that button displays the Add or Remove Buttons menu item, which lets you customize the toolbar.

⊕ Both the grabber and the toolbar menu appear on all the Windows toolbars.

As Word comes out of the box, it puts both the Standard and Formatting tool-bars on the same line at the top of Word's window. This is pretty useless, since it means you cannot see all of the toolbars. When that happens, a set of right-pointing arrows appears on the right side of the toolbar. Clicking those arrows displays a drop-down menu of the remaining items.

Refer to the "Moving toolbars" section later in this chapter for information on rearranging the Standard and Formatting toolbars to make them more useful.

Where are the toolbars?

Toolbars come and toolbars go. They appear when you use special Word commands or enter secret operating modes, and then they disappear. That's great, because Word has over a dozen toolbars and all of them on the screen at once would mean that you'd be using a toolbar program and not a word-processing one. That's not very productive.

Though most toolbars appear when they're needed (such as the outlining toolbar when you enter outlining mode), you can summon any toolbar you want by selecting it from the menu that appears when you choose View⇨ Toolbars. What you get is shown in Figure 29-4 — a list of all the toolbars Word has to offer.

✓	Standard
✓	Formatting
	AutoText
	Clipboard
	Control Toolbox
	Database
	Drawing
	Forms
	Frames
	Picture
	Reviewing
	Tables and Borders
	Visual Basic
	Web
	Web Tools
	WordArt
	Customize...

Figure 29-4: Word's submenu o' toolbars.

A check mark appears by the toolbars in use and already visible. To display a different toolbar, select it from the submenu to put a check mark beside it. Selecting a toolbar's name again removes the check mark, making the toolbar go away. You can use this select-on/select-off technique whenever you encounter check boxes.

✔ A quick way to get at the toolbars submenu is to right-click on any toolbar in Word. That action displays a pop-up toolbars submenu, from which you can switch various toolbars on or off.

✔ Toolbars can appear as a strip of buttons across the screen (like the Standard and Formatting toolbars), as floating palettes, or as buttons in their own wee windows. See the section "Moving toolbars" for more information.

✔ The ruler is not a toolbar, yet it's controlled through the View menu. To see the ruler or to hide it, choose View⇨Ruler. As with a toolbar, a check mark by the ruler item means that the ruler is visible; no check mark means that it has abdicated.

✔ Some Word toolbars don't appear in the View⇨Toolbars submenu. For example, the Merge toolbar appears only when you're merging documents (see Chapter 26); you cannot choose it from the menu.

✔ Having tons of toolbars sates the button gluttons, but too many toolbars leave little room on the screen for your all-important text. Typically, you only need the Standard and Formatting toolbars. Everything else is just for show.

Moving toolbars

You move a toolbar in Word by dragging it with its grabber, located on the far left side of the toolbar. When the mouse pointer changes into a four-way arrow thing (see margin), it means you can drag the toolbar hither or thither to move it around.

For example, you can drag the Formatting toolbar to just below the Standard toolbar, so that you can see them both when you use Word.

Be careful how far you drag, though. If you drag a toolbar into the document part of Word's window, it becomes a floating palette — a little mini-window that can hover over the top of all your other windows with its own Close button.

Figure 29-5 shows the Drawing toolbar as a floating palette. To move a palette, drag it by its title bar. To see its menu, click the down-pointing triangle by the toolbar's title (to the left of the Drawing button in Figure 29-5). And to close the palette, click its X close button in the upper-right corner.

To convert a floating palette into a toolbar, drag the palette to the top or bottom of Word's window. When you find the sweet spot, the palette changes to a toolbar.

Adding a toolbar button

Nothing is sacred: You can customize any of Word's toolbars. After all, it's *your* word processor (no matter what the licensing agreement says!). Seriously, if you find yourself using one command quite often, why not make that command a button on the toolbar?

As an example, I use the Small Caps text format quite a bit so a Small Caps text formatting button next to the Bold, Italics, and Underline buttons on the Formatting toolbar would be really handy for me. To add that button, or any button to any toolbar, follow these steps:

1. **Click the down-arrow at the far right end of the toolbar.**

   The down-arrow is found on *all* of Word's toolbars. You want to click the down-arrow on whichever toolbar you're adding a button to.

   A menu drops down when you click the down-arrow triangle thing.

2. **Select Add or Remove Buttons.**

   A huge pop-up menu appears, detailing the buttons available or already on the toolbar.

   If the button you want appears in the pop-up menu, select it from the list. You're done.

   If the button you want isn't there, move along to Step 3.

3. **Select Customize from the menu.**

   The Customize dialog box appears. (You can also summon this dialog box with the Tools⇨Customize command.)

4. **Click the Commands tab.**

   The Commands tab, as shown in Figure 29-6, comes forward, if it's not forward already.

5. Locate the command you want to add.

The commands are organized like the Word menus. So, if you want to add a text format, select Format from the Categories list, then find the format command you want in the Commands list.

6. Drag the toolbar button you've found up onto the toolbar.

This is the tricky part, though Figure 29-6 should help. When you find the command you want, drag its icon from the Customize dialog box onto the toolbar. When the mouse is over the toolbar, a large "I" thing tells you where the command will be inserted. Release the mouse button to drop the command onto the toolbar.

7. Continue adding buttons, if you like.

Repeat Steps 5 and 6 as necessary.

8. Click Close to close the Customize dialog box.

Your new toolbar is awaiting its first use.

✔ Adding buttons to toolbars makes the toolbars longer. You may consider removing some of the buttons you don't use, which is covered in the next section.

✔ Some commands don't have cutesy little buttons. In that case, the command's text appears on the toolbar. Nothing wrong with that.

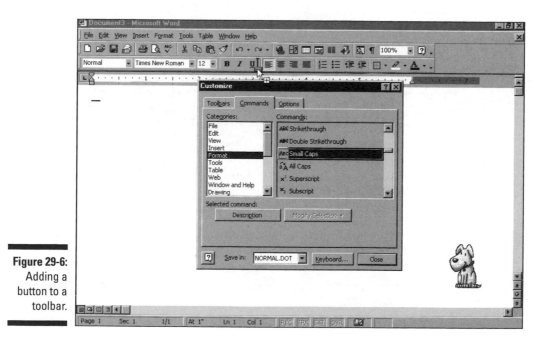

Figure 29-6:
Adding a
button to a
toolbar.

✔ A favorite button I usually add to the Standard toolbar is the Envelopes and Labels button. You can find it in the Tools category in the Customize dialog box. Clicking the Envelopes and Labels button lets you easily create and print an envelope in Word.

Removing a toolbar button

Removing a toolbar button is cinchy. Here's how to do it:

1. **Click the down-arrow at the far right end of the toolbar.**

2. **Choose Add or Remove Buttons from the menu.**

   From the huge pop-up menu that appears, choose the toolbar buttons you want to remove. Poof! They're gone.

   Keep repeating Step 2 until your destructive urges are sated.

3. **Press the Esc key when you're done.**

   This closes the menu.

If you think you really messed up and want things back the way Microsoft set them up when you first installed Word, then choose Reset Toolbar from the big menu that appears in Step 2 above. Word may ask if you're sure. Click OK to get back what Microsoft put there in the first place.

Zooming About

The Zoom command at the bottom of the View menu controls how big your document text looks. No, the command doesn't change the text size — that's done in the Font menu. Instead, the Zoom command controls how much of your text you see at once. Follow these steps for a quick demonstration:

1. **Choose <u>V</u>iew➪<u>Z</u>oom.**

   The Zoom dialog box appears, looking much like the one depicted in Figure 29-7.

2. **Select a Zoom size from the Zoom To area.**

   For example, 200% makes your text look real big — ideal for Grandpa. The Page Width option sets the zoom so that you see your entire document from left to right margins.

   You can set individual percent sizes using the Percent box on the Standard toolbar.

3. **Click OK to view your document at a new size on-screen.**

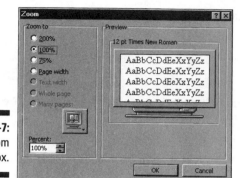

Figure 29-7:
The Zoom
dialog box.

✔ The Whole Page and Many Pages options in the Zoom dialog box are available only when you're in Page Layout view. Choose View➪Page Layout and then select the Zoom command to play, er, experiment with those options.

✔ When zooming takes you too far out, your text changes to shaded blocks, called greeking. Although not keen for editing, zooming out that far gives you a good idea of how your document looks on the page before printing.

✔ Way over on the right side of the Standard toolbar lives the Zoom drop-down list. Click it to set a Zoom size for your document quickly.

✔ If you have a Microsoft Intellimouse (or any other "wheel" mouse), you can zoom by pressing the Ctrl key on your keyboard and rolling the wheel up or down. Rolling up zooms "in;" rolling down zooms "out."

✔ Alas, you can only zoom in Word. The FreeCell game lacks a Zoom command.

Stop That Noise!

The Macintosh was really the first PC to fully utilize its little speaker. I remember a program — and I'm not making up this name — called MacPuke. It did nothing other than play the sound of someone retching every time someone ejected a floppy disk. Oh, I must have laughed and laughed. But after a while the sound got very annoying. I think I enjoyed removing MacPuke almost as much as I did installing it.

Word makes noise. And if that noise bugs you, you can swiftly turn it off. Here's how:

1. **Choose Tools⇨Options.**

2. **Click the General tab.**

3. **Select the Provide Feedback with Sound option to remove the check mark next to it.**

    This pulls the plug on the sound.

4. **Click OK.**

    Whew! Silence is such bliss. . . .

Part V
Creating Lotsa Stuff in Word

The 5th Wave   By Rich Tennant

"OK, TECHNICALLY, THIS SHOULD WORK. JUDY, TYPE THE WORD 'GOODYEAR' IN ALL CAPS, BOLDFACE, AT 700-POINT TYPE SIZE."

In this part . . .

*I*t looks so easy, doesn't it? Ever watch those chefs on the early morning TV shows? They just throw some ingredients together and *voila!* There's a wonderful, tasty dish there, which the show's host salivates over. I can do that too, you think, knowing darn well what the chef created and what you can do would look as dissimilar as sand and ice cream. Oh well.

This part of the book is about getting that extra edge. It's a cookbook of sorts, showing you some interesting tricks and techniques for making your documents look really good without having to suffer through a lot of learning. It's a fun, hands-on episode that, unlike the TV chef, will have you making great-tasting documents with a minimum of fuss. Go ahead. Salivate.

Chapter 30

Just Your Basic Letter and Envelope

- -

In This Chapter

▶ Making a letter in Word

▶ Configuring Word to print envelopes

▶ Adding an envelope to a letter

▶ Printing an envelope on-the-fly

- -

*U*sing Word to write a letter is kind of like using a jumbo jet to cross the street. Sure, it does the job, but it can be a little much. With all of Word's features, it's easy to forget that most of the things people use a word processor for are really simple. Take the basic letter and envelope.

A few years back, doing a letter on a word processor was no big deal. But doing the envelope? Not only was that a big deal, it was an ordeal. (Oh, a pun!) Anyway, this brief chapter gives you some tips and pointers on doing the basic letter and envelope in Word.

Writing a Silly Old Letter

Most letters start with two things right at the top: The date and the name and address of the recipient.

The date

To insert a date into any Word document, use the Insert⇔Date and Time command. Choose the format for the date from the list in the Date and Time dialog box; then click OK.

If you want the date shoved over to the right margin, press Ctrl+R after the date is inserted. Press the Enter key, then Ctrl+L to return to left-justified text on the next paragraph.

Whatever happened to manually typing in a date?

The address

Two lines below the date (press the Enter key twice), most letter-writing folks place the recipient's address. I've no idea why we do this, we just do. Type the address, press Enter a couple times, then type the salutation. Something like:

```
IDG Books
7260 Shadeland Station
Indianapolis. IN 46256
To Whom It May Concern:
```

You may notice that most salutations, such as "To Whom It May Concern," are stored in Word as AutoText entries; you need type only the first part and Word completes the rest if you press the Enter key. See Chapter 7 for more information.

The body of the letter

Typing the rest of the letter is up to you. Type away! La-la-la.

If the letter is longer than a page, consider adding page numbers. Use the Insert⇨Page Numbers command for that.

Finally, end the letter with a sign-off and your own name. You're done. The only thing left to do is add the envelope.

All about Printing Envelopes

To add an envelope to any document, you use Word's Envelopes and Labels command. This allows you to print an envelope on-the-fly or to "attach" an envelope to a letter so that they print one after the other. The following sections tell you everything you need to know.

Telling your printer to love an envelope

Every printer eats envelopes in a different manner. Some printers, why they even have fancy envelope feeders. Other printers have envelope slots. Still other printers have a pop-out manual feeding tray which somehow can be used to feed in an envelope. The following steps show you how to configure Word to properly print an envelope on your printer.

1. **Locate the envelope feeder/slot on your printer.**

   Notice exactly how the envelope is inserted: There is probably an icon printed or molded on the printer that tells you to insert the envelope in the middle, to the left, to the right, long-ways or whatever. Also check to see whether it's fed face-up or face-down.

2. **Choose Tools⊃Envelopes and Labels.**

   The Envelopes and Labels dialog box appears (I explain this dialog box in the next section). Make sure the Envelopes tab in the dialog box is up front.

3. **Click the Feed button.**

   This displays the Envelope Options dialog box, Printing Options tab, as shown in Figure 30-1.

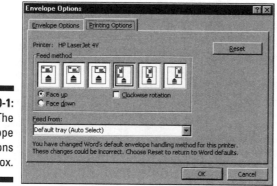

Figure 30-1:
The
Envelope
Options
dialog box.

4. **Select whether your envelope goes in face up or face down.**

   Click the appropriate Face Up or Face Down button.

5. **Select your envelope's orientation.**

   One of the six displayed Feed methods should do it.

   If necessary, click the Clockwise Rotation check box to flip the envelope 180 degrees.

6. **Click OK.**

   This closes the Envelope Options dialog box.

Now you're ready to create or print an envelope, or you can click Cancel to return to your document. Word knows about your printer and can properly print an envelope the next time you demand one.

Adding an envelope to your letter

A quick way to print an envelope with every letter you create is to attach the envelope to the end of the letter. Here's how:

1. **Create your letter.**

   Refer to the sections at the start of this chapter for more information.

2. **Choose Tools⇨Envelopes and Labels.**

   This step opens the Envelopes and Labels dialog box, as shown in Figure 30-2.

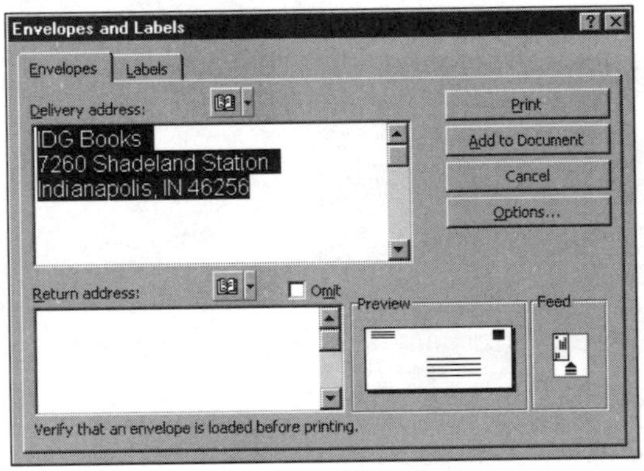

Figure 30-2:
The Envelopes and Labels dialog box, please.

If there is a proper address in your document, then Word magically locates it and places it into the Delivery address box. Ta-da!

If Word didn't automatically fill in the address, type it now.

Optionally, you can also type your return address in the Return address area.

3. **Click the Add to Document button.**

   The Envelopes and Labels dialog box goes away and you're returned to your document.

It may not be obvious on the screen, but the first page of your letter is now the envelope. (Choose File⇨Print Preview to see this wondrous thing.) When you're ready to print the letter, the envelope prints first, then the letter. All you have to do is stuff the letter into the envelope, seal it and apply postage.

- The letter and envelope print when you use the File⇨Print command for your letter (or press Ctrl+P or use the Print tool).

- Yes, you could create such an envelope-with-letter document as your main document in a mail merge. However, you're probably better off printing the envelopes all at the same time as opposed to feeding them in with every other page.

- Most printers prompt you to manually enter an envelope if that's what it wants you to do. After doing so, you may have to press the Ready, On-line, or Select button for the printer to continue. (My LaserJet just says "Me Feed!" and, for some reason, knows when I set in the envelope because it just starts going!)

- Check the envelope to make sure that you didn't address the backside or put the address on upside down — as so often happens to me. This last step is important because you can just repeat the above steps to reprint your envelope if you goof.

- If you have trouble remembering how the envelope feeds into your printer, draw a picture of the proper way and tape it to the top of your laser printer for future reference.

Printing an envelope on-the-fly

Whenever you need an envelope, for any reason, you can have Word whip one up for you. Follow these steps:

1. **Choose Tools⇨Envelopes and Labels.**

2. **In the Envelopes and Labels dialog box, type the address you want on the envelope.**

   If you want to format the address, type it in the document first. Format it, select it, then choose Tools⇨Envelopes and Labels. Beware though! Too much text may not fit on the envelope.

3. **Click the Print button.**

   Your printer may beep or otherwise prompt you to insert the envelope or it may just print it right then and there.

If printing envelopes is something you plan on doing a lot, consider adding an Envelope button to Word's Standard toolbar. Refer to Chapter 29 for more information on how to do that.

Chapter 31

Brochures and Greeting Cards

- -

In This Chapter

▶ Planning a three-part brochure

▶ Designing various document titles

▶ Using the Drop Cap command

▶ Printing a three-part brochure

▶ Printing a greeting card

- -

*I*f you want to create something in Word that will just *dazzle* someone, you've come to the right chapter. The information here isn't secret, and it definitely isn't advanced. It's just a collection of information already offered in this book, but with a *purpose:* to create a three-fold pamphlet or a greeting card. Go ahead. Amaze yourself!

Your Basic Three-Part Pamphlet

Some chores that you would think Word might utterly choke on it can handle with ease. Take the typical three-fold brochure, as shown in Figure 31-1.

Although Thomas Jefferson toiled away for days to pen the Declaration of Independence, Word and I whipped out a three-fold brochure in about three minutes. In another few moments, the brochure could be flying out of my printer — provided the British don't storm my office before then.

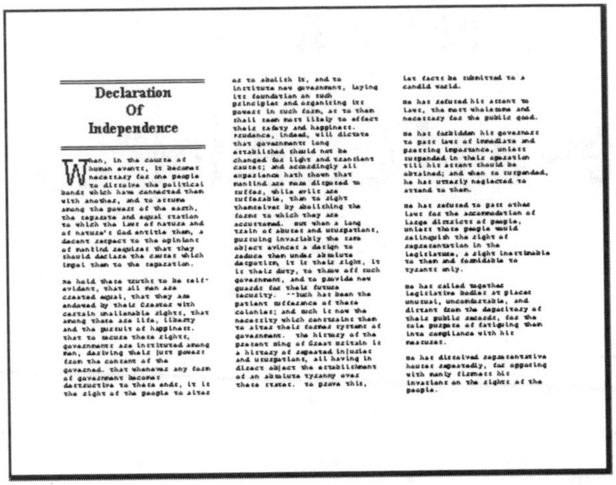

Figure 31-1:
A typical
three-fold
brochure
is a cinch
for Word
to make.

Building the pamphlet

A three-fold brochure is essentially a regular sheet of paper turned long-ways (landscape) and folded twice. In Word you do this in two simple steps — *after* you write your text.

It's always best to work on the writing first and create the document later. Also, Word works faster when it's in normal (non-column) mode. If you need to edit later, fine.

To turn a document long-ways, follow these steps:

1. **Choose File⇨Page Setup.**

   The Page Setup dialog box appears.

2. **Click the Paper Size tab.**

3. **Select the Landscape option from the Orientation area.**

   Behold, your world is 90-degrees out-of-sync.

4. **Ensure that the Whole Document menu option is selected in the Apply To drop-down list.**

5. **Click OK.**

To make the three columns for the brochure, follow these steps:

1. **Choose Format⇨Columns.**

2. **Select Three from the Presets list.**

   It's at the top of the dialog box.

3. **Ensure that the Whole Document menu option is selected in the Apply To drop-down list.**

4. **Click OK.**

Now your document is formatted for three panels that fold over on a single page. To get your text to print on both sides of the page requires a few more tricks, all of which are covered in the section "Printing the brochure," later in this chapter.

Giving your brochure a title

The best way to create a title for a brochure is to draw a table. Not only does a table have built-in borders, but it allows you to put bits of text to the right or left of the title without having to overly mess with Word's paragraph or tabs formatting.

Figure 31-2 shows three different titles done with tables. In each case, I used the Table drawing tool to create the title, plus any cells in the title's table. I added or removed borders and shading using the Table toolbar. (Use the figure for inspiration; Chapter 20 tells you the how-tos for tables.)

- ✔ The first image in Figure 31-2 is a single cell. Only the top and bottom borders have a line style. (Different line styles, by the way.)

- ✔ The second image shows a two-row, three-column table with no border style but background shading added. Each cell contains a different bit of text.

- ✔ The third image is a repeat of the second image, but with the table's borders displayed so that you can see what I did.

- ✔ The final image is yet another design. Notice how in this and other images, you can use two cells to hold information on the right and left sides of a line? That's pretty much the only way to do things in a table because you can't rightly use tab stops.

- ✔ And don't forget you can add graphics to the titles as well. See Chapter 22.

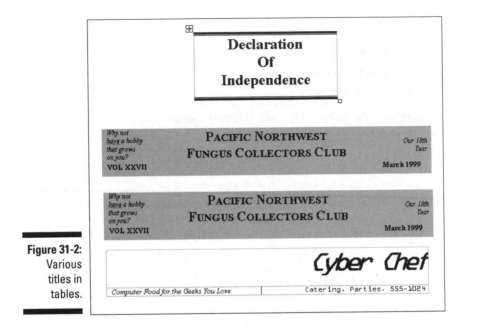

Figure 31-2:
Various
titles in
tables.

Starting a paragraph with a big letter (a drop cap)

A *drop cap* is the first letter of a report, article, chapter, or story that appears in a larger and more interesting font than the other characters. Figure 31-1 shows an example. Here's how to add a drop cap to your brochure (or just any old document):

1. **Select the first character of the first word at the start of your text.**

   For example, the O in "Once upon a time."

   It also helps if this paragraph is left justified and not indented with a tab or any of the tricky formatting discussed in Part II.

2. **Choose Format⇨Drop Cap.**

   The Drop Cap dialog box appears, as depicted in Figure 31-3.

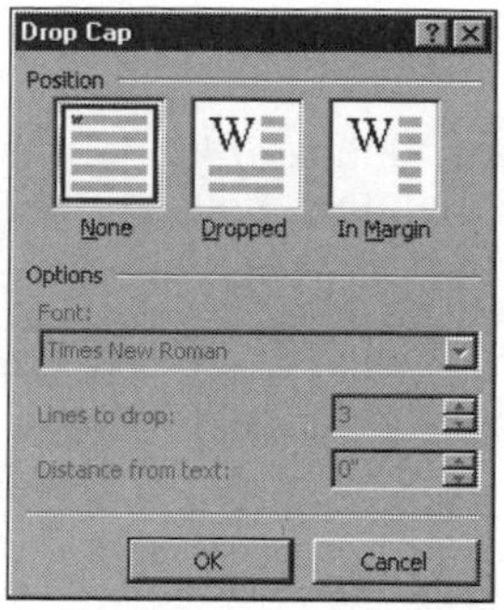

Figure 31-3:
The Drop
Cap dialog
box.

3. Select a drop cap style.

The first option, None, isn't a drop cap at all. The Dropped style is second, and the In Margin style is third. I prefer the Dropped style myself. Click in the box you prefer to select that style.

Select a font if you wish.

Oh, and you can mess around with the other options if you like. Especially if you're just starting a new novel, writer's block is a terrible thing. . . .

4. Click OK.

If you're not in Print Layout view, Word switches your document there so that you can see the drop cap in action.

The drop cap is highlighted and shown inside a hatched box with eight black handles. Yes, astute reader, just like a pasted-in graphic image. (See Chapter 22.)

5. Click the mouse in your text (not on the drop cap) and continue editing.

You're free to go on with your work.

✔ If you switch to Normal view (View⇨Normal), the dropcappe. letter appears on the line above your text. Funky, but that's the way Word does it. Don't try to fix it; instead, return to Page Layout view to see the drop cap more properly.

✔ You can undo a drop cap by clicking its box and then choosing Format⇨Drop Cap. In the Drop Cap dialog box, double-click the None position, and the drop cap vanishes.

Printing the brochure

Printing brochures is something best done by Kinkos or Insty-Prints, or some other printing professional. But if you're on a budget, you can do them yourself.

First print a sample brochure just to get the process down. Then you can print off a bunch of brochures in batches.

To print a sample brochure, follow these steps:

1. **Get the printer ready to print.**

2. **Choose File⇨Print from the menu.**

3. **Select the Odd Pages option from the Print drop-down list.**

    The Print drop-down list can be found in the lower-left corner of the Print dialog box. What you're doing is printing the front side of the brochure first — the odd pages.

4. **Click OK.**

The odd pages of your brochure print. If you have a one-page brochure, only one page spews forth from the printer. Otherwise you get only pages 1, 3, 5, and so on.

Now the tricky part:

Gather those pages up and put them back in your printer's feed tray *upside down*. You want to print on their backside. This is what may take a few steps. You need to ensure that the odd-numbered printed pages are oriented in the paper tray so that the even-numbered pages print properly. Don't be discouraged if this takes you a few tries. (And don't feel reluctant to use a Sharpie and write "UP" on one side of the paper tray.)

After you reload the paper, follow these steps to print the even pages:

1. **Choose File⇨Print from the menu.**

2. **Select the Even Pages menu option from the Print drop-down list.**

3. **Click OK.**

Check your results. If you have to try again, do so.

Another conundrum you may notice: The brochure may not fold the way you wanted it to. Don't worry! You can cut and paste the columns in your document later to match how the thing folds. That's not a big problem.

When you're ready to mass produce, simply repeat the above steps, but in the Print dialog box enter 50 in the Number of copies box. That way you'll be printing 50 copies of the brochure, front and back, each time. (Any more than 50 and you may run out of paper.)

Do-It-Yourself Greeting Cards

Greeting cards are simply a variation of the brochure example shown earlier in this chapter — with one special exception.

To set up Word to create a greeting card from a single sheet of standard letter-sized paper, follow these steps:

1. **Choose File⇨Page Setup.**

2. **Click the Paper Size tab.**

3. **Select the Landscape option in the Orientation area.**

4. **Click the Margins tab.**

5. **Check the 2 Pages per Sheet box.**

   This option is in the lower left corner of the dialog box. It tells Word to vertically split each page down the middle creating — aha! You guessed it — a greeting card.

6. **Click OK.**

Now your document is properly formatted. All that remains is for you to fill in the greeting card with text and maybe a few graphics. But there's a special way you need to do it!

The greeting card must be four pages long: two pages on the inside and two pages on the outside. (Only one sheet of paper is used, two "pages" per sheet.) Here's how the various pages shape up:

✔ **Page 1** is the inside left-hand page. Usually this is left blank. So in your document, you can press Ctrl+Enter to create a hard page break and leave that page blank.

✔ **Page 2** is the inside right-hand page. This is where you put your sappy message.

✔ **Page 3** is the outside "back" cover. This can be blank, or you can put wee tiny text at the bottom boasting of your word-processing prowess.

✔ **Page 4** ends up being the *cover* for the greeting card. Put a graphic or flowery text here.

Got it? If not, trust me, it all works out.

Fill in your greeting card accordingly.

To print the greeting card, you need to be tricky. Follow these steps:

1. **Choose File⇨Print.**

2. **Type** 1-2 **in the Pages box.**

   You want to print only pages 1 and 2 the first time.

3. **Click OK.**

Take the page out of the printer and put it back into the printer tray. Ensure that the page is in the printer tray *upside down,* so that the next page prints on the back side. (This may take a few tries, so be patient.)

Now print the backside:

1. **Choose File⇨Print.**

2. **Type** 3-4 **in the Pages box.**

   You want to print only pages 3 and 4 this time.

3. **Click OK.**

If everything goes well, you should be able to fold the paper down the middle and — *voilà!* — you have a greeting card.

✔ If you're into elaborate greeting-card formatting, consider using section breaks to divide the greeting card and not just the hard page breaks you get by pressing Ctrl+Enter.

✔ Watch out for fancy, thick paper. It tends to jam most laser printers. (If your laser printer has a single-sheet feed and a pass-through slot out the back, printing on thick paper may work.) Greeting card stock is difficult as all heck to get through an ink jet printer, too!

Chapter 32

Creating a Web Page

● ●

In This Chapter

▶ Saving documents in HTML format

▶ Working in the Web Layout view

▶ Animating your text

▶ Spicing up the background

▶ Using a Web theme

▶ Inserting a hyperlink

● ●

*I*n Microsoft's ceaseless effort to turn every product they produce into some type of Internet-something-or-other, they've tossed a rambling collection of World Wide Web (WWW or Web) features into Word. At first I rebelled against this. But now, after being brainwashed at a secret institute near Seattle, I've come to accept it.

Seriously, Word is heavy on the Web. And to be totally honest, if you're going to be building Web pages for the Internet, you're *not* going to be using Word. You'll be using FrontPage, Claris HomePage, Adobe PageMill, or some other specific program that does it much better. But if you're curious, or you merely want to create an HTML document because, well, it is the in-thing (you know), this chapter is the place you can call home.

✔ If you don't care about the Web or don't even know what HTML is, then you can blithely skip this chapter.

✔ This chapter (barely) covers Web page creation in Word. It does not describe how to "post" a page on the Internet. (Refer to a book specific to Web publishing for that information.)

Using Word as an HTML Editor

Whether or not you're connected to the Internet, you can use Word to create Web page documents, also known as HTML (HyperText Markup Language) documents. There are several different ways to do this, as described in the following sections.

✔ You can use all of Word's formatting commands to create your Web page. You can format fonts, paragraphs, insert graphics, tables, whatever.

✔ There is no reason under the sun to create an HTML document if you've never done it before or have no idea what's going on.

✔ On the other hand, HTML *is* a common file format and the documents saved in that format can be read by anyone on any computer with a Web browser.

The simple, almost goofy way to make a Web page

The simplest way to create a Web page in Word is just to create a Word document as you normally would, then use File➪Save as Web Page. Use the Save As dialog box (as normal) and, splat, you have a Web page document on disk. No sweat.

Of course, leaving this whole Web hullabaloo discussion at just that would make this chapter far too short to satisfy the folks in marketing.

✔ You can also use Word to load an HTML document, such as some Web page you may have saved to disk. Just use the Open command and choose the HTML Document option from the Files of Type drop-down list.

✔ If you want to save an HTML file as a Word document, choose File➪ Save as Word Document from the menu.

Using a Web wizard

Another way to create a Web page without really doing any work (and that would make marketing proud), is to use one of Word's built-in wizards. To do so, follow these steps:

1. **Choose File➪New.**

2. **Click the Web Pages tab.**

   You'll see several options for creating a Web page, a few Web page templates, and the Web Page Wizard. Ah-ha!

3. **Open the Web Page Wizard icon.**

Double-click the Web Page Wizard icon to open it.

Word may beg for its installation CD. Be prepared to insert it!

4. **Follow along through the wizard.**

Follow where the wizard leads.

Heed the various instructions and make the necessary choices to work through the wizard and create your Web page.

5. **Click the Finish button. You're done.**

Eventually the Wizard ends and your document is roughed-out on-screen. You now need to customize it.

6. **Edit the document.**

Find the present text, the `[Type some text]` stuff. Select that text by triple-clicking it once; then type in new text appropriate to your Web page. Then keep on editing and preparing the document as you normally do.

Using the Web view

If you do end up creating stuff for the Web, you should take advantage of Web Layout View — a preview mode Word uses to best show you how your Web page will look up on the Internet. So this is the choice you make if you start from scratch and don't use the techniques discussed in the two previous sections.

 To activate Web View, choose View⇨Web Layout from the menu, or click the Web View button on the lower-left corner of the document window (see margin).

Now you're ready to experience the thrill of a Web page as it happens in Word. Oh, goody.

The Whirlwind Roundup of Word's Web Tools

As you wander about the wasteland that inhabits the fringes of word processing, you'll encounter some of the wild plants and animals designed to make HTML publishing with Word a thing of grace and ease. I've collected specimens from that wasteland and share what I suppose are the most honorable in the following sections. Read on at your own whim.

The joys of animated text

Web page documents are alive, so why not threaten them with sharp objects? No, better still, prove to the reader that the document is alive by animating the text. Nothing gets a Web-page-reading person into a cheery mood like blinking, flashing or sparkling text. It says to the consumer, "Buy! Buy! Buy!"

To animate your text, choose Format⇔Font and click the Text Effects tab. There you'll see a scrolling list of various effects you can apply to text in a Web page document.

Go ahead. Go nuts.

Adding a swanky background

For word processing, you probably want black letters on a white background, unless you have a color printer and elect to use some colored text (sparingly). Not so with the Web!

The Format⇔Background command displays a palette of colors you can choose from for your Web page's background. You can even choose Format⇔Background⇔Fill Effects and choose background patterns, textures, or even photographs from the Fill Effects dialog box.

Go ahead. Go nuts.

Using a theme

What's the matter? Not feeling creative enough? Jealous of your co-workers and their fancy Web pages? Never fear! Just employ one of Word's pre-designed Web page themes.

Choose Format⇔Theme to display the Theme dialog box, as shown in Figure 32-1. Choose a theme from the long list and peruse its preview in the large window.

When you find a theme you want, click OK and Word automatically adjusts itself to those settings. All you need to do is type.

Go ahead. Go nuts.

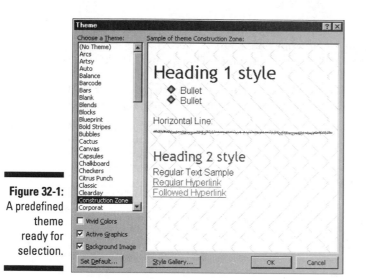

Inserting a hyperlink into your document

What is a Web page without hyperlinks? Well, it's a document! And then Word would be what? Anyone? Anyone?

Yes, Word would be a word processor. But that's not good enough, is it? Oh, no, it has to be — Look, there on the screen, it's a word processor, it's a text editor, it's a Web tool — it's SuperWord!

Follow these steps to stick a hyperlink to another Web page into your Web page:

1. **Select the text or graphic you want to use as a hyperlink.**

2. **Click the Insert Hyperlink button on the standard toolbar.**

   The Insert Hyperlink dialog box appears.

3. **Type the link into the Type the File or Web Page Name box.**

   You know, type the http thing or you can optionally type the name of a file on disk that would open when the link is clicked.

   Alternatively, you can use the File and Web Page buttons to insert a link. The File button displays an Open-like dialog box you can use to hunt down files. Clicking the Web Page button starts your Web browser, which you can use to find a Web page on the Internet (though this option is very tricky and would take too much space to explain here in detail).

4. **Click OK.**

   The link is created in your document. Notice that the text is underlined and in another color (probably blue). That's a hyperlink.

✔ To edit a hyperlink that you've already created, right-click on it. Then choose Hyperlink⇨Edit Hyperlink from the shortcut menu.

✔ You can also link to other parts of the same document. Use the Bookmark button in the Insert Hyperlink dialog box. Of course, it helps to set the bookmark first. . . .

✔ You cannot access a hyperlink to the Internet unless you're connected to the Internet. But be forewarned: Word doesn't assume that you're "just kidding." If you click a hyperlink, Word connects you to the Internet, especially if you're using Windows 98.

✔ Go ahead. Go nuts.

Chapter 33

Making Some Labels

*O*ne of Word's most esoteric duties is printing labels. Now this isn't too far out of the realm of word processing. The first time I printed up my own return labels was with WordPerfect 4.0 back in the dark ages. Unlike WordPerfect 4.0, however, Word 2000 has its own Label command and many exciting label options. This chapter discusses how to put them to use.

All about Labels

Because my handwriting is so darn lousy, I print labels with my return address on them and stick those on my bills and whatnot. I do it as a favor to the overworked men and women of the U.S. Postal Service. Of course labels can be used for more than addressing envelopes.

If you're curious about what types of labels are available, visit your local office supply store (or mega-warehouse). You can find all sorts of ingenious labels there, from the mundane "Hello, my name is" to labels you can use when creating your own CDs.

Ensure that you buy labels compatible with your printer. Laser printers need special laser printer labels. Some ink printers require special high-quality labels to hold the image. Impact printers need tractor-feed labels.

Transparent labels are also available, but if you have a laser printer watch out! Transparent labels must be made specifically for a laser printer, otherwise the heat inside the laser printer may melt the labels and you'll have a serious mess on your hands.

Of all the label brands available, I recommend Avery. Their stock numbers are standard for almost all computer programs. So if you buy Avery stock number 5160 or something similar, your software and printer know which type of label you have and in which format it is.

Printing a Sheet of Identical Labels

Here are the instructions for printing an entire sheet of labels in Word, such as your name and address for return mailing labels:

1. **Choose Tools⇨Envelopes and Labels.**

2. **Click the Labels tab.**

   What you see on your screen should look like Figure 33-1.

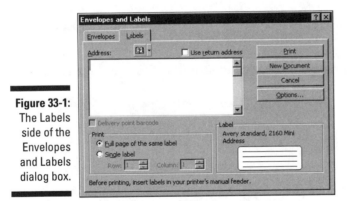

Figure 33-1:
The Labels
side of the
Envelopes
and Labels
dialog box.

3. **Choose the type of label you're printing on.**

   Confirm that the stock number in the lower-right corner of the dialog box matches the labels on which you're printing.

   If the numbers don't match up, click the Options button to display the Label Options dialog box. Locate the correct Avery stock number in the Label Options dialog box's scrolling list. Select it; then click OK.

4. **Type what you want printed on the label in the Address box.**

   Keep in mind that you have only so many lines for each label and that each label is only so wide.

   Press the Enter key at the end of each line.

5. **Click the New Document button.**

Ha! I bet you thought you'd click the Print button. No way! The labels are typically more ugly than you think and you may want the chance to spiff them up a bit before you print.

The labels appear in table format in your Word document. Figure 33-2 shows such a document. From this point on, you can work with the labels in your document just as you work with a table. (Refer to Chapter 20 for more information on working with tables.)

Be careful not to adjust the table's columns and rows! Everything is formatted just so. If you change something, the labels may not print properly.

6. **Format the labels (if you like).**

Press Ctrl+A to select the entire document (it's only a page long) and then change the font to something more pleasing. Refer to Chapter 11 for more information.

Don't mess with the margins or paragraph formatting. This is all carefully tuned to print on the labels you specified.

You can edit the labels. Sure, they all look the same, but if you like you can type in a few new names or other information in several of the little boxes.

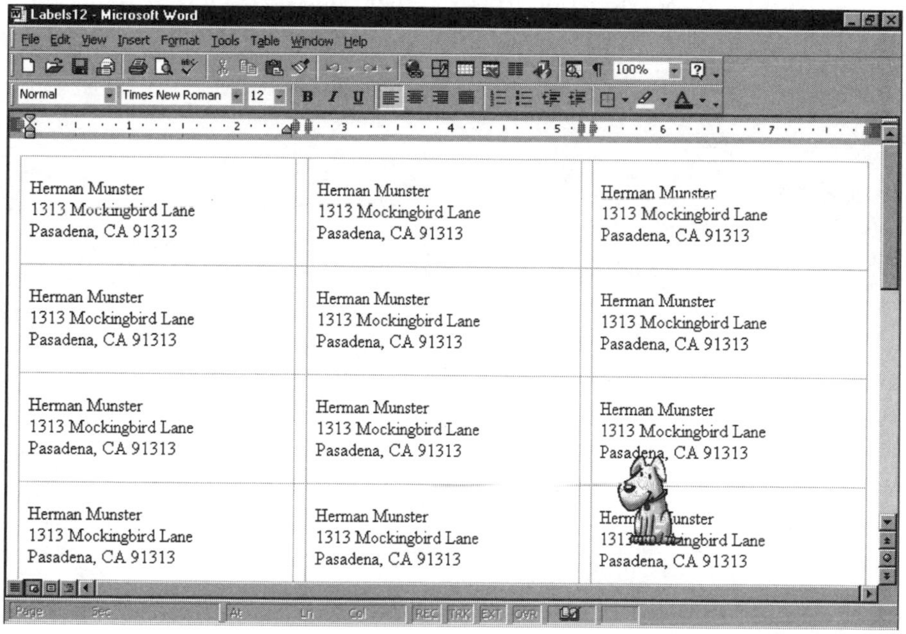

Figure 33-2:
Labels
await
inspection
in Word.

Herman Munster 1313 Mockingbird Lane Pasadena, CA 91313	Herman Munster 1313 Mockingbird Lane Pasadena, CA 91313	Herman Munster 1313 Mockingbird Lane Pasadena, CA 91313
Herman Munster 1313 Mockingbird Lane Pasadena, CA 91313	Herman Munster 1313 Mockingbird Lane Pasadena, CA 91313	Herman Munster 1313 Mockingbird Lane Pasadena, CA 91313
Herman Munster 1313 Mockingbird Lane Pasadena, CA 91313	Herman Munster 1313 Mockingbird Lane Pasadena, CA 91313	Herman Munster 1313 Mockingbird Lane Pasadena, CA 91313
Herman Munster 1313 Mockingbird Lane Pasadena, CA 91313	Herman Munster 1313 Mockingbird Lane Pasadena, CA 91313	Herman Munster 1313 Mockingbird Lane Pasadena, CA 91313

7. Print the document.

Make sure that your printer is on and ready to print and that you have the proper type of label-printing material in the printer, right side up and all that. Then print your document as you normally would. Click the li'l Print button and the labels soon unfurl from your printer ready for lickin' and stickin'.

- You do not have to save this document to disk, unless you just like the labels and want to keep them around. Press Ctrl+W to close the document and type **N**, no save.

- If you're serious about printing lots of labels, consider getting the label-printing program Avery distributes. I think it's called Avery Label Pro. Like any specific piece of software, this program does its job much better than Word's jack-of-all-trades approach.

- Printing a full page of different labels is something Word can do, but also something a database program does better. Even if database programs scare you, there are mini-mailer programs available that do nothing more than collect and print out various names and addresses.

- When you get into labels, you typically get into databases. If you need to print lots of differing labels and store and sort the names you print, what you really need is a database program.

Part VI
The Part of Tens

The 5th Wave   By Rich Tennant

Y2K FAULT TOLERANCE

In this part . . .

You think you're pretty good at Trivial Pursuit. And your aunt from out-of-town thinks she's pretty good too. You just *know* there will be some serious blood-letting if you play a game. So you round up the family into "teams," though it's really only you and her playing. And you both . . . bomb. I mean, weren't you two alive in the '60s?

When it comes time to play Microsoft Word 2000 Trivial Pursuit, take heart. This last part of the book contains my famous List of Tens. Not "top ten" lists, but merely lists and collections of thoughts whose number just happens to be ten. Ten of this. Ten of that. It's all here, or at least ten of them are.

Chapter 34

The Ten Commandments of Word

- -

In This Chapter

▶ Thou shalt not use spaces unnecessarily

▶ Thou shalt not press Enter at the end of each line

▶ Thou shalt not neglect thy keyboard

▶ Thou shalt not reset or turn off thine PC until thou quittest Word and Windows

▶ Thou shalt not manually number thy pages

▶ Thou shalt not use the Enter key to start a new page

▶ Thou shalt not quit without saving first

▶ Thou shalt not press OK too quickly

▶ Thou shalt not forget to turn on thy printer

▶ Thou shalt remember to save thy work

- -

And just where is Moses?" the rat-like character Dathan whines in the film *The Ten Commandments*. If it had been a story about word processing, Dathan could have gone on, "He says he's the deliverer, but from what? We can number our pages with the number keys. Look ye here while I type five spaces in a row. Behold! What good are Moses' tab stops, I ask you?"

This chapter contains the ten commandments of word processing, Word 2000 edition. These are the rules and suggestions I make throughout this book, condensed into one handy little chapter — much lighter than two of those tablet things Charlton Heston had to lug down that papier-mâché mountain.

Thou Shalt Not Use Spaces Unnecessarily

Generally speaking, you should never find more than one space anywhere in a Word document. Yeah, I know, most of us former touch-typists typed two spaces at the end of a sentence. With a word processor, that's unnecessary, so wean yourself from the habit.

Any time you have more than one space in a row in your document, you should probably be using the Tab key instead. Use the spacebar to separate words and to end a sentence. If you align lists of information, use the Tab key. If you want to organize information into rows and columns, use the Table command (see Chapter 20).

Thou Shalt Not Press Enter at the End of Each Line

Word automatically wraps your text down to the next line as you approach the right margin. You have no need to press Enter, except when you want to start a new paragraph. (Of course, if your paragraph is only a line long, that's okay.)

If you don't want to start a new paragraph but need to start a new line, then use Shift+Enter, the "soft" return command.

Thou Shalt Not Neglect Thy Keyboard

Word is Windows, and Windows is mousy. You can get a lot done with the mouse, but some things are faster with the keyboard. For example, when I'm working on several documents at once I switch between them with Alt+Tab. And stabbing the Ctrl+S key to quickly save a document or Ctrl+P to print works better than fumbling for the mouse. You don't have to learn all the keyboard commands, but knowing those few outlined in this book helps a lot.

Thou Shalt Not Reset or Turn Off Thy PC until Thou Quittest Word and Windows

Always exit properly from Word and especially from Windows. Only shut off or reset your computer when you see the "It's now okey-dokey to turn off this PC" type of on-screen prompt — never when you're running Word or have Windows active. Believeth me, if ye do, ye are asking for mucho trouble, yea, verily, woe.

Thou Shalt Not Manually Number Thy Pages

Word has an automatic page numbering command. Refer to Chapter 14 in the section "Where to Stick the Page Number."

Thou Shalt Not Use the Enter Key to Start a New Page

Sure, it works: Brazenly press the Enter key a couple of dozen times, and you are on a new page. But that's not the proper way, and you mess up your new page if you go back and re-edit text. Besides, pressing Ctrl+Enter is quicker. Doing so inserts a *hard page break* into your document.

Refer to Chapter 14, in the section "Starting a new page (a 'hard page' break)," for the details.

Thou Shalt Not Quit without Saving First

Save your document to disk before you quit. Shift+F12 is the key combo to remember. Or Ctrl+S is the one you don't even have to remember because it's so sensible. If only all of life — no, forget life — if only all of Word were so sensible.

Thou Shalt Not Click OK Too Quickly

Word has many Yes/No/OK-type questions. If you click OK without thinking about it (or press Enter accidentally), you can delete text, delete files, or perform a bad replace operation without meaning to. Always read your screen before you click OK.

Some dialog boxes have a Close button instead of an OK button. These buttons are typically used when you make some choice or reset some option, but you don't want to continue with the command. For example, you can change printers in the Print dialog box and then click the Close button to continue without printing.

And don't forget your handy undo key, Ctrl+Z!

Thou Shalt Not Forget to Turn On Thy Printer

The biggest printing problem anyone has is telling Word to print something when the printer isn't on. Verify that your printer is on, healthy, and ready to print before you tell Word to print something.

Never (or at least try not to) keep using the Print command over and over when a document doesn't print. Word tries to print once every time you use the Print command. So somewhere and sometime those documents will print, unless you do something about it.

Thou Shalt Remember to Save Thy Work

Save! Save! Save! Always save your stuff. Anytime your mind wanders, have your fingers wander to the Ctrl+S keyboard shortcut. Honor thy documents. Savest thine work.

Chapter 35

Ten Truly Bizarre Things

*E*verything in this program is bizarre, but some things are more bizarre than others. Below are listed what I feel are the ten most bizarre things, in no particular order. Read on. If you dare.

Using the Options Dialog Box

Choosing the Tools⇨Options command accesses the Options dialog box. What you get in this dialog box is ten — count 'em, ten — panels of various things Word does. The settings in the panels control how Word behaves.

The Options dialog box doesn't really contain any hints or secrets. In fact, you've probably been here a few times if you clicked any Options button in the various Word dialog boxes — no big deal, just, well, bizarre.

The Unbreakables

The two weird keys on your keyboard are the spacebar and the hyphen. They're weird because Word uses both to split a line of text: The space splits a line between two words and the hyphen splits a line between two word chunks.

There are times, however, when you don't want a line to be split by a space or hyphen. For example, splitting a phone number is bad — you want the phone number to stay together. And spaces can be annoying as well. For example, suppose that you work for the firm of Bandini, Lambert, and Locke and, by golly, Mr. Locke doesn't like to be left on a line by himself. If so, insert a nonbreaking (hard) space between each name to make sure that they're always together.

To prevent the space character from breaking a line, press Ctrl+Shift+spacebar instead of the spacebar by itself. That inserts a non-breaking space between two words.

To prevent the hyphen character from breaking a line, press Ctrl+Shift+- (hyphen) instead of the hyphen by itself. So type the first three digits of the number, and then press Ctrl+Shift+- and the phone number doesn't split between two lines.

The Document Map

I suppose the Document Map feature is there to help you see the big picture, especially if you use Word's Heading styles. Choose <u>V</u>iew⇨<u>D</u>ocument Map and a "pane" opens to one side of your document, listing a quick summary.

A scary weird thing you should avoid at all costs

Over many years of using Word, I've discovered one of the most annoying commands in the history of word processing. It's the terrifying menu item remover, something you may stumble over accidentally someday. (I hope you don't.)

If you press Ctrl+Alt+- (hyphen) in Word, the mouse pointer changes to a thick, horizontal line. That line is the menu item removal cursor. Just choose any menu item and — thwoop! —

it's gone, deleted, zapped, dead. And there's no way to get that menu item back, either. Deadly! Scary! Not even Rod Serling could dream up something that bizarre.

If you do accidentally press Ctrl+Alt+-, quickly press the Esc key to cancel that mode. Yikes! What kind of sick mind thought up that trick, huh?

This feature can be useful. In fact, since I use the Heading styles, the Document Map gives me a quick overview of how my document is laid out — like a mini-outline view. It's just a *bizarre* feature, which is why it's in this chapter.

Hyphenation

Hyphenation is an automatic feature that splits long words at the end of a line to make the text fit better on the page. Most people leave it off because hyphenated words tend to slow down the pace at which people read. However, if you want to hyphenate a document, choose Tools➪ Language➪Hyphenation. Continuously jab the F1 key when you need Help.

Various Send To Commands

Lurking in the File menu is the curious Send To submenu, where you find interesting e-mail and faxing commands: Supposedly something there lets you use Word as your e-mail editor and then instantly sends your document to someone else on your network or on the Internet. Sounds great, works terribly. Ditto for the Fax command, which is so painful it makes working a digital thermostat seem like fun.

Fear has prevented me from ever choosing an option in the File➪Send To submenu. I haven't any idea what the things in there do, nor do I want to know.

Random Statistics

This feature is something that you never use because it is a very unpopular thing. Besides that, it is a royal pain in the digit. Word tracks all sorts of statistics about your document. To see them, choose File➪Properties. Yoikles! That's just more information than I care to know about at any given time. Silly stuff.

Math

Did it ever dawn upon the Word people that math and English are two separate subjects for a reason? The math and English parts of the SAT scores are separate. Math and English are always taught as separate courses. So who needs a math function in a word processor? I don't know. Even if you do, it's still easier to calculate the numbers by using your desk calculator and typing them manually.

To use the Math command, you must first place your data in a table. Then highlight the row or column that you want computed. Choose Table⇨ Formula. Word suggests a formula type, or you can tell Word what you want done with the numbers. On second thought, I guess this woulda been kinda handy during algebra class. Anyway, Word puts the answer wherever you left the blinking toothpick cursor.

Macros

Macros are beyond the scope of this book.

Making a Cross-Reference

The Insert⇨Cross-Reference command allows you to insert a "Refer to Chapter 99, Section Z" type of thing into your document. This feature works because you've taken the Krell brain-booster and now have an IQ that can only be expressed in scientific notation. Fortunately, you may have also used the Heading style to mark text in your document that you want to cross-reference. Using the Heading style means that the Insert⇨Cross-Reference command works and sticks a "Refer to Chapter 99, Section Z" type of thing in your document — complete with an updated reference to that page should you overhaul your document.

The Office 2000 Optimizer

Word 2000 is a part of Office 2000, which is a part of Microsoft's new battle plan for making your computer run at tip-top speed. Part of that strategy means that Office has the ability to fix itself when needed. So, at random moments, you may see the Office 2000 Optimize program running. Don't let it freak you out.

A feature of the Optimizer is the Help⇨Detect and Repair command in Word. This command is used to fix any bugs or boo-boos that may creep into Word. So I suppose if Word is starting to behave like, well, like every other Microsoft program written, it would be a good idea to run that command.

Chapter 36

Ten Cool Tricks

Determining what's a cool trick (and what's not) is purely subjective. I'm sure that people who formerly numbered their pages manually think Word's Page Numbers command is a cool trick. I think AutoCorrect is a great trick. And I'm certain some two-fingered typist out there thinks the on-the-fly spell checker is keen. Now if the boys and girls in the Word labs could only come up with a handy tool that lets you take back something you said aloud, we'd all truly be blessed.

This chapter explains some of the neater Word tricks — mostly obscure stuff that I may not have mentioned elsewhere in this book. Some are simple and straightforward; some take a little longer for the human mind to grasp.

Typing a Fraction

Common fractions are easy to type in Word. The characters ½, ¼, and ¾ are available in just about any font. Choose Insert⇨Symbol to see the Symbol dialog box (see Figure 36-1).

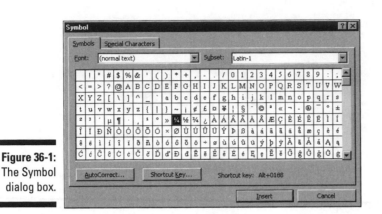

Figure 36-1:
The Symbol
dialog box.

To insert the proper fraction, locate it in the Symbol dialog box (they're all shown together in Figure 36-1). Click the symbol once, click Insert, then click Close.

Note that the characters displayed in the Symbol dialog box belong to a particular font. In Figure 36-1, (normal text) is chosen from the list, meaning those symbols are available in every font. To choose symbols from a specific font, select the font from the drop-down list.

If you have AutoCorrect on, Word automatically converts these three fractions for you. Otherwise, you'll need to build your own fractions using the superscript command. Here's how:

1. **Press Ctrl+Shift+= (the equal sign).**

   This is the keyboard shortcut for the superscript command.

2. **Type the numerator — the top part of the fraction.**

   For example, 4 for ⅘.

3. **Press Ctrl+Shift+= again to turn off superscript.**

4. **Type the slash.**

5. **Press Ctrl+= to turn on subscript.**

6. **Type the denominator — the bottom part of the fraction.**

7. **Press Ctrl+= to turn off subscript.**

There's your fraction.

Super- and Subscript Buttons on the Toolbar

If you plan on typing a lot of fractions, or the idea of super- and subscript text appeals to you, why not add those buttons to the Formatting toolbar?

Click the down-pointing triangle at the toolbar's far right end. Choose Add or Remove Buttons from the menu and a huge menu appears. Near the bottom are commands for Superscript and Subscript. Choose each one, then press the Esc key.

The superscript (x^2) and subscript (x_2) buttons are added to the toolbar for you.

Bullets and Numbering

Often, you need to drive home several points, and nothing brings them home like putting bullets in your text. No, these aren't the lead-propelled things used to kill tourists and innocent bystanders. Bullets are typographical ding-bats, like this:

- Bang!
- Bang!
- Bang!

To apply bullets to your text, highlight the paragraphs you want to shoot and choose Format➪Bullets and Numbering. You don't need to dawdle in the dialog box; just double-click the type of bullets you want and your high-lighted text is all shot up, nice and neat. (You can also click the Bulleted List button on the Formatting toolbar.)

You can also apply numbers to your paragraphs. When you see the Bullets and Numbering dialog box, click the Numbered tab to bring that panel forward and then click OK. (Or click the Numbered List button on the Formatting toolbar.)

Lugging Blocks Around

Here's a weird trick: Select a paragraph of text, or any old chunk of text. To move that text up one paragraph at a time, use Alt+Shift+↑. Every time you press Alt+Shift↑ the block moves up one paragraph.

The Alt+Shift+↓ shortcut moves the selected block down one paragraph. Interesting, no?

I believe you may find these keyboard shortcuts handy for moving chunks of text that would take the mouse a while to master.

AutoSummarize

In the category of "how the heck did they do that?" comes the AutoSummarize tool. Just like those prehighlighted used textbooks in college, this tool takes any document and immediately fishes out all the relevant points, highlighting them on the screen. I have no idea how this tool works, but it's pretty keen — for Word, that is.

To AutoSummarize your document, choose the Tools⇨AutoSummarize command. Heed the steps on the screen. In a few minutes (longer if the computer is unplugged), the AutoSummarize dialog box appears. Click OK. (You can peruse the options in the AutoSummarize dialog box on your own, if you like; clicking the OK button generally does what you want it to do.)

Splat! Your document then appears on the screen with relevant parts highlighted in yellow. Also visible is an AutoSummarize floating palette, which I have yet to figure out.

To return to normal editing mode, click the Close button on the AutoSummarize palette. Your document returns to normal.

No, it's the AutoSummarize tool that makes it bright and sunny outside.

Select All

There are times when you want to block the whole shooting match; highlight everything from top to bottom, beginning to end; select the entire document. When you want to do so, click the mouse three times in your document's left margin. Click, Click, Zowie! There it is.

Oh, and you can hold down the Ctrl key and press the 5 key on the number keypad. Zap, Zowie! There you go.

Oh, and you also can press F8 (the Extended Text key) five times. Zap, Zap, Zap, Zap, Zowie! There you go again.

Oh, and the Edit⇨Select All command does the same thing. Press Ctrl+A. Zowie!

Inserting the Date

Word's date command is named Date and Time and hangs under the Insert menu. Selecting this option displays a dialog box full of date and time formats, one of which you're bound to favor. Click OK to insert the current date, time, or both.

Sorting

Sorting is one of Word's better tricks. Once you understand it, you go looking for places to use it. You can use the Sort command to arrange text alphabetically or numerically. You can sort paragraphs, table rows, and columns in cell tables and tables created by using tabs.

Always save your document before sorting.

Sorting is not that difficult. First arrange what needs to be sorted into several rows of text, such as:

```
Greed
Envy
Lust
Wrath
Sloth
Pride
Gluttony
```

Word sorts by the first item in each line. So just select all the lines as a block, then choose Table➪Sort. The Sort Text dialog box appears. (Yes, the Sort command is in the Table menu, though your text need not be in a table.)

Mess around in the dialog box if you need to, but as Word tosses it up on the screen, the dialog box is set to sort your text alphabetically. Just click OK to do so.

Automatic Save

When the Auto Save feature is active, your document is periodically saved to disk. This isn't the same as pressing Ctrl+S to save your document. Instead, Word makes a secret backup copy every so often. In the event of a crash, you can recover your work from the backup copy — even if you never saved the document to disk.

To turn on Auto Save, choose Tools⇨Options. Click the Save tab to bring that panel up front. Put a checkmark by the Save AutoRecover Info Every option. Then enter the backup interval in the Minutes text box. For example, I type **10** to have Word back up my documents every ten minutes. If the power is unstable at your home or office, enter 5, 3, 2, or even 1 minute as the backup interval. Press Enter to return to your document.

With Automatic Save, you won't recover all your document in case of a mishap, but you get most of it back.

Cool Characters

You can use the Insert⇨Symbol command to stick odd and wonderful characters into your document. Quite a few Windows fonts have a few weird and wonderful characters in them. The Symbol font is full of neat stuff; the Wingdings font has all sorts of fun doodads; even the normal font, Times New Roman, has several cool characters in it.

You can insert any of these funky characters into your document at your whim. Simply put the toothpick cursor where you want the symbol to appear, choose Insert⇨Symbol, point at the cool character you want inserted, and click your mouse.

Chapter 37

Ten Things Worth Remembering

*T*here's nothing like finishing a book with a few heartening words of good cheer. As a Word user, you need this kind of encouragement and motivation. Word can be an unforgiving, but not necessarily evil, place to work. This book shows you that having a lot of fun with Word and still getting your work done is possible. To help send you on your way, here are a few things worth remembering.

Let Word Do the Work

There's so much Word can do. Even so, some stubborn people still insist upon doing things their way because, well, that's just the way things get done around here. Wrong! You can use a handy Word command to do just about anything, and you'll never remember the commands if you're afraid to try them.

Have a Supply of Diskettes Ready

You need diskettes to use your computer, even if you have a hard drive! You need diskettes for backup purposes and for exchanging files with other PCs running Word, such as between home and the office.

Keep one or two boxes of diskettes available. If your PC has a ZIP drive, then have a few of those disks ready as well. Every so often, copy or back up your working documents to those disks.

Keep Printer Paper, Toner, and Supplies Handy

When you buy paper, buy a box. When you buy a toner cartridge or printer ribbon, buy two or three. Also keep a good stock of pens, paper, staples, paper clips, and all the other office supplies (including diskettes) handy.

Keep References Handy

Word is a writing tool. As such, you need to be familiar with and obey the grammatical rules of your language. If that language just happens to be English, you have a big job ahead of you. Even though they are an electronic part of Word, I recommend that you keep a dictionary and a thesaurus handy. Strunk and White's *Elements of Style* (Allyn & Bacon) is also a great book for finding out where the apostrophes and commas go. If you lack these books, visit the reference section of your local bookstore and plan on paying about $50 to stock up on quality references.

Keep Your Files Organized

Use folders on your hard drive for storing your document files. Keep related documents together in the same subdirectory.

Remember the Ctrl+Z Key!

The Ctrl+Z key is your undo key. If you're typing away in Word, press it to undelete any text you mistakenly deleted. This command works for individual letters, sentences, paragraphs, pages, and large chunks of text.

Save Your Document Often!

Save your document to disk as soon as you get a few meaningful words down on the screen. Then save every so often after that. Even if you're using the AutoSave feature (discussed in Chapter 36), continue to manually save your document to disk: Ctrl+S.

Use AutoText for Often-Typed Stuff

To quickly insert things that you type over and over, like your name and address, use an AutoText entry. Type your entry once and then define it as a glossary entry under the Edit menu. Then use the shortcut key to zap it in whenever you need it. See Chapter 27 for more about AutoText.

Use Clever, Memorable Filenames

A file named LETTER is certainly descriptive, but what does it tell you? A file named LETTER TO MOM is even more descriptive but still lacking some information. A file LETTER TO MOM, APRIL 23 is even better. Or if you want to be brief, try 4-23 MOM LETTER. (Or just throw them all into a MOM folder.) You get the idea here: Use creative and informative filenames.

Don't Take It All Too Seriously

Computers are really about having fun. Too many people panic too quickly when they use a computer. Don't let it get to you! And please, please, don't reinstall Word to fix a minor problem. Anything that goes wrong has a solution. If the solution is not in this book, consult with your guru. Someone is bound to be able to help you out.

Index

(continued)

• *U* •

Notes

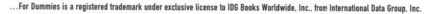

YOUR ONLINE RESOURCE

WWW.DUMMIES.COM

Discover Dummies™ Online!

The *Dummies* Web Site is your fun and friendly online resource for the latest information about ...*For Dummies*® books on all your favorite topics. From cars to computers, wine to Windows, and investing to the Internet, we've got a shelf full of ...*For Dummies* books waiting for you!

Ten Fun and Useful Things You Can Do at www.dummies.com

1. Register this book and win!
2. Find and buy the ...*For Dummies* books you want online.
3. Get ten great *Dummies Tips*™ every week.
4. Chat with your favorite ...*For Dummies* authors.
5. Subscribe free to *The Dummies Dispatch*™ newsletter.
6. Enter our sweepstakes and win cool stuff.
7. Send a free cartoon postcard to a friend.
8. Download free software.
9. Sample a book before you buy.
10. Talk to us. Make comments, ask questions, and get answers!

Jump online to these ten fun and useful things at
http://www.dummies.com/10useful

SURF THE NET

WWW.DUMMIES.COM

For other technology titles from IDG Books Worldwide, go to
www.idgbooks.com

Not online yet? It's easy to get started with *The Internet For Dummies*®, 5th Edition, or *Dummies 101*®: *The Internet For Windows*® *98*, available at local retailers everywhere.

IDG BOOKS WORLDWIDE

Find other ...*For Dummies* books on these topics:
Business • Careers • Databases • Food & Beverages • Games • Gardening • Graphics • Hardware
Health & Fitness • Internet and the World Wide Web • Networking • Office Suites
Operating Systems • Personal Finance • Pets • Programming • Recreation • Sports
Spreadsheets • Teacher Resources • Test Prep • Word Processing

IDG BOOKS WORLDWIDE
BOOK REGISTRATION

Register This Book and Win!

We want to hear from you!

Visit **http://my2cents.dummies.com** to register this book and tell us how you liked it!

- ✔ Get entered in our monthly prize giveaway.

- ✔ Give us feedback about this book — tell us what you like best, what you like least, or maybe what you'd like to ask the author and us to change!

- ✔ Let us know any other *...For Dummies*® topics that interest you.

Your feedback helps us determine what books to publish, tells us what coverage to add as we revise our books, and lets us know whether we're meeting your needs as a *...For Dummies* reader. You're our most valuable resource, and what you have to say is important to us!

Not on the Web yet? It's easy to get started with *Dummies 101*®*: The Internet For Windows*® *98* or *The Internet For Dummies*®, 5th Edition, at local retailers everywhere.

Or let us know what you think by sending us a letter at the following address:

...For Dummies Book Registration
Dummies Press
7260 Shadeland Station, Suite 100
Indianapolis, IN 46256-3917
Fax 317-596-5498

BESTSELLING BOOK SERIES